The Color of Rain

A KANSAS COURTSHIP IN LETTERS

JOHN W. FEIST

Inquiries should be addressed to:
John W. Feist, 2335 Dale Drive, Falls Church, VA 22043, USA, or jwfeist@aol.com

ISBN (print): 978-1-7357497-3-0
ISBN (ebook): 978-1-7357497-4-7
ISBN (audiobook): 978-1-7357497-5-4

Book design and production: Domini Dragoone, www.DominiDragoone.com
Cover images: Tetyana Kovyrina/Pexels, and from the author's personal collection.
Letters and all interior photographs from the author's personal collection.

PUBLISHED BY

Contents

WHAT FASTENS ATTENTION, in the intercourse of life, like any passage betraying affection between two parties? Perhaps we never saw them before and never shall meet them again. But we see them exchange a glance or betray a deep emotion, and we are no longer strangers. We understand them and take the warmest interest in the development of the romance. All mankind love a lover. . . .

. . . The lover never sees personal resemblances in his mistress to her kindred or to others. His friends find in her a likeness to her mother, or her sisters, or to persons not of her blood. The lover sees no resemblance except to summer evenings and diamond mornings, to rainbows and the song of birds.

—RALPH WALDO EMERSON, ESSAY V, "LOVE,"
ESSAYS: FIRST SERIES

Miss. Irene. Webb.

Nortonville

Kansas

aug 21

THE LOVE LETTERS YOU are about to read are real. They are untouched except for minor deletions for brevity, light use of pseudonyms, and a very few silent corrections of grammar and punctuation. The narration is fictional but informed by my examination of newspaper and photography archives; conversations with the letter writers' descendants and study of their genealogical notes; and walking the ground the lovers' footsteps must have traveled in Horton, Nortonville, and Lawrence, Kansas.

In both letters and narration, the full names of Frank, Irene, their parents, and Frank's sons are real, as are the names of locations. Other names have been changed.

I REALIZE THIS IS NO TIME FOR LETTERS

LETTER MAILED FROM ST. JOSEPH, MO.
REC'D AUG. 20, NORTONVILLE, KANSAS.

Aug. 19, 1896

My dear Miss Webb:

I write you a few lines this morning to tell you Mrs. Wilson died last night at the Embrey hospital here in St. Joe. As Mr. Wilson was alone and wholly unprepared for such a sad event, he scarcely knew what to do when the hospital officials would not allow him to keep Mrs. W. at the hospital until he could take her home. As we were with him we insisted on bringing her to our home until he could make his arrangements, so they have been here since last night. He will take her home this morning at 10:30 and the funeral will be probably tomorrow afternoon. He requested me to write you, as he knew how fond she was of you. It is very sad. May our Father be pitiful to the little orphan children and comfort him is my prayer, and I'm sure it's yours as well.

Lovingly, your friend,
Delia Alton

FRANK WILSON AWAKENED TO a new existence. His realization came through glimpses of what no longer existed. His Allie's adoring eyes. Her smile. Her arms holding lilac branches. A newborn. And then, lit in the hospital's electric light from overhead, he saw tangles of Allie's hair matted in sweat against her cold forehead. Still dressed in yesterday's clothes, he bolted from bed.

He had to send himself away. He fled his friends' guest bedroom and clambered up the attic ladder to hide. His jaw stiffened under his down-drawn mouth. His mind cried, "No, please." He could no more stop his tears than he could stop his knees from sinking to the rough floor. He hurled bursts of sobs into the attic's oven of yesterday's air. Gasping, he inhaled each one, coated in Missouri dust, for later use.

When his thoughts returned, he returned, down the attic ladder, down the bedroom stairs, to the Altons' parlor, its wallpaper the color of tea. The Altons were not yet there. He raised dusty hands to slide tears off his cheek-bones. He managed only to smudge his face and sting his eyes.

Sunlight streaked into the room. Prisms in a window's edge spread magenta and indigo beams across the flat lid of the coffin made of raw lumber. Its sole beauty had been its availability late the day before. It rested unevenly where boots had creased Delia Alton's Persian rug. Beside it, higher, gleamed the polished black curve of a baby grand piano. On the piano lid a ruby-colored vase held ripe-smelling paperwhites. Delia's cat traced a figure eight between Frank's legs. The room was quiet, except for her purr.

Delia descended the stairs and stood at the doorway to the parlor. "You had a very bad night," she said softly.

"You heard?"

"Enough to know that much. Tell me if you'd like something to eat before you go. I wrote the letter you asked me to. We'll mail it right there at the depot when we take you. Are you sure there is no one else I can write to?" Frank brought his lips into a tight, unbent smile and shook his head. His shirt was wilted with night sweats. His tie was straight. His collar chafed. His wiry hair was unkempt.

"No? Would you prefer to be here alone? Very well, I'll be in the kitchen or upstairs. Be sure to call me if there is anything I can do. I'll leave bread and fruit on the table. Ethan will be back in an hour or so with the wagon and driver. It's early, we have ample time to make your train."

Frank could not converse in the carriage Ethan Alton drove behind the green wagon to the railway station for his train home. Frank had brought Allie to the St. Joseph hospital twelve days before she died. Their family doctor had run out of anything meaningful to do or say about whatever it was that put her in bed a week before that. Between visits to her bedside, Frank had talked with the Altons about sickness and mortality until he, too, had run out of meaningful things to say. Today, the Altons did converse but accepted his silence. He looked from one side of the street to the other. A normal day. But the sun-splashed houses, buildings and people he saw were water-colored contrivances not from his world.

The Altons sat with him in the St. Joseph terminal until his train yanked him toward home, toward two sons, their thirty-seven-year-old father now widowed. Their mother would be buried beside two infant siblings in a graveyard which he was later to design as a more formal cemetery. It was now an unshaded patch of hill in the northeastern Kansas town of Horton, founded just ten years before.

The train crossed the railroad bridge over the Missouri River to the Kansas side and started to speed up its run toward Horton, putting soot into the cloudless sky. The tracks of the Chicago, Rock Island and Pacific Railway would not pass such a waterway again in their transit of the vast Kansas wheat fields and prairie grasses. But, for the next three hours, Frank's journey would be only fifty miles across wrinkled hillocks of sorghum, oat and corn fields, and over streams lined with willows and cottonwood trees. Soon farmsteads came into view that he knew by name. He had financed those farmsteads. He was banker to these farmers. Today he saw that his fields of collateral needed rain badly.

Seeing familiar crossroads and steeples brought back thoughts of the girl he fell in love with. The smile he fell in love with. Allie lived the love commandment. She held a constitutional belief in the goodness of others. She delighted in her encounters with everyone without reservation or exception. Whoever felt her smile felt improved. Frank did so daily. It was not some occasional, wordless expression to signal mood or assent. It was the emblem of her soul. Her smile was her distinctive song, regular as dawn, constant as breath.

Frank had seen life leave Allie. He had watched the swarm of nurses drift away while he stood stationed at the foot of her bed. A doctor he had never met before declared, unnecessarily, that she had expired. It hurt to hear it. It hurt to smell the still, sultry air. What exactly she died of had not been evident or ever explained. I'll forever wonder *why*, he thought. No, please . . . not on the train. He stiffened. His mouth bent downward. He stifled himself. The whistle shrieked.

"I'm sorry to hear about your loss, Frank," said Mr. Dixon, the station-master and telegrapher at Horton's immense locomotive manufacturing works and maintenance roundhouse. Frank nodded and lifted his straw hat, exposing reddish, short-cropped hair to roasting air that didn't move. The two friends watched in silence as a porter and the undertaker, Mr. Lubie, helped Mrs. Wilson off her freight car and into a wagon. Before taking up the reins of the mule, Mr. Lubie gnawed at his palm for a splinter from the rough corner of her coffin.

Frank heard Turk's nicker at the hitching post, the carelessly parked buggy pinching his sweaty flanks. Frank touched Turk's frothy withers and looked around for Mr. Edwards, who had discovered shade at the gable end of the station. Frank scowled and drew himself to his full height of five feet seven inches. Edwards's voice caught on dust as he said, "I ran him a bit. Didn't want to be late."

Frank let Turk walk the buggy up the baked station road to the corners of Main and Front. When they passed the narrow stone building housing the Homestead Bank, two men stepped outside its door and placed their hats over their chests. Frank nodded in acknowledgment, a lump in his throat. Frank Wilson, Scott Henderson and Phillip Latham had founded Homestead Bank ten years before. His partners had expected his passage by, but had not come for him at the station. In harvest month it was better that they stay at the bank to greet farmers making deposits or paying down crop loans. Frank's mind lay ahead to two boys he would have to face directly. They would want him to explain. How was he to do that?

Once inside the shaded barn in the north yard of Mina and High Streets, Frank broke the silence and said to Mr. Edwards, "I'll rub down Turk myself. You're on for the day. What I want you to do next is go in the corncrib and scoop the cobs from the pile they're in to a pile against the opposite wall. After that, lime the privy pit."

"Crib don't need it," said Edwards after a pause. The corncrib would be about like the Altons' attic.

"And Turk didn't need a run on this kind of day."

Frank, still in a tan gabardine suit, brown-striped shirt, suspenders, and brown shoes laced along high ankles, dried, rubbed and currycombed the family horse. Eventually he could think of no further reason not to go into the house.

As he pushed the front door open, Frank found Harold and Wallis standing stiffly inside the hallway. Harold, at five, was a miniature Lincoln, black-haired, Roman nose, and gangly with limbs longer than his shirt-sleeves and trouser legs. Wallis, eleven, had his father's ginger hair and, while athletic, was somewhat more rounded than his brother. Allie's mother stood between them, gripping their hands. No one spoke. Mrs. McCall's eyes were sullen and accusing.

Wallis suddenly sat down on the thin, blue-and-gray kilim hall runner and wailed. Frank clenched his teeth against the inevitable. No. No, please.

MAILED AUG. 21, 1896, FROM NORTONVILLE, KANS.
RECEIVED AUG. 22, HORTON, KANS.

My dear Mr. Wilson,

I realize this is no time for letters, and I know you have no heart or time to read idle words, but oh, please, let me tell you how my heart goes out in sympathy to you tonight. Your precious wife was my true, loyal, helpful friend—ever ready to help and sympathize with me. I loved her as a sister. Her nature was so true and beautiful—and I know beyond a doubt that tonight she is with her darling babes in that happier world where there is no more illness.

I pray our Heavenly Father to comfort you and to care for Wallis and my sweet baby Harold. I should have gone to Horton today had I received Mrs. Alton's letter in time. Now everything is over and you want to be alone.

I cannot express my sympathy, dear Mr. Wilson, but if I can do anything in any way for you, you will let me know, won't you? Can I help you any by going over? Remember I am eager and anxious to do even the smallest thing to testify to my love for my dear loving friend. I cannot realize she is gone. She had so much to live for and to be happy for.

I cannot write more now. Believe me

Your sincere friend,
Irene Webb

IRENE HAD WALKED TO carry her letter to the Nortonville station, three miles north of the Webb farm. The men had all the horses in the fields and she could not bear to wait a day to post it. Mailing the letter gave her legs a purpose. On the way home her pace was slower. Allie's friendship could not be replaced. She would be unable to grieve at her friend's funeral. She tried to think of passages she would read to herself in a solitary memorial in her bedroom. John Donne, certainly. "Death, be not proud . . ." She would have to look it up. Then, her mind drifted to how she might compose more lengthy condolences to Mr. Wilson in a second letter. She returned to the farmhouse with heavy steps.

Inside, her mother was napping on the living room rug in her slip, as she and Irene customarily did in the middle of summer days. Irene stepped around her mother, also named Irene, and went to rock in the blue chair in the kitchen. She peeled a Jonathan apple and cut thin, crisp slices which she covered in salt for her lunch. She had difficulty swallowing. Life is so everyday, she thought. And for her, life came as the pullets, the Guernsey cow, the garden, and the wash. And the unexpected.

How *does* it go? She put down the paring knife and plate. She went upstairs to her room and opened a book. Here it is. "Death, be not proud, though some have called thee / Mighty and dreadful, for thou are not so."

Augusta Irene Webb lived with an ailing father, Hiram, and mother. She was the youngest of seven children raised on the farm. She looked after her parents and whichever of her four brothers and two sisters came home for a spell. From time to time the farmhouse was also filled with cousins from two Webb families in nearby Valley Falls, and the nearly daily visits by Irene's niece, Maggie Rea, who lived in Nortonville. Despite her genuine affection for family, Irene did, at times, ache for privacy so lacking when family filled the house. When she found the time to read or just reflect there was no place under the roof to do so without interruption.

Irene had a naturally regal look because of her straight carriage and quiet, thoughtful visage. She was slender and plain-looking to some—a small, unremarkable nose, a muted smile, a wide chin with a soft fold beneath it that suggested more maturity than her twenty-six years, and gray eyes the color of rain. She wore her light brown hair pushed up loosely to a braid encircling the crown of her head. She was humble and simple, like the

Mennonites who farmed a cluster of alfalfa fields south of the Webb's land. The Webbs admired but did not emulate the Mennonite ways.

Hiram and Irene Webb were very much of the world. Over the years the nearly five hundred acres of market crops and cattle they had accumulated had allowed them to provide comfortably for their children. Some had started farms of their own. Others, including Irene, had gone to college. But over recent years Hiram's health required him to pay for more and more labor on the farm and with the livestock, with dwindling returns for the family.

Irene was a teacher, but one with neither school nor pupils at the moment. She had studied liberal arts at Kansas University in nearby Lawrence. To enter the teaching profession she had attended The State Normal School of Emporia, Kansas. Her teaching certificate did not hang on a wall in a schoolroom but rather rested in a box covered in blue-and-white gingham her mother had made years ago. It had a sliding lid and had once held two dozen fourteen-inch candles. It was large enough to hold Irene's diploma, notebooks, sketches of domino combinations, and letters home. In it was also a brochure on a Gorham silverware pattern, Versailles, Irene had long admired. The box served to hold fond memories of school, and wistful dreams of a home and family of her own.

There had been a school, three years before, in Horton. After graduation, she had been accepted to teach there without pay, as was customary for a first teaching job, but with room and board provided by someone on the school board. For her, it was provided by Mr. and Mrs. Wilson in the two-story yellow house with white trim on the corner across from the school. In it were a stove in the kitchen that used combinations of corncobs, kindling, and coal; a storm cellar under the pantry next to the kitchen; a well with sweet, soft water next to the kitchen door; a corncrib; a wraparound front porch with a swing; and four bedrooms and a sleeping porch upstairs. The front yard rose slightly from the rutted roadway that was High Street as it passed through Horton. On this road, Nortonville lay thirty-three miles to the south, and Hiawatha sixteen miles to the north, the county seat of Brown County, Kansas.

That was in 1893. From the moment she had arrived in Horton, on New Year's Day, Irene had felt she was coming to her true place on Earth. She had been put up in a large bedroom on the second floor with windows facing south and east. From that room she could look across to the brick schoolhouse as she dressed for the day. She relished her classes there and especially those moments when a student seized upon an insight through her reasoning. Inside the Wilson household, her days were filled with companionship and the antics of a two-year-old boy and the quieter presence of his brother, older by six years. Allie Wilson had gladly accepted Irene's enthusiasm to help with the boys and the routines of home life. To Irene, it meant joining a new family. That family came to include, on occasion, Allie's mother and sister, who also lived in Horton. Pearl, the sister, worked at the bank.

Allie and Irene came to be more than companions and soon thought of each other as sisters. Frank had never before seen eyes the color of rain.

Frank Wilson was a dominant presence when at home. Two or three times a week, he became an impresario of evening readings from classical literature. The living room held a pair of five-foot-wide bookcases, dark oak with lead-mullioned glass doors, which flanked the door to the dining room. In it, he had gradually accumulated assortments of histories, essays, poetry, and the complete works of Shakespeare by subscription edition from a Philadelphia publisher. The Wilsons would read aloud from these books after the children had been put to bed. They took enormous pride in the fact that they had just completed the four-year Chautauqua course of reading.

Frank quickly brought Irene into these readings and the glorious discussions that followed. Allie was an earnest reader, but had not the same insights that Frank and Irene were quick to find when they read together. Irene was a poignant Cordelia to Frank's aloof Lear. Irene listened politely as Allie soldiered through Juliet. Those winter evenings glowed for the three companions.

Harold became attached to Irene within the first few weeks. One weekend afternoon as he cooed in Irene's arms, Allie smiled and said, "Irene, don't feel as though you need to always fuss over the children. You're welcome to enjoy your leisure as you wish. You are so considerate. You won't spoil the boys but you might spoil me."

"Oh, I am enjoying just being in the house and helping any way I can. It seems like a holiday compared to wintertime on the farm. I hope I'm not in your way."

"Hardly that," Allie said. "Tell me, Irene, how many girls were there at university when you were there? Not in Emporia, but at Lawrence."

"More than I had expected, actually. A little over a third overall, I'd guess."

"I finished high school," said Allie, "and Frank and I did the Chautauqua. Now it doesn't sound like so much compared to you at university and teacher's college on top of that."

"Mrs. Wilson, you are not only well educated, but you apply it in everyday life at home and when you and Mr. Wilson talk about the bank. I'm envious of your practical ways and wisdom. Not much chance of that for me in the middle of five hundred acres of corn and cattle."

"Nice of you to say. Please call me Allie," she said. "I never spent much time on a farm. So, you and I have our learning from different aspects. Did you ever take a fancy to one of those college men?"

Irene said, "Well, college has its social side. Mine wasn't much to talk about."

"I'd like to hear about the social side, Irene. It's hard to picture you that way."

Irene laughed and said, "It'll put you to sleep. But I'll be glad to have a gossip, Allie."

"What's the most gossip-worthy social occasion you had in Lawrence?"

Irene studied her face. Allie's smile invited trust. "Well, there is no doubt as to what that was. But it's something I didn't even tell my mother."

Allie still smiled.

Irene laughed and said, "It was in September, my last year at university; the year before I went down to Emporia. A carnival came to Lawrence, or rather to the outskirts. I had a chance to go to it with three young men, but on a Sunday, and we would be out after my landlady's curfew. I knew she wouldn't allow it, but I went anyway. When we got there we realized why Chancellor Snow had declared the carnival unsuitable for students. It was. It was a flimsy excuse for a whole lot of sleaze going on in tents. But we made the best of it and learned a few things not offered at KU. Eventually I did have to get back to the boardinghouse. I had left a downstairs window unlatched, but when I got there it had been locked up again. I had to use the front door. The landlady was waiting for me. She threatened to evict me. She threatened to write to Chancellor Snow. If she had done so, then my friends would have been at risk of expulsion same as me."

"Oh, Irene, that sounds dark. What happened?"

"My brother Alfred and cousin Charlie came down from Topeka and talked to her. Somehow they convinced her that the consequences would be way out of proportion to the indiscretion. Charlie took a chance and suggested an increase in rent for the rest of the term. It was settled at that."

"And you told no one?"

"I did tell my sister Lydia. She's about your age. So only Alfred, Charlie and Lydia know, and now you. I guess you're my sister now."

Allie laughed and her eyes glowed. She said, "I believe I like that idea very much," and gave her a quick hug. "Now, am I barred from repeating your tale to Mr. Wilson?"

Irene thought a moment, smiled, and said, "I couldn't ask you to withhold anything from your husband." They both laughed at that.

That spring, Irene embraced Easter Redemption as at no other time before or since. But right around then Allie began to feel uneasy over the facility with which Frank and Irene could breathe such life into the pages, and their exchange of glances when a scene sparkled.

"You are an actress," Frank commented after one lively reading.

Irene said, "Oh, I just try to interpret what is written."

Frank put the book back in the oak bookcase and said simply, "I believe that's what an actor does. It's a second act of creation. There is artistry in your voice."

"Wallis, did you enjoy this one?" Irene asked.

"It was nice to hear, but I didn't get it. What was the dream?"

Irene said, "I won't leave you in the dark over it. I will explain it after school tomorrow—you and I will break it down. You could even learn one or two beautiful passages."

Allie said nothing. She had begun to look forward to the end of the school term.

At the end of the term the school board made no offer of permanent employment. Irene feigned relief that she would be free to return to Lawrence in the fall for postgraduate literature classes at the university. The three friends pledged faithful correspondence and frequent rendezvous at holidays.

She made only one brief return visit to Horton, but the atmosphere was not quite the same.

And now, the postal service had brought Delia Moore Alton's news that shattered any lingering hopes of reuniting with the blissful surroundings of Irene's Horton family. Irene rearranged the contents of the box to make a place for Delia's letter.

WRITTEN AUGUST 27, 1896.
RECEIVED NORTONVILLE, AUGUST 28.

Miss Irene Webb, Nortonville, Ks.

Dear Friend:

I rec'd your very kind letter in due time, and I cordially thank you for the loving tribute to the memory of my dearly beloved wife, and also the tender expressions of sympathy in the hour of my greatest trial. Allie was a faithful and devoted wife and mother, her best thoughts and efforts being for her husband, her children, and her home. Her own comfort and pleasure were last to be considered. Our home, once so complete, is now broken and desolate. My loss is indeed great, but that of the children greater. I am fortunate in having my mother to step into our household and take charge. We have a splendid girl, for our general housework, who has been with us some time and will likely remain with us, and thus we are trying to keep our home as near like it formerly was as is possible under the circumstances.

I contemplate a short trip to Ills. with the children next week, but if I go I will return not later than 15th prox. After this date I shall be at home, and would very much appreciate a visit from you at any time that would best suit your convenience. I know of no one who has a better faculty of making the fireside bright and cheerful than you. Allie was indeed your true and loyal friend.

I regret that you did not receive Mrs. Alton's letter in time to be present at her funeral. I also regret that I have not the space and time to tell you in detail all about her last illness, but I have received so many letters that I have been unable to find time to answer them as fully as I should like.

I trust that I may see you soon, when I can tell you so much better than I could write. I would like for you to bring your mother and make us a nice visit at such time in the near future as may best suit your convenience.

With kind regards to your mother and yourself, I am

Your sincere friend,
F. M. Wilson

WALLIS CAME TO FRANK in the kitchen to help dry the dishes. Frank's mother, Amanda, had taken Harold upstairs for a story in bed. He said, "Papa, do you know about Mama's clothes in the closet next to my room?"

Frank managed to calm his voice. "Oh yes. We should take those away."

"Don't throw them away, though."

"No, Wallis, I'm not doing that with any of her things. Actually, you can help me here. I've been thinking to give some of the things to the church, of course. But I also had the idea the other day to have Miss Deutsch make a quilt for me with pieces of Mama's clothes. Would you like to have a quilt like that of your own? Don't feel you have to if you'd be uncomfortable."

"Papa, I like that idea a lot. Could I have it this winter?"

"When I spoke to her she said it should go fairly quickly. I should ask Harold if he wants one."

"Let me ask him. He's my brother. He'll tell me honest if it would spook him. He might not say it to you."

Frank smiled, and dried his hands on the dishtowel Wallis was holding. He beamed at his son and said, "You do that, son. That's the best way."

"But I think he'll want one too. Will Gramma Wilson and Gramma McCall get theirs?"

Frank paused. He knelt to be at eye level. Wallis's chin trembled twice, then held firm. "Wallis, I'm thinking this is just for the Wilson men. That is, if Harold wants one. If he doesn't, just you and I will have them. How does that sound?"

Wallis nodded gravely and said, "Yes, that's how it should be. Can you read to me?"

"I want to write a letter first. I'll be up in about an hour. What do you want to hear?"

"That poem. The long one in India."

"I'll be up in about an hour with 'Gunga Din' then. Now scoot."

MAILED SEPTEMBER 15, 1896, VALLEY FALLS, KANSAS.

Mr. F. M. Wilson, Horton, Kans.

My Dear Friend,

I was much pleased to have your very kind letter some two weeks ago. I was about to write and ask you to bring the children and come to visit us for a time if you felt that you cared to when your letter came. Mrs. Wilson always intended coming to visit us. I am so sorry she did not come. I, too, regret very much that I did not attend the funeral.

I feel so sorry for Wallis, poor boy—no one knows his feelings. Wallis has rather a strange nature—he will bear his sorrow heroically, but it will be very hard on him. I presume he is in school. I wonder if there is a kindergarten in Horton now. How nice it would be if there is to let Harold go for awhile.

Thank you very much for your kind invitation to visit you. I should like to come and perhaps I can sometime during the fall or winter. I do not contemplate teaching this year, so I shall have more time at my disposal than heretofore.

Sincerely Yours,
Irene Webb

WRITTEN SUNDAY, OCT. 4, 1896.
RECEIVED NORTONVILLE, OCTOBER 5.

Miss Irene Webb

My Dear Friend:

. . . I am indeed lonely. The world seems cold and uninteresting to me now, and if it were not for the boys, who are a great comfort to me, I should feel despondent. I realize that I have a double duty and responsibility now, however, and I shall not shirk it.

I am glad to hear that you think of visiting us, and as this is the most delightful season of the whole year to my notion, I think you would find it a good time for you to come. Allie & I always intended to visit you, but like many other good intentions, this was not fulfilled.

I have not given up my intention to visit you but at present am unable to say when it will be. I think I will wait until after your visit to us, which I trust will be soon. In the mean time I hope to hear from you frequently.

It seems to require no effort upon your part to write a good long letter, and if you will favor me with such, I will assure you that I will appreciate them, and while letter writing is a great task for me, and I cannot promise you an interesting correspondence, I will endeavor to the best of my ability to show my appreciation. I have delayed answering your letter longer than I intended for the reason that I have been kept very busy since my return and Mr. Phillip Latham has had a 2 weeks vacation leaving double work for me to do.

Hoping to hear from you very soon, and assuring you of my highest esteem, believe me to be

Sincerely Yours,
F. M. Wilson

BY 10:30 IRENE HAD wrung and hung a week's worth of her father's and brother Alfred's long cotton underwear on the clothes wires that stretched from the eves of the back lean-to across the chicken yard to the stable. A quickening westerly breeze set the heavy, damp legs lumbering crookedly so that more than once she had been head-swiped as she leaned over to gather another victim for her gallows. Actually, it had been one more time than had been entirely amusing, although the pullets had not ceased their chuckling. *Well,* she thought, *why in the world would anyone rather be standing in a classroom exploring sonnets when one could be breathing damp, piss-stained cotton underwear under a bright sun? And why would a high-collared, starched shirt, brooch, and tight-waisted, long black skirt more suit my frame of mind than a gray day-dress and apron? And who wouldn't prefer . . . oh, stop it!*

I haven't dressed that way every day since Horton, she thought. Frank was always in suit, vest and tie at home, so Irene tended to keep herself dressed as for school. Besides, it seemed appropriate with Wallis running around the house.

Allie's two closest friends had drifted away over the years: one to Chicago and the other, Delia, to St. Joseph. She came to relish companionship with Irene. The two women shared confidences as personal as Irene had with her own sisters. Allie did not confide her growing displeasure over Frank's glances at the young schoolteacher. Allie had never known Frank to have a roving eye, so what kind of eye is this? she found herself wondering. But Frank was never less attentive to Allie, upstairs or downstairs, and she could not find cause to fault either of them. Especially since Irene was so genuinely eager for Allie's company and so willing to help with Harold, whom Irene called "my baby."

Irene thought of Wallis as "my mystery" but never said it out loud. She imagined she might bridge the gap of silence with dominoes. After a few games to break the ice she decided to add a layer of schooling. The college in Emporia had taught her to use dominoes as a handy, rigorous tool for teaching number combinations.

"Oh, you drew the double six! Now you'll give me a thrashing. So, Wallis, how many spots on the double six?"

Wallis frowned and said, "Your move." His lips told her he was counting.

"You can see it faster than you can count it out. You know your tables from school. What's six and six?"

Wallis, who had finished counting, said, "Twelve. Still your move."

Irene placed the six-three tile against Wallis's and said, "How many white spots on the table in total?"

"Can I go now? I feel like going outdoors."

Irene held her tongue a moment, and then said, "I'll put the pieces away. We will set them up this way when you're ready. We will finish the game." Irene saw in Wallis his father's stubbornness and occasional abruptness. Wallis looked so much like Frank that it took her breath away.

Oh, that Frank. Irene had seen in him so many of the ideals she had put by in her mental pantry of men. In her mind she had sorted: great men she had read about; great men she had actually known—a much smaller group; all others—the largest group. Take, for example, Frank's ability to talk about his bank business, great books, and the business of the home, practically in the same breath. Allie could keep up with these quick switches whereas Irene found them mysterious. She also found them intriguing and masculine, coming as they did from a head covered in wiry red hair. He made Irene a part of the family, and she was glad to be in it. Even though it was Allie's family, as she would have to remind herself.

Such reminders occasionally would also come from Allie, in a disappearing smile, or exhales audible only to ears on alert to uncertain boundaries. Once, and only once, Allie felt the instinct to utter a territorial warning. At the end of a play reading one evening, as the conversation turned to deconstructing a scene that Frank and Irene had felt caught up in, Allie said, with a smile but distinctly, "Miss Webb, I wonder if I may have the remainder of the evening with my husband?" Irene retreated to her bedroom with burning ears. Frank and she read far fewer plays together after that.

Irene put away Frank's most recent letter in the box in her dresser, and looked in the uneven mirror above it. She fussed with a wayward strand. So he wonders if he'll have time to go here or I'll have inclination to go there. Well, Mr. Wilson, this farm girl has ample patience but also has her own yearnings not entirely addressed in letters and letters and more letters. And certainly addressed not at all by the menfolk of Nortonville, Kansas, who don't know I exist on this farm. Thirty miles of muddy road should not be that difficult for you and me, not in this day and age.

Yes, Mr. Wilson, my Caballero, by all means let us write our letters. And let us speak in our letters about how we might enjoy making the short trip between our realms. And I shall begin to add letters, and hopes, to my hope chest.

SUNDAY, OCTOBER 18TH, '96.
RECEIVED IN HORTON, KANS., ON OCT. 20, 1896.

Irene Webb to F. M. Wilson

Dear Friend,

Your very kind letter came some days ago and was read with interest and pleasure. My letters you will find to be very poor excuses but if you derive any pleasure from them, if they will in any degree cause you to feel less lonely or brighten the winter days a little, I shall be pleased to write to you. . . .

No doubt, Mr. Wilson, "the world does seem cold and uninteresting to you"—how my heart goes out in sympathy to you. I presume it seems almost cruel to you sometimes to see others happy and to realize that the bright star of your home has faded. But do not become despondent—you have your two boys to live for and to be happy for. They are at an age when you will be greatly interested in directing their education and in implanting in their young minds the principles of manly boyhood. I am truly glad that Wallis has outgrown his naughty habits. I was confident he would. I have always predicted a brilliant future for that boy and I see no reason that my prophesy should not prove true. To be sure he will sadly miss his devoted mother's tender words of advice, but the foundation is already firmly laid and he will never forget her nor her wise counsel. . . .

I do not know when I can go to Horton. I should greatly enjoy a visit there, but now that I am at home I find my father and mother loath to spare me even for a brief visit. My father is not strong these days, but I think he is improving. He is under the Dr.'s care and has been for months. . . .

The members of my family and my friends seem to think because I am not going to school, not teaching, that I have plenty of time to visit. I find that housework is quite as busy work as any other, although not so confining. . . .

Very Sincerely Yours,
Irene Webb

P.S. People say a woman's letter is not complete without a postscript so I shall add one. You remember Miss Harris do you not? She is married and lives in Kansas City. I saw her in June. I fear her married life has not been as happy as it might be. Mr. King is still in Chicago. He is now a full-fledged lawyer and is getting along very well, I have understood. I heard from him soon after Mrs. Wilson's death and he expressed great sympathy for you and wished to be remembered to you. What are you reading? I have been reading nothing but the magazines and daily papers lately. I must take up some more solid reading soon. . . . Did you attend the Topeka festivities? I did not. I wanted very much to go to Kansas City last week to see Joseph Jefferson in Rip Van Winkle, but I could not go. I hope you went. It would certainly be a rare treat to see the versatile old actor who never fails to delight his audience.

Again I must tell you Good Bye. I wish I could see you all tonight. I hope you are all well and happy.

Irene Webb
Please do excuse the fit of these envelopes.

TWO BANK PROBLEMS KEPT Frank awake at night. He resented the way Latham had up and left the place to run itself for two weeks. And he could see that the lingering depression was keeping money tight, and tight money was holding back business in Brown County.

He had a notion how to cope with tight money close to home. He had even had a printer in St. Joseph print up pocket-sized bank IOUs "to bearer" in one-dollar denominations. They were in storage now. He had heard it worked elsewhere and this would be a pretty good time to float the scrip. Latham said it would be a bookkeeping nightmare. He didn't feel like taking Latham head-on over this. His spells of grief, when they came on, just shut down his capacity to function. He would postpone the scrip but he knew he shouldn't. Pretty much everything was on downslope.

Frank Wilson, the last-born of five children, was eleven when Joseph and Amanda Wilson had moved their family to Holton, county seat of Jackson County, Kansas, from Carthage, Illinois, in a covered wagon. When he was thirteen, his parents, married for twenty years, had divorced. At sixteen he quit school to read law with a two-man Holton law office. At eighteen he went to work at the Holton bank and set his career sights on finance rather than the law: there was greater advantage to lending the money to buy cows than to occasionally replevy a cow upon default. At twenty he started his own bank in the corner of a drugstore in Havensville, Kansas, with very little capital, and his life started picking up momentum. He made daredevil money deals in a boomtown economy centered on Havensville's thriving cattle market. His business model resembled more a temple money changer's than a bank's.

At twenty-two he married Allie McCall, her family originally from Georgia. In 1887 the lure of the boosters of the newly founded "Magic City" of Horton drew them into a dream to create a Chicago-on-the-prairie. There, Frank, Scott Henderson and Phillip Latham assembled $50,000 in capital to win the US Comptroller of Currency's charter for the first national bank of Horton, doing business as the Homestead Bank, beating out a competing group by just a matter of hours in a telegraph race.

Now, everything had changed and his mother, Amanda, was back in his daily life at close quarters.

"You should find yourself someone, don't you think, Frank," Amanda said on Halloween eve when the boys were away marauding. It was a declaration, not a question. He had sensed this was coming and still hadn't been able to ward it off. Amanda took a keen interest in matches following her own divorce. He paused. He pursed his lips and made a measured response.

"I know you need to get back to Holton. We're all pretty well back to normal, thanks to you. We can do fine. You can come back Thanksgiving and Christmas."

Amanda stood up, briskly folded her apron and put it away. "That's not what I asked you."

Frank made a vague, swatting gesture with his left hand. "I'll take a look in the Sears and Roebuck," he muttered.

Amanda planted her feet squarely in front of Frank, looked him in the eye, and stated: "I am talking about the other half of this new letter-writing campaign that seems so absorbing to you. The Miss Irene Webb of Nortonville you're so fond of talking about. When am I going to get to meet Miss Webb? Are you simply going to keep on writing letters like this till you have yourself a book?"

Frank shrugged. "It's way too soon for what you're talking about, Mother."

Amanda folded her arms and said, "Soon was last week, Frank, and if it's not the Webb girl there are plenty of women here in Horton for you to think about. Believe me, they're thinking about you."

Frank now stood. "Allie and I were married fifteen years. In my mind, I still am. I can't stress that strongly enough." Why couldn't his very own mother understand that? He had told her this before.

"Your father and I were married for twenty years. I *know* I'm still not."

Frank took three quick strides away, turned back, and said, "Mama, I saw what you and Papa went through. With you, the love died but Papa didn't. Not like that with me. There is a world of difference." He lowered his voice and stepped to her again. "With me, Allie dies every morning. Listen to what I just said: *every morning,* Mother. But the love didn't die, and it never will."

Amanda's face softened. She nodded, taking Frank's hand. "What I think is, Allie's ghost got inside your head in the form of her mama keeping blinders on you. Mrs. McCall has hung that ghost out there with the tack, watching to see if you're slipping out to trot with some fillies. Look, Frank, she has never thought highly of me and has been pretty plain about it." She turned away as she remembered. "Oh, she had such harsh words for me at Allie's grave. She was distraught, of course, and there was no reason to tell you about it." She turned back to face Frank.

"The poor woman saw her daughter go away with you to St. Joe and never come back. She blames you for that, but won't ever tell you to your face because her other daughter works at your bank. And she blames me for you, and she had no hesitation telling me so out there under the blazing sun in the graveyard. Blames us for what exactly I'll never know. Maybe she thinks I couldn't raise you right, or that the shame of my divorce infected you so you couldn't properly care for Allie. I know it doesn't make a speck of sense, but I've learned what a divorced woman has to put up with, Frank."

Amanda's chin trembled. She sat again. Her voice caught as she said, "So don't go thinking you're the only one with grief. She wants me out of your life and especially your boys' lives. You can't tell me you are not smart enough to have figured that out. She comes around here almost every day to smile at the boys and scowl at me.

"Naturally she has her friends and neighbors, and naturally she gives them an earful at the drop of a hat. Those friends and neighbors are your bank customers, Frank Wilson, and her daughter is your teller. And they're folks I run into every now and again." Her voice was barely audible. "So, as I said: 'soon' was last week, Frank."

Frank sat next to her and patted her shoulder. "It is reprehensible that she hurt you. But please understand that I'm in no hurry, Mother."

She smiled and said evenly, "Then I guess I'm in no hurry to get back to Holton." Frank kissed her cheek before she stood and left the kitchen.

As Frank waited for his sons to come home for bed, he did reflect on his mother's words. He could certainly see that remarriage was inevitable, and he was beginning to think Irene would top his list of possible brides. But he could not bring his mind to bear on that now. Just two months ago he was married. He could not yet fathom that his marriage was truly over. It was easier to accept Allie was dead than to understand his marriage was too. He would be unable to act decisively until he could reconcile those opposing forces in his mind. The best he could think of to do was to explore his growing fondness for Irene through correspondence and actual visits.

When he could find the time to make the trip, that was.

My Dear Friend Irene,

. . . You assure me that I will find your letters "very poor excuses," but you will excuse me if I take issue with you and declare to you that they are full of interest and I am quite sure that I shall derive much pleasure from them. . . .

On 10th inst. we are to have John Dillon and I presume this will be as good an attraction as we ever get here. If you will come over about that time we will attend his performance. I don't know just how you feel about making us a visit just now but if you feel that there is any impropriety in it I will release you from your promise.

For my own part I see no impropriety in it and I seldom consider what the public will have to say concerning my acts. We would enjoy your visit very much I assure you, and will make it as pleasant for you as we can while you stay. . . .

I wish you lived in Horton, or very near Horton, so that I might see you often.

Trusting that I may soon have the pleasure of a visit from you, and hoping that your father's health is much improved since you wrote of his illness, and with kindest regards to both your parents, and assurances of my highest esteem I am

Sincerely Yours,
F. M. Wilson

"WHEN DO YOU THINK to go to Horton?" Maggie Rea asked as she and Irene folded spanking-clean sheets from the clothesline. They stood ankle deep in fallen yellow cottonwood leaves and wrapped in bright sunshine. Maggie Rea was just half the age of her Aunt Irene, or "Aunt Tot" as the family referred to her. Maggie Rea's mother, Mary Elizabeth, was Webb before she became Mrs. Jerret McVey of Nortonville. The McVey family farmed acreage in the section adjoining the Webb farm and also in Delaware County near Valley Falls. Both families had been early settlers in the region.

"What do you mean, go to Horton?"

"Well then, when do you think he's coming to Nortonville?"

"How do I know when he can take the time for a folly like that?"

Maggie Rea whooped and stomped in a circle of leaves with laughter. She had pudgy cheeks which matched a generally prosperous appearance; she had a weakness for anything with flour and butter in or on it. She was shorter than Irene, whom she adored, and wore her dark brown hair just as Irene had worn it the last time they were together. Irene loved the girl, but having her around constantly sometimes affected Irene as summer nettles did.

"Oh, how stupid of me," Maggie Rea said between jets of giggles. "That's right, Horton got picked up by a tornado and moved to the coast of the South China Sea. And you can only get there by train and then steamship and then dugout canoe through smelly, snaky marshes. But you can't spare time either from teaching Latin and electricity to eighth graders in the new brick schoolhouse they named for you west of town."

Irene carried a basket of folded sheets upstairs to the linen press. She thought it might finally be time for the family to consider committing Maggie Rea to that special hospital in Topeka.

Maggie Rea called after her, "Aunt Tot, want a game of dominoes? After that I'll stay and help you snap beans and put up cucumbers."

Oh, Irene did love this girl. They didn't just "play" dominoes. It made her glad that Maggie Rea wanted more "lesson games."

"You set them up, I'll be down in a minute."

Irene knocked and looked into her father's bedroom. He was sitting up, an opened Bible upside-down and tented next to him. When he smiled at Irene, his long, thin, salt-and-pepper beard parted like a curtain and his eyes widened. "Irene! Come to take old Hiram to brand the cattle?"

Irene giggled. "May I bring you anything, Papa?"

"New lungs from Canada, sweet girl. Who did you see?"

Irene sat beside him, ready to report. "Jenny Wrens. A pintail drake out by the stock pond. Two adult thrushes and a juvenal. Hawk, but too high to tell what kind. Oh, and a Rufus-throated Maggie Rea got in the house when I opened the back door a while ago. Who did you hear?"

"Catbird under the eaves. Sparrows. The wrens you saw. And, just after sunup, cranes very high, moving south. From the time it took 'em to pass, there must have been hundreds."

"I thought I heard geese . . ."

"No, cranes. You remember. Far away. More rolling and throaty. How's Maggie Rea? And don't start in about the asylum, the state can't afford her."

"She's brilliant and spoiled and dear. Come down and see her. You can do with a walk."

"I'll be there directly. I love you, Irene."

"I love you, Papa."

THAT SAME EVENING, IN Horton, Frank and Amanda cleared the table and cleaned up the kitchen. Amanda winked at him and said, "When do you think to go to Nortonville?"

"I know, I know. You made your point a week ago. Are you going upstairs now? If you are, would you look in on the boys and ask them to come back to the table? I'm trying to get some ideas for their Christmas wish list."

Amanda smiled broadly and said, "Of that, I approve a hundred percent," and climbed up the back, winding stairs that led from the kitchen to the upstairs hall. Frank arranged writing paper and pencils on the round, black oak dining room table. He heard the boys stampeding on the front stairs. Or, rather, Harold was doing most of the stamping because Wallis slid down the bannister.

"Gramma said you needed us, quick march. What's wrong?"

"Nothing's wrong, Wallis. I have something for you to do. You know how I've been doing a lot of letter writing lately. Well, I'm going the station to mail another one and I thought I might as well mail yours to Santa Claus at the same time."

"Papa! This is kind of early, isn't it?" said Wallis.

"Not really. Shouldn't take you long. At least I hope it won't. I've told you about being greedy."

Harold sat very still. Tears formed in the corners of his eyes. "I can't write a whole letter."

"I'll sit right here and help you spell things out. You don't have to be fancy. Even just a list would be fine."

"I want Mama," said Harold. "So do I," Wallis echoed.

"Well, I like that you said that but you know it doesn't work that way."

Wallis gnawed the end of the pencil and then set about to build up his inventory of cast-iron fire wagons and baseball gear. He said, "Can it be a trip to Kansas City?"

Frank said, "Put down RR Tickets, KC. Better give a date. And why."

"Around my birthday. There's a huge, big magic show. I'm putting down dominoes. Would you play dominoes with me? Miss Webb used to when she was here. It helped me with my numbers."

Frank said, "If Miss Webb played them with you, I certainly shall as well."

Harold whispered something in Frank's ear, and Frank carefully wrote *Pony*.

"What kind?" "Cowboy kind." Then he whispered again.

"Really?" Frank whispered back. "Pants? That's not a toy, but very well. What kind?"

Harold spoke animatedly into Frank's ear and pointed to his knee. "Knickerbockers?" whispered Frank. "Actually, I think there are some Wallis has outgrown somewhere . . ." Harold stamped his foot and whispered again. Frank nodded and said, "Oh. New ones. Never Wallis's." Frank picked up the pencil and made notes with a smile. "What else?" Harold went quiet. Then he said, "Two of them."

"Knickers?"

"No, ponies."

FRIDAY, NOVEMBER 6TH, '96

Mr. F. M. Wilson, Horton, Kansas

Dear Mr. Wilson,

I shall waive the conventional ten days or two weeks usually observed in letter writing and endeavor to answer your charming letter very soon this time. I should very much enjoy going to Horton for the occasion of John Dillon's performance, but I fear I shall not be able to do so. It is most kind and thoughtful of you to anticipate and appreciate my feelings in regard to making you a visit at this time—though to be frank about the matter it had never occurred to me that there might be any impropriety in my going. Your remark, however, has set me to thinking and I have come to the conclusion that I would better not go and I beg you to release me from my promise.

If you are disappointed you are not more so than I am as I have looked forward with a great deal of pleasure. The more I consider the matter in your letter the more I think I cannot go. I appreciate how you feel about it. Society has certain iron-clad rules, as it were, and there are always those in small towns who are greatly interested in their neighbors' affairs. I fear my visit might be somewhat embarrassing for you and for that reason I now ask you to "take the will for the deed." I do not know when I can go to St. Joe. . . .

Very Sincerely Yours,
Irene Webb

THE ROCK ISLAND WORKS' steam whistle sounded every day at noon in Horton. The whistle could be heard on every street in town. The streets had been laid out as a grid in which Front was the dividing line running east and west and Main was the dividing line running north and south. South of Front sprawled the train tracks and works along the Delaware River. After Front, going north, the streets were Vera, Florence, Beatrice, Mina, Mabel, Frances, and North. The streets east of Main were High, Trenton, Lenora, Netawaka, Yuma, and Park. The ones west of Main were Arthur, Grant, Lincoln, Logan, Harper, Stanley, Morse, and Hancock.

When the noon whistle sounded on November 7, 1896, Miss Elizabeth Hamlyn set out from her home at Main and Florence carrying a covered dish of mashed, creamed sweet potatoes she intended for eligible widower-banker Mr. Wilson at High and Mina. The day was warm and the wind was light out of the southwest. She was overdressed for a Saturday. Amanda Wilson greeted her at the door and told Harold to scoot out to the barn and fetch Papa. Frank was harnessing Turk to the carriage for a family jaunt to the river and a picnic. Wallis was loading his fishing pole and tackle.

At 12:25 Miss Faith Daldrup walked from her front porch at North and Arthur Streets with a casserole of shepherd's pie, and Frank and Wallis walked to their front porch to greet Miss Hamlyn. Frank smiled broadly and listened carefully to a detailed report on her health. Miss Daldrup rounded the corner of North and High as Amanda carried the sweet potato casserole to the north porch. Amanda returned as Frank was complimenting Miss Hamlyn on her front-yard display of geraniums. "I admire them every day on my way to and from the bank." His words pleased her more than he could have known. Once, her ambition had been to grow the finest geraniums in Horton. In September her ambitions grew to include a husband with a bank.

At 12:48 Miss Helen-Marie Trojovsky let the kitchen screen door slam behind her as she left her house at Yuma and Mabel Streets carrying a covered tray of perogies for Mr. Wilson. Miss Hamlyn was still sitting on the swing with Frank and Amanda when Frank happened to look up to see Miss Daldrup approaching a block north on High Street. He shot a look at Amanda who stood quickly and invited Miss Hamlyn to see the new quilt Miss Deutsch had made for Frank. They both were touched, remembering familiar patterns and fabrics from Allie's wardrobe in the quilt.

At 1:15 Miss Nerva Dunn closed the front door of her house on Logan Street and began walking east on Mina carrying a two-crusted blackberry pie which she hoped Frank Wilson would find memorable. That was when Miss Hamlyn sighed and said she should "get back to home and start raking leaves." Amanda suggested it might be shorter for her to go down the back stairs and out the kitchen door. On the stoop of the south porch, Amanda invited Miss Hamlyn to return next Monday for a supper with the family "and more of a visit."

On the front porch Frank struggled to help Miss Trojovsky in a discussion with Miss Daldrup over the election. She was no match for Miss Daldrup's vehemence for Morrill, although she felt in her heart that McKinley was the better choice. She decided that her own better choice was to go home, so she bade farewell to the Wilsons. Amanda accompanied her a few steps and suggested that she return the next week for a quiet dinner, "say, on Thursday?"

Miss Dunn had reached Mina and Main just as Miss Crawford was coming out her side door of the corner house carrying a lidded, ten-inch oval Wedgwood deep-dish of scalloped potatoes with scallions and crumbled bacon. She and Miss Crawford chatted about chores and errands and fleeting time, and discovered that they were both out to bring a little something to Mr. Wilson. And his sons. Miss Dunn reminded Miss Crawford that she was Wallis's teacher. "I've taken extra care with the boy, now that he's an orphan. I've made an extra effort to keep *Frank* informed on Wallis's progress, which is excellent and a credit to *Frank* as a widowed father."

Miss Daldrup had accepted Amanda's invitation for supper with the family the next Saturday. Instead of returning on High Street, she chose west on Mina and north on Main for her walk to North Street. She met up with Miss Dunn and Miss Crawford just as they were crossing over to the north side of Mina on their short stroll to the Wilsons'. Miss Daldrup had a fleeting notion to forewarn the ladies that the Wilsons had company. On second thought, she decided to let them fend for themselves.

At 2:10, after the blackberry pie and scalloped potatoes had joined the perogies and other covered dishes on the north porch, Miss Dunn sat down at the parlor grand to play a medley of Stephen Foster favorites. Miss Dunn took the high part, Amanda and Miss Crawford doubled on the alto line, and Frank's was a strong tenor lead. Wallis despaired of getting much fishing in that afternoon.

Shortly after 3:00 a knock on the door interrupted the impromptu song-fest. Frank opened the door to greet the widow Mrs. Leighton who had been baking all day. She had walked from Vera and Netawaka with a basket of small bran muffins she called "gems" because of their size. Frank welcomed her into the parlor to warm greetings from Amanda and polite ones from the others. Miss Crawford's hand started for the basket to sample a gem, but Mrs. Leighton deftly moved closer to Frank and said with a twinkle, "Can you find a warm place for these?"

The Misses Dunn and Crawford and widow Leighton remained for another hour. Who would be the first to leave? Mrs. Leighton thought to herself that since she was the last to arrive and had traveled the farthest it shouldn't be she. Miss Crawford knew she had only a block to walk so that she could go whenever it suited her best interests. The case of Miss Dunn was complicated by the fact that she was Wallis's teacher. So, when the Seth Thomas clock in the living room stroked the half hour, she gathered her things and began her good-byes. Amanda walked her to the kitchen door and invited her to a return visit for supper next week. "No, better make it the week after that, say on the Monday?"

Miss Crawford managed to keep bantering to allow Miss Dunn time to get well beyond Main and Mina. She complimented Mrs. Leighton on her sensible choice of white summer shoes on such a warm November day. She happily accepted Amanda's invitation to return for dinner with just the family the week after next—toward the latter part of the week.

Mrs. Leighton, satisfied for having outstayed the others, said she should probably be getting back. Frank asked, "Would you like Wallis to walk with you? It'll be getting dark." Wallis was gladdened to hear that she could manage on her own. At the door, Amanda suggested that she come again, "for dinner this time, say the Saturday after Thanksgiving?"

Miss Hamlyn had just finished raking her leaves when Miss Crawford sat down to begin a long letter to her friend Delia Moore Alton in St. Joseph about the events of the day.

Frank unhitched the carriage, unpacked Wallis's fishing gear, and settled Turk for the night. Amanda organized labels of the contents and makers of the covered dishes, with notes about her invitations to return for a family supper. Wallis put away the cast-iron, horse-drawn toy fire equipment he had gotten out to show to Miss Dunn.

The family sat down at the round, black oak dining room table for a cold supper from their picnic basket just as the St. Leo's bell rang six o'clock.

MAILED NOV. 23. RECEIVED IN NORTONVILLE, NOV. 23.

Miss Irene Webb, Nortonville, Kansas

My Dear Friend Irene:

When I rec'd your kind letter of 6th inst. and learned that contrary to my suspicion, it had not occurred to you that there might be any impropriety in your paying me a visit at this time, I very much regretted having mentioned the matter. I feel guilty of a breach of etiquette, for which I sincerely beg your pardon. I suspected that this was your feeling, and that you hesitated about mentioning it, hence my awkward effort to release you from your promise, which has resulted in the loss of your visit. I am sure that my disappointment was greater than yours could be for I have looked forward to your coming with much pleasure, yet not without misgiving, lest I should fail to entertain you as you deserve, and as I would like to do.

Now as neither of us see any impropriety in your visit, and we have a mutual disregard for the criticisms of society, I think we might arrange for your visit at such time as may best suit your convenience. I am very anxious to see you I assure you. I hope you will consider yourself sufficiently invited and urged to come so that when it suits your convenience you will not hesitate to announce your coming. . . .

You observe that I usually select Sunday evening for this correspondence. It's now 11 o'clock, and as the fire is getting low I fear I shall catch cold if I don't stop. I am glad to hear that your father is improving, and trust that he will soon regain his usual health. We are all well excepting colds.

Mr. and Mrs. Henderson expect to spend Thanksgiving in Lawrence, so that I shall probably remain at home that day.

With very kind regards, I am

Sincerely Yours,

F. M. Wilson

ON THE MORNING BEFORE Thanksgiving the sky above Horton was a Romanesque clerestory of blue cobalt glass. Some forty Canada geese pierced the stillness, descending to a field of cornstalks across the river half a mile south of the Homestead Bank. The call of the geese came to ground unobstructed by sounds from the locomotive works, which had closed for the holiday. The three customers, the teller, and two officers of the bank paused their conversations and listened for the entire eleven minutes it took the formation to circle and settle into the granary of strewn field corn. Who could not smile? An already-sparkling day had brightened with the short chorale.

When St. Leo's bell struck twelve, Frank shook everyone's hand and wished Thanksgiving happiness. He gave Pearl McCall, his teller and sister-in-law, a hug and whispered, "Our Allie is surely happy this day."

Pearl responded with a silent squeeze and warm smile. Pearl was five years younger than Allie and more robust in physique. Measles had struck Allie as an infant in the exodus from the burning of Atlanta. That hardship and fright had added to her mother's resentment over aspirations extinguished by the Union Army. But Allie and Pearl had refused to inherit hatred from their mother, whether over the tragedy of Atlanta or the tragedy of Allie.

Frank locked the front door of the bank and struck out north along Main Street, the bright sun warming the nape of his neck. Frank felt a liking of life that had eluded him for several months. He looked in the front window of the funeral home and waved to Mr. Lubie. He crossed the street to shake hands with Eric Thornton who was standing in front of his blacksmith shop. Eric shoved his right palm down the side of his leather apron before extending it to pump Frank's hand in a grip that could have bent a nail. Eric said,

"Good paint, no? Glad it's on before winter. Couldn't have done it without the loan. You here for pay it back?"

Frank stood flexing his fingers and admiring the shop's fresh coat of paint—white with black trim and lettering—and said, "No, Mr. Thornton, you just bring in payments when you can. Spring will be fine since business is bound to slow down in winter. Just came over to wish happy Thanksgiving to you and Helga and the girls. How old are they now?"

"Janet turned fourteen last week. Tonya's eleven. I let 'em paint the back of the place, at least as far up as the haymow. Tonya bossed the job like always. She thinks highly of your Wallis. Missus is fine. Sure too bad about your Missus. You thinking to court anybody?"

"Never know, Eric. Never know. I expect no time soon. Winter coming on and all. Lot more on my mind right now."

Eric stood quietly, then tapped Frank's chest with an index finger the size of a trout and said, "No bank business more important than you get a good woman, Mr. Wilson. You let money take over your life, maybe you get to where you can't . . . you know . . . stand like a stallion." Eric threw his head skyward and roared a long, rolling laugh until his knees weakened and he had to lean on the hitching post.

Frank chuckled and waited for the blacksmith to collect himself. Then he said, "Sound advice, Eric. Sure wouldn't want that. Hah! No sir! Well, look, I'm mighty glad we had a chance to talk. You've got a fine family there. And don't worry about the loan. I mean, it wouldn't do for money worries to take over your life. Poor Helga, if that ever happened!" At that, Thornton lifted his head for another howling laugh, and could hardly return Frank's wave as he continued on his way north on Main.

This had been another morning that Frank had wakened not watching his wife die. And this morning was the second or third time so far in November like that. He inhaled deeply. Someone was burning leaves. He saw that Elizabeth Hamlyn's geraniums were still standing. Elizabeth was attractive, he thought, and, um, what else? She brought a casserole to us. She has a clever hand with watercolors. She's always writing a strong letter to the editor. She's about my age. But . . . well, that's pretty much all. I don't feel any spark there.

But I do with Irene. High time I paid a call. Afraid she might be seeing someone. Or engaged even. Can't take anything for granted. She is fine in every way. I mean, the eyes alone. And bright and quick and deep all at the same time. Saw that when she was here with us. Couldn't say anything, of course. I mean, Allie. And I never really thought about her like that. Not with Allie right there. Well, if I did I made myself stop. Irene's from good stock. Goodness, they've farmed there since before the War. She's the perfect age for bringing new children into my life. If I'm to remarry at all, then I would want that. And she is so pretty.

Frank stopped in front of the Presbyterian church on Main. On Sundays Frank, a Protestant, took from churches as from a smorgasbord. He was not one to split doctrinal hairs, and sought out good choirs and short sermons. He did enjoy the thrall of Easter service at St. Leo's.

Looking up at the steeple, he thought, Allie, what do I do? Silence and bright sunlight were the only replies. Yes, not going to get any help out of the blue. Have to sort it out alone. I wonder how Irene feels?

He turned and walked around the rear of the church to where the pioneer headstones stood, some tipped at an angle. It was a country church before Horton was even built. He sat on a bench under a maple tree with scarlet leaves. Well, Frank, he thought, just how do you really feel? Have to start with that. The rest doesn't matter without knowing that. Not what are all her good points and her rain-gray eyes: how do you feel?

I could easily love her. I could easily ask her to live in Horton with me. Married to me. Not married to anyone else. Oh, God! Absolutely not that. So, that's that. Court her. Get engaged if you're lucky. Long courtships and short engagements. Could take a year. Boys would be older and could get used to the idea. She'd have all that time without disruptions to get prepared. Give everyone in her family and mine time to plan. He waited, half expecting some kind of sign telling him these were dangerous thoughts. He heard only doves and a distant calf bawling. Yes, I'm thinking I could fall in love again. I could with Irene. He stood up and thought, You'll never know just sitting around. Have to recognize it's time to get something started. Not going to get any younger.

Frank circled the church back to Main. He started up the sloping Mina Street to High Street and his home on the corner. God love you, Allie. I know I still do. Oh, this is hard.

I love the spirit that lived inside your fragile body. Your strength was in your spirit more than in your frame. That spirit and your constant smile were always enough to prevail over whoever chose to contradict you. Henderson would shake his head and say your smile actually brought customers to the bank. You smiled when our children were born and, after tears, when half of them died. In the end I could not protect the spirit behind the smile. What you said to me in that hospital will live in me forever,

"You are my only smile a day."

AT NOON ON THAT day, Irene had said, "Mother, I want to invite Mr. Wilson for a Sunday with us just as soon as he can get here. He'd be here through dinner and I'd spend quite a bit of time with him and him alone."

"That would be grand, Irene, but this isn't a good time for me or your father to be having company in right now." Mrs. Irene Webb had given life to ten children, three of whom were buried before they reached their third years. When not occupied with her own childbearing, she had seen to the labors of the mares and cows of the farm. She was slightly taller than her husband, Hiram, and the upward tilt of her head with its full, snow-white hair would have reminded one of a Romanoff countess had anyone in Nortonville, Kansas, given any thought to what a Romanoff might have looked like. She had a beautiful, mezzo-soprano singing voice that had enchanted Irene since childhood. Her breath had not been able to sustain long phrases for the last four years, however. Her climb up the stairs was more labored. Her shoulders slumped. Dresses she had worn for years were now loose around her.

"Mother, there is no better time than right now . . . before winter brings more sickness on top of what's already come. Before the weather sets in and puts a halt to everything till next year sometime. The men in Nortonville either see right past me or don't fancy what they see. I'm not going to meet a man like Mr. Wilson in Nortonville, and I'm not even sure I can get him to come for a Sunday. Mary Elizabeth got married and she's got her own family.

Lydia got married. You're forever saying, 'Baby Tot: last but not least.' What am I now, Mama? Last, and little Cinderella girl on this farm?"

Her mother bowed her head and held out her arms. Irene walked into her embrace which she held during a long silence. My baby Tot, now a strong, capable woman with her own life to lead. My Hiram so sick. Six children out of the nest, and soon, maybe even last-but-not-least. It hurts to think of living alone. Oh God . . . dying alone. She shivered. The back of her throat ached. Then she lifted her head and shook off a craving to cling.

"What a brilliant idea, Tot," her mother said with enthusiasm. "As yours always are. You are absolutely right, it's time we had company. Had family around. We need to have a Sunday dinner like we used to. Sweep and scrub the place of summer dust and sickly air. This banker friend: you've always spoken so highly of him and he did so much for you in Horton. Of course this is the perfect time to show him our Webb hospitality. And you are also absolutely right, there aren't many like him in this town, Nortonville's only banker being profoundly married as it is. I'll have a talk with Hiram. He'd do anything for you, Tot."

Irene brushed dampness from the corner of her eye with her hand and said, "I'll write that letter to Mr. Wilson right now and mail it in the morning. You explain to Papa that we're inviting Mr. F. M. Wilson for company next Sunday or the one after that."

"Tot, when you were there with the Wilsons that year, did you have the notion that he could be taking an interest in you?"

Her mother's face was impassive, but she thought something of the sort must be behind this flurry of letters and insistence on inviting him for a visit.

Irene gave her an honest shrug and squeezed her hand. I hope so, she thought to herself, and went to her room to tend to her correspondence.

Dear Mr. Wilson,

I should like very much indeed to visit Mrs. Alton this week and meet you there but I fear it will be impossible. Neither Papa nor Mamma are well and I do not feel that I should be gone from home until "the folks" are stronger. . . .

I think I have a very good substitute for our brief visit at Mrs. Alton's. It is this—that you spend next Sunday with us. While our visit at Mrs. A's would doubtless be very pleasant yet the associations would recall very vividly to your mind your great sorrow and the grief you suffered there. I am sure our visit will be pleasanter here—that is, if you will be content with a very quiet visit. I cannot promise you any attraction—save a very plain Sunday dinner. I think the best route to come is to leave Horton on that 4:30 p.m. train Sat., spend the night in St. Joe and come to Nortonville Sunday morning. Train leaves St. Joe about 7 and arrives at Nortonville at 9. Unless it is storming I shall be pleased to meet you.

If it is, anyone can direct you to Hiram Webb's. Please let me hear that we may expect you.

Sincerely,
Irene Webb

Miss Irene Webb, Nortonville, Kansas
Dec. 10, 1896

My Dear Friend Irene,

I rec'd your letter yesterday morning. You certainly have a good excuse for not leaving home at this time and I cheerfully excuse you.

Your suggestions, and your kind invitation for me to visit you next Sunday meet my approval, and I cheerfully accept the invitation. I think I shall act upon your suggestions as to route, and be with you Sunday morning. I had often wondered how I could visit you, in the time which I ordinarily have to spare, but never succeeded in figuring it out.

I have no idea now how I will get back home, but you have so kindly figured out a way for me to go, that I shall trust you to find a way for me to return. I assure you that I shall appreciate a quiet day with you at home, very much more than a meeting at St. Joe. My principal reason for suggesting the latter was, that I could see you, knowing your fondness for a good theatrical attraction, and your intention to visit Mrs. Alton anyway, it occurred to me that it would be pleasant all around.

Sincerely, your friend,
F. M. Wilson

CHAPTER TWO

LIFE SEEMS TO HAVE A SWEETER

AND DEEPER MEANING TO ME

SINCE I LAST SAW YOU

MORNING ONE

On the morning of Sunday, December 13, 1896, sunlight arrived at Nortonville Station just an hour ahead of the westbound Atchison, Topeka and Santa Fe long-train of passenger and freight cars out of St. Joseph, Missouri. Irene sat in the buggy, hands in a woolen muff, face steaming into a pale yellow scarf, head covered in a tight-fitting red woolen hat, and watched frost patches dissolve into the station's roof and unshaded wooden platform.

She clenched against the clangs and chuffs and bangs of the arriving train. Then Frank stepped to the platform, a tan leather valise in one hand and paper cone of long-stemmed red roses in the other. He looked around briefly before the locomotive's escaping steam enveloped his entire frame. But he had glimpsed her and was soon walking from the cloud toward her, wearing a full grin. The separation of three and a half years had not dulled their ability to speak in unison,

"Here, these are for you . . ."

"Here, this is for you . . ."

Irene handed him a heavy, oozy yellow pear from the tree her father had planted for her, and accepted his roses as he settled next to her. They looked at each other through smiles and hearty hellos. She could not stop looking at the red-bristle mustache she had never seen before; nor could she stifle a short laugh. Surprise deprived her of words, so she resorted to pointing—actually touching his lip. He lifted his eyebrows. She blushed. He intoned, "Winter approaching, I grew a mustache."

He beamed in triumph—he had scored an ablative absolute! Irene groaned and smiled. So, this is how it is to be, she thought, this game all over again, from the very start. The two of them had discovered mutual fun trading sentence constructions at breakfasts until Allie, not able to keep up with the game, had asked them to stop—for the boys' sake. She shot him a look that said, "I'll get you," and flicked a rein across Bluebelle's haunches.

He then took a conciliatory tack. "You look wonderful, Miss Webb, as beautiful as ever."

She looked directly ahead, reached into her coat pocket, and handed him a single sheet of paper. "Attend," she commanded.

Frank, who had hoped for lighter banter, studied the sheet with care. It contained names. *Hiram, father. Irene, mother. Lydia Melisa, sister ten years older, now Miller, husband Henry, living in Atchison. Stephen and Dennis, older brothers, Valley Falls, wives can't come. Alfred, brother, two years older but, to me, my baby brother, nicknamed "Ton" and I'm "Tot" and it doesn't matter why. Ton lives in Topeka; wife Bessie. Mary Elizabeth McVey, Nortonville, husband Jerret, daughter Maggie Rea.* Frank began to adjust his other hopes of spending unhurried time with Irene this weekend. "Will they all be there today?" he asked.

Irene thought, *This is the best I can do with Mother, Mr. F. M. Wilson. It boiled down to either all family, and you, or no one, not even you.* "Probably most of them, I'm not sure. You can learn the deceased ones later," she said with a grin.

Frank said with a sigh, "Ah, thanks for keeping it a small gathering."

She laughed and said, "Well, we might have had Uncle Doctor Webb but he couldn't come today. He's the only doctor in Nortonville. That's a good-looking scarf. The roses are perfect."

"Thank you. I should abstain from this pear but it's delicious."

Bluebelle and the buggy were now about halfway between Nortonville Station and the Hiram Webb place. The black, stiffly furrowed fields bore a soft lawn of October-planted winter wheat, giving the landscape a scant mossy look. The stream near the road moved darkly under a thin skin of ice. Quail called from piles of brush and slash at the edge of the plowing.

Frank decided he should address a matter of importance before they became engulfed in Webbs. He said,

"Irene, I know we haven't been in touch much since you left Horton. You wrote that beautiful thank-you letter. I know Allie never answered it. I didn't feel right making a separate correspondence, of course, and so here we are and I don't know what you've done since you left. Did you go back to university?"

Irene frowned over what Allie's thinking might have been, and replied simply, "Yes, thank you. I did the semester after my visit that Christmas, but not after that. Then I came back to the farm. Much as I enjoyed being in Lawrence, and in classes, there is always so much to do here, and my parents are beginning to slow down. Every day is so filled that it's actually a relief to be away from the worries of exams and papers. Have you had other teachers boarding with you and Mrs. Wilson since I left?"

"No. Actually, Mrs. Wilson decided that we wouldn't be offering that accommodation to the school board. You were the one and only."

"Allie decided?"

"Well, she and her mother pretty much made up their minds that school business didn't mix that well with personal life. I'm away at the bank all day, so I can't really have much say in the matter. But the two of them seemed sure that home life would be easier for Allie that way."

Irene looked straight ahead. Her smile had disappeared. She was subdued by the implications of the new information about Allie. She thought, So Allie was uncomfortable when I was there. We were so close. She was jealous? Seems so. How terrible if she carried that to her grave. I can't tolerate that thought. Still, she was determined to not be sad today.

"Anyway, we can go into that later." Frank paused. "I want to ask you something else right now." Frank's eyelid twitched.

He swallowed. He mustered a smile, and asked, as if for directions to the next farm, "Are you seeing someone now, Miss Webb? Is there a man in your life?"

Irene smiled. She tried to sound nonchalant. "No, Mr. Wilson. My life is pretty uncomplicated here."

"No more adventures to carnivals with miscreant admirers?"

"You!" she exclaimed. "I'll thank you to pack that anecdote off to oblivion."

She turned to him and said more warmly, "But I'm very glad to see you today and for you to meet the family."

"And would you favor the idea that I might continue to pay you calls and keep up our correspondence?"

"That would suit me very well, thank you. Here we are. This is our paradise. Home sweet home. That's my father coming to help with Bluebelle. You've got a whole lot of pear juice on your face." She lowered her voice to unloose her projectile: "Hiram approaching, the mustache goes soggy."

Frank grinned broadly as he shook Hiram's hand, then relaxed his grip when he discovered how weak Hiram's was. Mrs. Webb quickly joined them and said, "Welcome to the place, Mr. Wilson. We are so sorry for your loss, and regret we could not have known Mrs. Wilson ourselves. Irene has always spoken very highly of her. Anyway, it's a pleasure to meet you finally. We appreciate your warm hospitality for Irene when she taught in Horton. Come in and meet the family. You don't have to remember all the names. It's more than I can do myself at times. No, really. And when a name slips my mind I just call them Fred." They both laughed.

The quickness with which Frank could sum long columns of figures was matched only by his quick study of names. He moved easily among the Webbs and asked pointed questions about farms and businesses in Valley Falls, Atchison, Nortonville and Topeka, as appropriate. Hiram gave a strong-voiced and overlong grace. The "very plain Sunday dinner" took thirty minutes to just pass from hand to hand in platters of cold meats, fried chicken, bowls of creamed, mashed root vegetables laced with butter, rolls and cornbread, sliced radishes and apples sprinkled with cinnamon, and hot coffee. The banter was companionable, the laughter genuine, and Irene's prayer that none of her brothers would tell a banker joke was answered.

Hiram moved to a chair next to Frank, which Ton had vacated to join a horseshoes match on the side lawn. He said, "Mr. Wilson, tell me what Horton's like. I was there only once and that was eight years ago."

"Well, there is no doubt it has grown since then. But those of us involved in what goes on there day-to-day realize that the claims of the promoters ten years ago were wildly unrealistic. Oh, we've done a lot. The population was four hundred when I moved there in 1886. Now it's ten times that. We finally finished lining the streets with elms that are now head high or taller.

The town's spirit is tied to the Rock Island works, Mr. Webb. That's what pushes us. But I don't see us ever becoming a 'Chicago' that was all the talk back when you came over. The farms around the town have their ups and downs, as I'm sure you know very well yourself. Our bank is lucky. We get railroad payday deposits and we make land and crop loans to hard-working farm families."

Hiram was quiet for a moment, then coughed. He said, "That still sounds more bustling than our lives on Section Eight. Webbs pioneered these parts. We added on by whatever surpluses we got, not much from borrowed money. I admire bankers, not like some folks. I burned our one small mortgage about the time Ton and Tot came along. Right now, we've got about five hundred acres free and clear. We'll go mostly between field corn and soy beans, some in cattle. We're close to the railroad and the Missouri markets. Our ups and downs have been mostly ups, Mr. Wilson, so we've been blessed.

"I think I'll go upstairs for a lie-down, if you'll excuse me, Mr. Wilson. Irene very much admires you, sir. I can see why. Very glad to have met you."

He and Mrs. Webb retired to the upstairs bedroom. In the shank of the afternoon, the Valley Falls Webbs began to move off in the receding sunlight of the solstice to their homes.

Frank gave a quizzical look to Irene since it was she who had figured out his return schedule. She had arranged that he would be taking the Atchison, Topeka and Santa Fe's last train eastward that evening to St. Joseph and staying with the Altons again, returning to Horton on Monday morning at 10:30 on the Rock Island Line. The afternoon was slipping away, so it then became imperative for Frank and Irene to bundle up for the ride to Nortonville Station. Irene insisted that Frank carry an enormous wicker basket of fried chicken, rolls, pickled vegetables and cucumber salad for the Altons and Frank to enjoy later that evening. She also filled Frank's ear with congratulatory messages to the Altons on their new house and abundant Christmas greetings. Feeling some pressure of the schedule, Frank and Irene stepped quickly into the late-afternoon dusk, and Irene set Bluebelle to a brisk trot to the station. He regretted having to leave before saying goodbye to the Webbs directly.

Frank managed to take Irene's right hand from the reins for a few moments and hold it in both his hands. "Today has been a wonderful reunion with you, Irene. You have never looked lovelier to me than today. You reflect your mother's grace and your father's wit and wise character. You have made me feel glad to be alive."

Irene replied, "I could not have imagined a better first visit from you, dear friend. You mustn't try to turn my head—it might be so easy that you'd have to deal with the consequences. This is a wonderful beginning. I know we both feel that same sentiment."

Suddenly she retrieved her hand, whooped, and gave a full stroke of the reins to Bluebelle, who broke into a run. She gestured westward with her head where Frank saw a plume of gray smoke in the distance. Since the loco-motive would take on water and fuel at Nortonville, there was no danger of actually missing the train. Still, Irene made sure that Bluebelle did her part of the plan.

At the station there was no time for long good-byes. When Frank stood at the top steps of his car to look back, Irene made a broad gesture with her pointed index finger to her upper lip, and then a melodramatic movement with her fist there, pulling at something and flinging it away high into the dusk. A beguiled Frank grinned, and nodded.

Miss Irene Webb, Nortonville, Kansas
December 20, 1896

My Dearest Friend Irene,

One week ago tonight I was with you in person, and in spirit. Tonight I must content myself with the presence of the spirit only. This has been another beautiful Sabbath day, and how I have wished that I might spend it as I did last Sabbath. It is needless for me to tell you that I enjoyed my visit very much, my reluctance to leave was quite sufficient proof. I felt very much ashamed of myself that in the excitement of my departure, I so far forgot myself as to leave your home without bidding farewell to your father and mother, and thanking them for their kind hospitality.

I trust that you, who knew the condition of my mind, and the thoughts which were uppermost there, will pardon the neglect. I feel highly honored by the attentions shown me while in your home, and I shall not soon forget the event. Indeed I trust that the events of that day shall never be forgotten by either of us, for they mark the beginning of a friendship between us, closer, and dearer, than that which has heretofore existed, and we have been good friends ever since we first met.

I have always held you in very high esteem, and admired your beautiful character, and am sure that Allie shared me in this esteem and admiration, though I am not sure but that my admiration for you, at times may have aroused a slight feeling of jealousy upon her part. I would not mention this except as an answer to the question which you put to me last Sunday evening, which I left but partially answered.

You could not fail to see that my visit last Sunday was one of great pleasure, not however unmixed with sadness. You have been the subject of my thoughts almost every hour of every day since we parted. How I wish that you lived in Horton so that I might see you every day, and be with you often.

If there is anything in the old adage "Absence makes the heart grow fonder" I presume that our hearts will have a splendid chance to grow in that direction. I do not believe in that doctrine however.

I reached home at noon last Monday, having an uneventful trip, and finding all trains on time. I called on Mr. Alton and delivered your message. He seemed pleased to know that you would visit them, and suggested that it would be very convenient for me to run up to St. Joe while you are there, to which I readily assented.

I hope that your father and mother are both improving in health. Give them my kindest regards.

Wishing you all a Merry Christmas I am

Yours affectionately,
F. M. Wilson

"DID YOU KISS HIM?"

"That's a complicated question, Maggie Rea. Moreover, it is impolite."

"I guess you didn't cover that in university. I thought you might at least kiss him for a start, Aunt Tot. And then maybe go on to have his babies and after that go work in that bank, counting out the money. Or maybe I should just kiss him."

"I am smartly dressed and you have on bib overalls the cat won't sleep on. Get yourself decent if you still want to go with me to town to mail my letter."

"I'll take it in myself, you just stay here where it's warm. I'll run all the way."

"I'm going to walk down the stairs and out the door."

"I'll only be a few more minutes. Could you iron your black skirt and let me wear it to town?"

"There's an article somewhere on my dresser on that hospital in Topeka. You should read it. The people there are very kind."

Her smile let cold morning air stun her teeth as she set off for the station.

Mr. F. M. Wilson, Horton, Kansas
December 23, 1896

My dear Mr. Santa Claus,

Your beautiful Christmas greeting came safely yesterday morning. I could not imagine what in the world such an enormous box could contain—I thought of most everything and finally concluded as I rode along with my curiosity almost overwhelming me that there must be a corner lot or something along that line in it. I carried the box into the house and began undoing it—At first I found only paper and paper—then some more paper. I concluded my corner lot wasn't there but another layer of paper was removed and my exquisite present was revealed. It is perfectly lovely and I am so pleased with it—only I think you should not have gotten anything so very expensive. The mirror is the most beautiful one I ever saw and I shall always prize it very highly. Please do accept my sincere thanks for your remembrance. I trust you had a happy Xmas. We had a very happy time. My brother Ton and his wife Bessie are still with us and will remain till Monday. I received Mr. Alton's address and have written them of my plan. If my coming will be convenient for them I shall go either New Year's or the Saturday afterward. I received a great many beautiful gifts of which I shall tell you at another time. I have such a lovely box of flowers. Also a beautiful palm and quantities of holly and mistletoe.

Sincerely,
Irene Webb

MRS. MCCALL STRUGGLED WITH the twisted handles of a cloth bag that held an acorn squash and cans of evaporated milk, soup, and spinach. She shifted the bag to her left hand and rattled the front doorknob of the house at High and Mina. Annoyed to find it locked, she descended the broad steps of the porch and made a right turn to try the door to the kitchen. She elected to walk close to the evergreen shrubs next to the house rather than use the road. As a result, her shoes crackled patches of leftover snow and occasionally slipped, nearly sending her to the ground. Finally she scuffled up to the stoop of the south porch and turned the doorknob.

The door opened and she pushed into the kitchen as she had every day for fifteen years. Frank's mother flinched and blurted, "Oh! You gave me a fright! You got a wolf after you and can't knock?"

"Very well, thank you, and you?" said Mrs. McCall as she lowered herself into the kitchen rocker. "Such a warm welcome. And yes, I would enjoy a cup of tea. And no, I can't stay for supper, but that's kind of you." She gave Amanda a smirk.

Wallis, who had been helping Amanda roll out and cut biscuits, was slowly edging his way to the door to the north porch. "Wallis, where have you been? I haven't seen you since you shoveled my sidewalk after the storm. Have you spent your dimes already?"

"Hi Gramma. No, I put them in the piggy bank. Well, I got a little behind in school so that's why I haven't been by."

"Really? What classes, Wallis?" He squirmed and looked at Amanda, who frowned. He said, "Math."

"And no one around here's helping you with that? Like I do? Not even the banker? So busy, I suppose. Can't see what's going on under his own eyes.

"Goodness, Mrs. Wilson, are those meant to be biscuits? You need to roll them thinner. Let me show you." She heaved herself to her feet and reached for the rolling pin. Amanda snatched it away, saying,

"Do you mind? We prefer ours light and flaky. Do you want to put any of your things on the north porch? Not have to carry 'em back home all at once?"

"I might at that. Wallis, why don't you bring them to me tomorrow."

Amanda moved to stand between Mrs. McCall and Wallis, flour-covered fists on hips. "Because, Mrs. McCall, Wallis will be here tomorrow helping with getting the house ready for Christmas. Your things will keep fine on the porch. You can stop by in a couple of weeks to collect them. The kettle should be hot. You know where we keep the tea. All ready for Christmas?"

"It'll be a sad one for us without Allie, that's for sure. Appears you'll be here, not in Holton. That'll be nice for you. You livin' alone and all. I'm happy to coach Wallis in his math. Where'd he disappear to?" Wallis had slipped out from behind Amanda and decamped to his room.

Amanda said, "Wallis is as bright as a pin and can take care of himself when he puts his mind to it. He can do better than most on his own. I don't hold with doing a child's work for him and I'll thank you not to as well."

Mrs. McCall snorted, "When did you get the charter to take over how Wallis gets along in school? I've got the knack with numbers and there's no harm in showing it to him."

Amanda put down her rolling pin and faced her, fists on hips again. "There is if you do all the answers and he doesn't learn it himself. It so happens his teacher told him that his tests in class aren't matching his homework. The homework that he does over at your place. Or that *somebody* does."

Mrs. McCall took a step closer and thrust her fists on her own hips. "Well, Mrs. Wilson, I don't see that what he does at my place is any of your business at all. You should be glad someone sees to the lessons he has to turn in. I don't hear anyone sayin' you're much good at that. That'd be Miss Dunn who's his teacher, right? My Allie was on the board that hired that girl. I think I know her a whole lot better than you or anyone else from Holton does."

Amanda tilted her head, squinted, and said, "Don't get me riled up, Mrs. McCall!"

Mrs. McCall twisted her mouth, leaned forward, and growled, "You rile yourself up. Riled over nothing. Your son sits there in his bank on top of the savings of this entire town. You sit here all cozy, soaking up the affections of this family. My daughter's family! Your own home is empty and loveless! You sit here and pass judgments on me! About how I deal with my own grandsons! And my Allie, who made this home and raised these boys, my Allie lies stiff out in that frozen ground! *You haven't earned the right to be angry!*"

The women glared at one another.

Wallis appeared in the door and announced, "Papa's coming up Mina Street. Just thought I'd say."

Amanda went to the rocker and picked up the other grandmother's coat. She hung it over the crook of her elbow and said, "Yes, and it's starting to get dark out. Might do well to start on home."

Amanda stood stock-still, unsmiling. Mrs. McCall hesitated. She said, "Mrs. Wilson, we'll continue this later. I'll be back for my groceries myself. Real soon." She took her coat and pushed her arms through the sleeves. She took Wallis by the hand and they walked to the front door just as Frank was coming up the porch stairs.

"Merry Christmas, Mrs. McCall. You leaving already? Come have a cup of tea to warm up."

"I'm plenty hot without tea, thank you, Mr. Wilson. Plenty hot, believe you me. Merry Christmas." She brushed past Frank and headed north on High Street.

Frank came into the hallway. What was that about? he wondered. He shrugged and glanced up at the mirror over the hall table. He turned his head left and right. Not bad. Better without the mustache, too. "What a good-looking fellow, don't you think?"

Wallis giggled and said, "Papa, Miss Johannes came by. She brought a covered dish. She and I put it out on the north porch."

Wallis helped Frank off with his overcoat. Frank put the mail and some loan papers from the bank on the table. He said, "That's nice of her. So what's in it?"

"She said she made extra stuffing and we need to keep it cold. I told her the north porch is where we keep things like that. She went out there and said it was perfect. No heat from the house. She put it on the long table under the window."

"Oh. I suppose it's next to the other ones."

"Gramma Wilson covered those with dish towels, remember?"

Frank laughed. "Right. Well, I'm sorry I missed her. Did you ask her to stay a bit?"

"Yes, I did. She sat in the rocker. We sort of ran out of things to talk about. I think she was hoping to see you. She said she'd come by in a day or so. She left a little while ago."

"You're a polite boy, Wallis. I'm proud of you. A lot more agreeable than you were a couple of years ago."

"That was before Mama died. I'm trying to act more grown-up now, like you told me."

"Well, you certainly have improved. You should still have fun, you know."

"I know. But I mess up sometimes."

"What do you mean? Like, for example?"

"Aw, never mind. Can I go?"

"Yes. Tell me if there's something you need to talk to me about."

"I will." Wallis took the front stairs two at a time.

Frank thought how much more mature Wallis had become after Allie's death. Wallis had wept openly and often. Not like Frank who wept in solitude. He could never find pat answers to Wallis's questions about her: Why? Where is she, really? What is heaven, really? So Frank stuck pretty much to platitudes. Frank had nearly drowned in platitudes.

The Book of Common Prayer was his best source for his own comfort, and seemingly for Wallis and Harold as well. "Hear what comfortable words our Saviour Christ saith unto all who truly turn to him. Come unto me, all ye that travail and are heavy laden, and I will refresh you." Explaining to Harold such things as "travail" and "laden" helped divert the conversations from morose sinkholes.

Frank longed to be refreshed more often. The days at the bank were long, and then managing the household and raising two sons made for another day's work when he returned home. Amanda helped, but not when it came to the strain of those questions. He shook off the dreary thoughts and tried to put Christmas into his mind.

He opened a letter from Nortonville.

Mr. F. M. Wilson, Horton, Kansas
Wednesday night—10 o'clock
December 23, 1896

My Dear Friend,

. . . I am glad you enjoyed your visit with us. It all seems very strange to me as I recall the hours we spent together. Very strange indeed. How I wish I might see you tonight—There are so many things I want to tell you and this old pen moves so much slower than my thoughts. I shall be ever so glad to see you at Mrs. Alton's and I trust that our mutual friend will be considerate enough to let us entertain ourselves at least one evening when I can feel free to talk to you of those things which I feel you ought to know.

One or two of your questions were answered only in part if I remember correctly. Somehow my mind was not as clear that night as it usually is. I think you understand what I am trying to say, don't you? I thank you from my heart, my Dear friend, for your beautiful tribute to my womanhood. It never occurred to me that I am any better looking than any other girl. You must not indulge in heroics; you may cause me to become vain! I am very much astonished to know that you even suspicion that Allie ever felt as you suggested. Really, I think you are mistaken. If she did feel so it was most noble and beautiful in her never to reveal her feeling to me. She was always so lovely to me. She was my ideal of all that is pure and womanly and good. I never dreamt that she ever had the shadow of a jealous feeling. I always appreciated your admiration for me. I regarded it as the same kind of admiration which I have always felt for you and that kind of a feeling will ever be an inspiration for good to a true man or woman. May we ever be worthy of such my dear friend. As I told you in my little note yesterday life seems to have a sweeter and deeper meaning to me since I last saw you. I believe you entirely sincere and good and true. I hope the occasion of Christmas may not be as sad as you feared. I know you are lonely and everything suggests your sweet wife to you—but dear heart, do not grieve too deeply. Do you know I always feel at such a loss to know what to say to people who are sad? My heart goes out to them in sympathy but I can't tell them my feelings. Some people know just what to say and how to say it but I am not one of those fortunate ones. I thought of you Sunday night and I felt that you were writing to me. I dreamed too that night about you. I'll tell you my dreams someday if you will promise not to tell—will you? . . .

. . . I think I shall go to Atchison and St. Joe next week but I cannot tell definitely until I hear from Mrs. Alton. . . .

How kind of Mr. Alton to invite you up. I send a Christmas kiss to the children—will you deliver them for me.

Sincerely,
Irene Webb

P.S. Do you mean to say that I resemble The Girl Everybody Likes? Do you like a girl whom everybody likes? Let's see. This is logical—Major premise. You like the girl whom everybody likes. Minor premise. Irene is like the girl whom everybody likes. Conclusion. Irene is like the girl whom you like. You will admit that both premises are true and if they are true you can't avoid the conclusion—See! From present appearances we are going to have an ideal Christmas. I enjoy this weather as much as the sunshiney days. I hope that 1897 may bring to you only the best of everything.

Irene

Miss Irene Webb, Nortonville, Kansas

My Dearest Friend Irene,

Your beautiful Christmas letter was rec'd by me upon my return from Holton Christmas night, and was I assure you the most highly prized gift received by me. . . .

I found a sprig of Mistletoe in your last note. I guess you thought this sprig was dead, and couldn't talk. I thought once I heard it trying to speak to me, but when I got out my book, and begun the study of its language, I concluded that I was mistaken. I feel quite sure now that this sprig was quite dead before you mailed it to me.

I know you wouldn't send me a real live sprig that could talk.

I am glad to know that you appreciate my little gift. I don't know whether it can talk or not. I failed to inquire before sending it. If you find that it does, and it doesn't talk real nice, please return it and I will have its fangs removed. I am sure however that you will find much beauty if you look at it closely. I didn't see it when I looked into it, but I am sure that you will have no difficulty in finding it.

I am glad to hear that you expect to visit Mrs. Alton so soon, and I heartily join you in the hope that they will permit us to be alone. You will let me know of your arrival there and when it will be most agreeable for me to spend an evening with you. Saturday evenings would be most convenient for me but possibly next Saturday would be too soon after your arrival. I leave it all to you however, and I will try to come when it best suits you. I am so anxious to see you again. How I do wish that I could see you every day. I wish, but wishes are vain.

We'll have to build a private telephone, or something along that line. Excuse me I guess if we had such a line we would keep it in constant use, that is if you would do the most of the talking. I am a good listener and could promise you an audience. I shall be delighted to hear the many things which you have saved up for me, and especially all about your dream, which will be a close secret between us. I promise to tell you all my dreams, and I must hear yours. Do you believe in the fatality of dreams? They certainly have a great significance and I am anxious to hear your first one.

The kisses which you sent to the children for Christmas were cold when they arrived, but I warmed them over and delivered them. I was sorry they were not fresh and sweet, as I know they were when started. I wish some enterprising Yankee would invent a means of transmitting kisses without the loss of the flavor and fragrance. I would buy the first one for sale. You have disposed of "the Girl everybody likes" in a very logical manner, and the conclusion is irresistible. I confess in full. You have cornered me.

Wallis went to Powhattan yesterday morning to visit a boy friend who invited him out for a jack rabbit chase. We expected him home last night but he has not yet returned. He is doubtless wild with delight, and concluded to remain until tomorrow. The rabbits up in that locality are numerous, and the sport is immense. They hunt with dogs only, and do not attempt to shoot them. The Andrews Opera Co. rendered the Mikado here last Wednesday night. This is the 4th time I have seen the Mikado, but I do not tire of it. The Opera is my favorite amusement. Light-comic opera is my preference.

I heartily agree with you that Mr. Alton is a very nice man. He is certainly a model husband if I know anything about him. I don't know of any man among my acquaintances who treats his wife with more courtesy and consideration.

Well my dear I must stop. If I were with you, I wouldn't be in a hurry about it, but I expect you would send me to bed if you knew what time it is. So Good Night!

Very Affectionately,
F. M. Wilson

Mr. F. M. Wilson, Horton, Kansas
Atchison, Friday Evening, January 1, 1897

Dear Mr. Wilson,

I herewith enclose Mrs. Alton's letter. I guess there are no secrets in it. If there are you will keep them. I came down here this morning and will go over to St. Joseph tomorrow afternoon. I think Monday or Tuesday evening would be a suitable time for you to visit us. On account of my Father's health my visit at St. J. will have to be somewhat brief. I feel that I cannot leave him to stay longer than Wednesday or Thursday. I talked with Mrs. A. over the telephone this afternoon and she insists upon my staying a month with her. A month! Just think of it—Wouldn't you pity her? My Sunday letter came on Monday night and was read with the usual pleasure and interest. If you want to make evening dates you might come up to St. J. Sunday evening. Any evening will suit me and I should remain over next Sunday—a week from this coming Sunday—if I thought Papa could spare me. I shall answer your lovely letter in person so will tell you Good Night and Happy New Year. Write me a note when to expect you at St. J.

Sincerely,
Irene Webb

Care E. K. Alton, St. Joseph, Missouri
Jan 3d, 1897

My Dearest Friend Irene:

All things considered I think Tuesday evening will suit my convenience best, to visit you and if there is no preventing providence, or something along that line, you may look for me, at Mr. Alton's home about half past seven o'clock. If prevented from going Tuesday, I will be there Wednesday evening at same hour. If you find since your arrival in St. Jo that some other evening will suit you better for my visit than Tuesday, please don't hesitate to so inform me, by letter, or wire, and I will conform to your suggestion. I don't know that it will make any material difference to me as regards date.

What crisp, earnest, winter weather, this winter of '97 is starting out with. A very decided, and to me not unwelcome change from the latter end of '96.

The only sad thought in connection with it, is that so many of our fellow creatures, are so poorly provided against its bitter blasts. It seems to me, that the poor, were never more in evidence, than at the present time, though our land abounds with plenty. I didn't start out to write you a letter, merely a note, and as I left Harold out on the hillside coasting, I must stop and go look after him. He gets so excited over the sport that he does not realize that he is cold.

With sincere affection,
F. M. Wilson

Mr. F. M. Wilson, Horton, Kansas
Homestead Bank
January fourth

My dear Mr. Wilson,

If you could arrange to so do, we would be very glad to have you come up for a few days this week. Miss Webb is here for a little visit, and there are some good things at the Opera houses especially Wednesday evening—I think you would enjoy the little vacation, and we would all be glad to see you. Mr. Alton is out of the city on business or he would have written you.

Very truly your friend,
Mrs. E. K. Alton

[*Over, in Irene's hand*] P.S. I had two letters from my Mother this morning. One written Sat. The other Sun. In the first she said Papa was so poorly they would perhaps send for me today. In the second however she said he was much better—I. W.

The postman has just brought your letter. Mrs. A. says it will be all right for you to come tomorrow—Tuesday. Possibly I shall go home Wednesday if Papa is still poorly—Until tomorrow Good Bye.

Irene Webb

MORNING TWO

On the morning of Tuesday, January 5, 1897, Frank rose from a small guest bedroom of Ethan and Delia Alton's newly built house overlooking the river in north St. Joseph. His train had arrived late the night before. He had slept fitfully, uncertain what he might say to Irene on this trip; uncertain he could express feelings on the rise. He finally decided to just dress for the day.

In 1886, the *Chicago Times* reported St. Joseph, Missouri, to be a city of 60,000 inhabitants, eleven railroads, seventy passenger trains each day, 170 factories, thirteen miles of paved streets, the largest stockyards west of Chicago, and a wholesale trade as large as that of Kansas City and Omaha combined. In that year, Delia Moore, now Alton, then twenty-five, had moved from St. Joseph to Horton, Kansas, with her family. Her father, "Gus" Moore, had been named the first works manager of the Rock Island Line's locomotive shops.

There, Delia made friendship with Georgia-born Allie McCall Wilson, who had arrived in town with her new husband a few months later. Delia was, and remained, a graceful, compelling, organizing force, whether for an impromptu Sunday brunch or a committee to review proposed city annexations—Horton's Pallas Athene. She made Allie her confidante and the Wilson house the high temple. In 1892, Gus Moore was promoted to oversee expansion of the St. Joseph terminal. With this new station in life, Gus could resume being called Augustus, and Delia could turn her full attention to an advantageous marriage. In consultation with a select search committee she selected Ethan K. Alton, a rising executive in his uncle's prominent wholesale dry-goods business. She then steered the expansion of that business as it proceeded to clothe and outfit the expanding populations of the prairies and plains.

Although Frank tried to make his way to the kitchen noiselessly, he was soon joined by Irene. Her hair pinned in a bun in the back, she wore the rewards of yesterday's shopping with Delia: a slim, long black dress, mushroom-colored silk blouse with covered buttons, and a timepiece broach. She grinned at him. Frank looked at her and held his breath a moment. He made a circling motion with his index finger. She turned around twice and curtsied. He made his eyes wider and put his hand over his heart. She started to giggle. He then lifted his finger to pursed lips, and she covered her mouth with both hands. He stepped next to her, leaned to kiss her, and she wiggled her fingers without uncovering her lips. He kissed her fingers. She wiggled them again.

Frank said, "We should be in bed."

"That's the first thing out of your mouth? Don't be fresh, Mr. Wilson," Irene said with a smile.

Frank returned the smile and lit the wall sconces of town-gas. Irene drew water into a large, spouted kettle. Frank soon had a fire roaring beneath the kettle of cold water. Wordlessly, Irene spooned ground coffee into a blue-and-white enameled pot, and set cups and saucers of Delia's blue willowware.

Frank yawned and said, "Why can't you sleep?"

Irene sat next to Frank at the spacious kitchen table and said, "At home I would have just now finished milking the Guernsey, Mr. Wilson, and starting a pot of coffee as I am now. I slept well last night; sorry if you did not." As the kettle began to rumble, but not actually boil, Irene carefully poured hot water into the pot, followed by the crumbled shell of an egg and a pinch of salt, gave the whole mixture two vigorous stirs with a wooden spoon, and set the pot to settle and steep. Soon the aroma of her coffee filled the entire house.

Frank tilted his head upward and then from side to side. "I hope you noticed?" Irene let out a short laugh, nodded, and touched her fingertip to his smooth upper lip. Before he could purse his lips over her finger, she withdrew her hand and said,

"It's an improvement, Mr. Wilson. But then, I suppose there are women of Horton who must surely grieve for it. I've been meaning to ask you about that since our last conversation in which you showed such interest in my social calendar. Mrs. Alton tells me that her friends in Horton tell her that the path to your home is a pilgrimage for unmarried women bearing casseroles. I don't remember reading accounts of that in your correspondence to me—has it just become too commonplace to mention? Or have you taken a fancy to one or more of them?"

Frank, a student of cavalry tactics, took to higher ground at the first sign of ambush. "The community has shown remarkable support for our family, Miss Webb. The teachers at the school, as you must remember, hold the boys in fond regard, as do the church women who are always in search of a worthy mission."

"Mine was a somewhat more specific question about fond regard, Mr. Wilson. Have you now thought of a reply?" Her eyes twinkled as she tried to set a stern jaw.

At that, Frank charged the light brigade. In a breathless stream he blurted, "Miss Webb, no. Yes, I mean. Look, my only interest is in you. You alone. Other girls can't compare. No one. They can't match your wit and I can't keep you out of my mind."

She beamed at him. He brought his head closer to hers. She tilted her face upward. He flushed and said, "Irene, I—"

"Aren't you the early birds! Do pour me a cup of that heavenly coffee." Delia's voice came from the hallway. Frank's shoulders sagged. Irene giggled, jumped up and greeted Delia at the kitchen door. Frank blanched and walked to the sink without knowing why. When he turned back, one foot failed to cooperate and he had to take two hops to maintain balance, if not composure.

Delia stared at him and allowed her jaw to drop. She pushed a chair to him to lean on. "I must tell the girls in Horton that they'll have to get up at a much earlier hour if they expect to catch a banker in these parlous times. You look haggard, Frank. Is that from late-night trips to the Altons to evade the womenfolk of the Chicago-of-the-Plains? I suppose I should step to the *new telephone* right now and raise the alarm that their quarry has slipped into Nortonville territory and gone native. Frank, you did notice the *new telephone* in the dining room, right? But then, you must have your own, although I don't have your number."

"We're considering one at the bank," Frank said as he returned his chair to the table and sat.

"Waste of bank deposits," said Delia. "Business requires deliberation and the solemn, written word. No, the future in telephones is gossip and trivia."

Frank's haggard look lightened when Mr. Alton came into the kitchen. Chairs scraped as he and Irene rose to greet their host. Toronto-born Ethan Alton stood just over six feet tall and his long black hair was combed straight back until it met the nape of his neck. He had rowed competitively at Princeton and his compact physique still showed it. His smile was genuine and broad. He said,

"Shirred eggs, brown bread toasted, soft butter. Wilson will join me. Thank you, Del. And open the Concord grape jelly Miss Webb brought us of her own making. And some of that coffee I've been smelling. Is that from the pricey new French press device? Wilson and I will take lunch at the club. He's off in the morning. Miss Webb, you grace the breakfast table with elegance. Are you up to another day of plunder?"

"Thank you, Mr. Alton, and I hope to be able to keep up with Mrs. Alton as she has invited me to accompany her in visiting the children's wing of the hospital and then the first organizing meeting of the new Associated Charities Committee. And I gather that her little niece, Fiona Moore, will be joining us tonight and for a few days' stay."

"And don't forget," said Delia, "We are all going to the theatre tonight, including Fiona."

"Right, Del. Mind, three minutes on the eggs. Miss Webb, a day like that will put you in need of sherry tonight. Your mother still ensconced, Wilson? Suppose it can't be helped; two boys. Still. There's the other one, too, Allie's mother, right? Del tells me they're a pair to draw to!"

"Your eggs, Ethan." Delia gave Frank a sympathetic look and said, "Word has traveled, Frank. I hear that Mrs. McCall's bitterness over Allie's tragedy has not subsided, and that having a rival grandmother taking her daughter's place in the home is not helping. How do you manage?"

"It seems telephone lines elongate the rumors that run through them," said Frank, looking directly into Irene's eyes. "We all manage very well, thank you, and it's a comfort having two grandmothers to lessen the boys' loss. However, I acknowledge that they have parenting instincts that occasionally clash."

Irene returned his gaze and said gently, "And you stand tall in the center of it all, a Gibraltar rock for your impressionable sons and diplomat among all who bring good intentions to your door."

Ethan stood and declared, "Well said, Miss Webb! That buttons it then. Try not to exhaust the stricken children, Delia love. Looks to be a brilliant day. Meet us at the theatre at six, Del, and a homey, light supper here afterward."

On the doorstep, as they were leaving, Alton turned to Frank and said, "First-rate girl, Irene. Delia and I are charmed. Look, Wilson, besides those obvious charms, look at it this way: Let's say you take a wife—and let's say it's Irene—the dueling grandmothers have to clear out and there's a new life in the lives of Harold and Wallis. As it is, all they have is what's done and gone and bound to be stuck in the past. Two vast improvements. All in a single stroke. Hard to see things from that angle when they're right on top of you."

Frank thought, Yet another call to remarry, yet another good intention.

IT WAS LATE WHEN they had finished the homey, light supper. The Altons tactfully made excuses and retired upstairs to allow Frank and Irene to finish the unspoken conversation that had caused their heads to touch so often during the performance. Fiona Moore was already practically asleep.

Frank's affection had grown beyond friendship. He had fallen in love. That morning he felt an unexpected urgency to tell her so which had remained with him the entire day. But before he could broach that subject, he felt he should finish what was started by the Altons about his mother and Mrs. McCall and their effect on the boys. As they sat at the kitchen table, touching hands occasionally, Frank told her exactly what his mother had told him about Mrs. McCall's unpleasantness at graveside. Irene did want to hear about it—*but another time.*

Her eyes brightened as she squeezed his hand and said, "I am not daunted by their strained relationship. At any event, to be forewarned is to be forearmed. Now, dear friend, where were we when we were interrupted over coffee this morning?"

"Irene, I'm glad we're alone and can speak freely. Your comment this morning about Gibraltar rock and diplomat filled me with pride, and more. Your words connected us. They gave me encouragement to be open with you. I only hope I can match your eloquence. I probably should have made notes to speak from but I did not. Much as I admire poetry and drama, I cannot rightly recall a single verse from literature now when I want it most. Irene, know that I love you. I love you romantically and as a suitor. I hope to be your suitor, and I hope that our future holds a lifetime of romance." He sat mesmerized by rain-gray eyes.

She said in a low, firm voice,

"I came to the Altons in high hopes to be with you again. My feelings have also grown but I had no plan to say anything. You say you wish you had prepared notes before coming here; does that mean you did not expect to declare your intentions here and now?"

Frank made no reply, no gesture.

"In any case your heart must have been prepared. Your words, if spontaneous, have unlocked my tongue. I told you that December evening that you could easily turn my head. Well, you have. So hear my secret heart, Frank. My dear, dear man, I am floating with happiness to hear your words. I don't need passages from literature to feel what your heart tells me. The novels, the plays, the poetry are simply for those times when we do not hear such words directly. I have never before heard such words spoken to me. Your earnestness surpasses the rhyme and meter of all the poets. I love you, Frank. I love your words to me tonight. I love your words in your letters. And my love for you is also romantic love. I have never before uttered that to anyone, and can imagine saying it only to you—over and over and over."

He leaned closer. She touched her fingertips to his cheekbone, then his upper lip. He allowed her to trace his lips until she tilted her head. When her eyelids closed, he kissed her. He could never have imagined how vividly her kiss amplified the words of love he had just heard.

"Again," she whispered. Frank was eager to comply. She turned her head slightly and said, "No, I meant say it again." Frank tilted his head. "I love you, Irene." She shook her head. "No, not that part . . . you know . . . the part about as a suitor."

"Ah. I love you romantically. I love you as a suitor."

"Exactly. That's it."

"And you said . . . ?"

"I said hooray!"

"Not to me, you didn't."

"I said, 'I am floating with happiness.' Now, the part after that."

Frank thought. "Was it, 'I love you'?"

"No. Just now, about the Gibraltar rock."

"Ah. That it connected us."

"Yes. I loved that. Side by side, supporting one another no matter what."

"Well, for the most part, but I'd keep you away from danger. The unruly sort of danger so commonplace down in Viniti and Haden, for example."

"Then, Frank, please just stay away from those places for my sake."

Frank kissed her.

Irene made a sound that could have been a purr and nestled closer. "Say the other part." Instead of answering, he kissed her again.

There, in the guttering firelight, they spoke their hearts again and again until Frank realized that he had to get some sleep.

He said, "There is no escaping the reality that I must return to Horton in the morning. I shall think of you every day, darling. See your face. Hear your voice. While you're in St. Joe, please find a photography shop and have your picture taken. I would treasure it. If I could, I would put you in my pocket, take you with me on that train, and never let you go. I must content myself with recollections of this moment. And now that I'm your suitor you must not hesitate to ask anything about me."

Irene nodded slowly. "I'll have the photo taken when I get back home. I think of you every day now, dear man. Your words tonight give me purpose."

Sleep came to Frank quickly and deeply that night.

POSTED ST. JOSEPH, MO. HORTON, KANSAS, JAN. 6, 1897, 5:30 P.M.;
REC'D HORTON, 6:00 A.M., JAN. 7

Mr. F. M. Wilson

My Beloved Friend,

The messenger boy delivered the tickets for "Pudd'nhead Wilson" which you so very kindly secured for us. The courtesy was entirely unexpected—but nonetheless greatly appreciated by Mrs. Alton, Miss Moore and myself. Please do accept our thanks for your kindness. We shall greatly enjoy Pudd'nhead, I am sure, and we only regret that you cannot be one of our number. Mrs. Alton says she fears you overestimate any kindness she may have shown you. She was a little worried after you had gone this morning for fear you might have taken her little joking about too much to heart and that perhaps you thought she would mention something about it in her letters to her Horton friends which she says would be the farthest thing from her mind. There is an undercurrent of fun in Mrs. A's make up that she cannot resist.

Dearheart, is it not all strange, so strange—I wonder if it is right for me to feel toward you as I do. I have only followed the dictates of my heart—my mind seems to be entirely subjective—I wish you could understand just how I feel. I cannot tell you. My whole life seems changed since I have known that you love me. How strange that I should give to you in so short a time that for which others have sought for years to gain. I have tried to be a good girl all my life—I have done many wrong things which I wish were undone. I guess everybody has—and now I feel that life henceforth is a new thing entirely. I shall be happy and contented at home as any place else in the consciousness of your love—I shall be worthy of only your best—your very best. I am writing upstairs in the cold and must go down before I get too cold—I can see your dear face and hear your last words "I shall think of you every day, darling." I shall see your face and hear your voice—till we meet again.

Lovingly,
Irene

Miss Irene Webb, Nortonville, Kansas
Sunday eve, Jan 10/97

My Darling Irene,

Your beautiful letter of last Wednesday reached me on time, and was devoured with more than usual relish. I am sorry that Mrs. Alton imagined that I took her so seriously, for such was farthest from my thoughts. I appreciated her joke, and never for a moment took it seriously. I have no knowledge that any of my Horton friends or acquaintances, are aware of my visits with you, or even my correspondence, as no one has yet ventured to so intimate in my presence. While I do not invite and court public criticism, I do not shrink from it, or seek to avoid it as some do. However it will be a very strange thing indeed if it is not very generally known about town. While I have taken no pains to conceal the facts, I have likewise refrained from advertising them, but have never for a moment supposed that my actions were unknown to those who always know what is going on about them. . . .

Let me again assure you Irene, that I love you with all my heart. My love for you is growing, day by day, as I trust yours for me is doing. I hope that we may know one another thoroughly.

It is now about 10 o'clock and the boys have fallen asleep. I must close and put them to bed, so Good Night.

Your affectionate lover,
Frank

CHAPTER THREE

HIS HAS BEEN A LIFE FILLED WITH KINDLY DEEDS

MAILED 14 JAN. 1897, 6 P.M., NORTONVILLE.

Mr. F. M. Wilson, Horton, Kansas

My Beloved Friend,

I came home Thursday morning to find my father feeling very poorly—he grew worse the night I left home and tho. Mama wrote to me every day he would not let her tell me his real condition as he knew I would come home immediately. I noticed a great change in him the few days I was away from him. My brother and his family from Northern Oak, Iowa were here when I came, having arrived the day before. There seems to be no apparent change in my Father's condition from day-to-day, tho. we can see that he is growing weaker all the time. It seems almost unendurable to see him gradually slipping away from us and not be able to do anything for him. His physicians think water is collecting around his heart and unless he responds rapidly to their present treatment his life is a matter of only a short time—indeed we may expect the change any time. Dear, kind, patient Father, we can't spare him and I know that you join us in the prayer that he may not be taken from us. Desolate indeed will be the home that has sheltered all of us all our lives without his grave, kind face. His life has been a constant benediction to his family and to the community where he has lived so many years. To my mind his has been a truly successful life: a life filled with kindly deeds; a life free from envy and full of hearty good will toward his fellowmen. I never knew of his doing an unmanly act in my life. Surely he has scattered roses for his reaping bye and bye. If he can only live till summer comes I believe he will get strong. We have sent for Dr. Martin of Topeka, a specialist on diseases of the chest. He will come this evening and spend the night with Papa.

My head and hands and heart have been full since I last saw you, dearheart, but in the midst of everything I have found time to think of you and to reflect on our last meeting. Do you know, I had no intention of revealing my heart to you that night. I wonder why I did? I guess it must have revealed itself. Yes, I'm sure it did! I remember we were sitting before the grate and I was wondering if you could hear the violent throbbing of my heart, when suddenly—it was all over—my secret which I thought I was guarding so closely was confessed! How strange! How strange!

How little do we know of what is in store for us in this life.

Your last letter, dearheart, is typical of your true character as I see you: Frank, open, manly and sincere. Yes, I presume I had a better opportunity to know you than you had to know me. I want you to see me and know me as "others see me." I want you to know that I am only a real, live, human American girl. I do many things that are wrong. I do not live up to my ideal of right, but I try to. Like yourself I am fully aware of my greatest faults and I firmly resolve every day to overcome them. Sometimes I succeed and often I do not. Thank you for the permission to ask concerning your life—the same privilege is granted you—tho. there isn't much to know in my case.

Mrs. Alton and Miss Moore must have thought I was more interested in Mr. Frank Wilson than in the play we attended. I do not think Mrs. Alton has to have an Irish house fall down on her before she understands matters pretty thoroughly. Mrs. A. told me many strange things while I was there—some of which I told you. I have had no time to think and ponder over them. Mrs. A. regards you as a very dear friend of hers and I trust she feels the same toward me.

So you are comparing me with other girls. I'm glad that you are, though. I tremble lest I shall fall in the comparison. You are unlike Emerson in that he could not find any resemblance to anyone else in his Sweetheart. Some thought she resembled her mother. To him she suggested only "long evenings or diamond mornings or the song of birds." I must close now and go to work. With every good wish. Believe me

Sincerely Yours,
Irene

POSTMARKED JAN. 15, 1897, 5 P.M., NORTONVILLE, KS

Mr. F. M. Wilson

My Beloved Friend,
Dr. Martin performed an operation last night for the purpose of drawing the water from the heart cavity. The operation was not entirely successful and we are in the greatest anxiety over the reaction which is now taking place. Dear Father I fear is soon to leave us.

Irene Webb
Friday, 9 A.M.

Miss Irene Webb, Nortonville, Kansas
Home, Sunday, Jan 17/97

My Darling Irene,

I still hope that your worst fears are not fully justified and that he is not soon to be taken from those who love him so dearly. He certainly cannot be tired of life, or feel that he is a burden to those around him, although he has lived out the average allotted time to man, for he has so lived and provided for his family, and for his own declining years, as to best enjoy that period of life, which unfortunately is so burdensome to many.

I am sure that all that loving hands, and hearts, and skill, can do for him will be done. I fear that you have denied yourself much needed rest, to write me these beautiful long letters. I know that you have much to do, and shall make all due allowance, if your correspondence should be less prompt, and less lengthy, knowing full well that you will more than make up for the loss, when time is more at your command.

Wallis will pass from his present grade, to the next higher one, tomorrow, but Miss Nerva Dunn will still remain his teacher. She seems to think very well of Wallis, and reports that he is doing good work this year. About 6 weeks ago, at the last examination he received one unsatisfactory mark, in one of his studies; he felt so badly about it that he did not bring his card to me for examination and signature, but took it to my mother who signed it for him. Miss Dunn noticed that I had not signed the card, and at once surmised the cause. It had not occurred to me, until she informed me of her suspicion, that Wallis had any motive in presenting his card to my mother instead of to me.

We are getting along at home very nicely, considering the fact that harmony does not prevail between the two grandmothers of the children, as I told you when I last saw you. The question has worried me, not a little, and I have tried hard to find out where the fault lies. I am now pretty well convinced that my mother unjustly censures Mrs. McCall. It has been a matter of much regret to me that my parents, after some 20 years of married life, and with a family of 5 children, found it necessary to become divorced and separated. This is a subject upon which I am very sensitive indeed, and I have never permitted anyone to engage me in conversation upon the subject.

I am not at all satisfied that Mrs. McCall is attempting to influence the children, or to create a prejudice against my father and mother, in their minds because of the lots they drew. Whatever may have been said, at or about the time of Allie's death, I have concerned myself but little about it, and shall not let it worry me for a single moment. At that time however my mother formed such a dislike to them that I fear she is the victim of a violent prejudice. I also believe this is being fed by false reports, made to her, by meddlesome people who do not have good foundation for their reports.

Our housekeeper, Alice Vance, is entirely free from any feeling of prejudice one way or the other. She can see no difference in the conduct of Harold & Wallis, whether they make frequent visits to McCalls' or not.

Neither can she see that they are wanting in respect for my mother, except when she herself is responsible for it, but she has repeatedly noticed that when the children return from McCalls' house, my mother treats them with indifference, and thus provokes the feeling, of which she complains.

For some time I have suspicioned that these facts existed, and that the imagination was responsible for much of the trouble, but I felt a great delicacy in confiding my secret to anyone. But believing the importance of a right understanding of the facts fully justified me I discussed the matter fully with Alice, with the result that I found my own judgment, fully coincided in, by hers. You will perhaps wonder why it was necessary to consult Alice, why I did not have the same opportunity to observe events that she did. It was because I could see nothing in the conduct of the children, when I was at home, that justified the belief, that they were being taught to disrespect Mother, and I wished to know if their conduct when I was absent, differed from that when present.

I cannot believe it right to teach the children disrespect for either of their grandparents. I could not find it in my heart to do so, even though I believed them guilty of the charge, I have made no effort to keep the children away from McCalls' and there is scarcely a day that they are not there. Wallis often takes a meal there, and sometimes stays overnight. Allie's sister Pearl has recently purchased a piano, and Wallis loves music. I trust that this letter is not growing uninteresting to you, my only excuse for thus enlarging upon this matter is that having told you something about it when last I saw you, I felt anxious for you to know the more recent developments.

To you I now talk freely of matters that I would not think of discussing with others. From you I have no secrets.

Since you have come into my heart, you have taken complete possession of it. I believe you possess in a rare degree all those charms, personal, social, intellectual, and moral, which I prize most dearly, and which so admirably equip you for a bosom companion. When I first told you of my love for you, I remember that you asked me if I had such intention in my mind when I left home to visit you. I believe I left this question unanswered at that time, but I don't mind telling you now that I had no such intention. Upon the contrary I had quite determined to not do so upon that occasion, feeling that it would not be quite proper. I did however, and I have not since regretted it.

I do not feel that I am wanting in respect for the memory of my dear departed wife. Quite the contrary is my feeling. I have a duty to the living as well as the dead. My whole aim is to do my duty. I hope I may be made to know my whole duty. No other thoughts have occupied so much of my mind during the past 5 months.

You say I am unlike Emerson in that he could find no resemblance to anyone else in his sweetheart. Well I don't know whether I am or not. It is said that love is blind, and I am ready to concede that its eyesight is somewhat impaired, but in Emerson's case we must allow something for his poetical license. In that respect he has the advantage of me.

Believe me,
Your sincere lover, Frank

FRANK LEANED INTO THE north wind and tried to turtle his head into his black woolen coat collar against the sting of pelting snow. It had started about noon. Despite good intentions he had been unable to lock up and go home when everyone else at the bank had left: too many loans pending. And each of the mortgage loans meant poring over abstracts of title. These were summaries of the chain of title prepared by a father-and-son firm in Hiawatha, pages upon pages, in thick rolls bound in twine. Transfers by deed were not hard to follow, but transfers of fractional interests through probate or divorce made painstaking work. Most bankers hired an attorney to go through them and give a title opinion. Frank was stubborn and frugal. He had done this work as an apprentice lawyer, so he did it himself now. That work was a thief of time. He always had a pile of unread abstracts in his office.

He finally left after a few hours. Now the snow was such that he could not move faster than a trudge on the rutted, unlit Main Street, each step a deliberate effort. At Main and Mina, he cut across Miss Crawford's yard to gain a few steps, even though he and she had often spoken of their annoyance with others who cut across corner lots. Force of nature, he thought, and assumed her forgiveness. The shortcut had meant soft snow spilling into his shoe-tops to further chill his numb feet.

Ahead he saw the gaslights and candles of home. He stamped his shoes dutifully on the stoop of the small south porch before opening the kitchen door. He stood just outside the door, removed his coat, and flapped it in a vain attempt to free it from its white crust. Inside the kitchen he sank into the rocking chair and inhaled the aroma of chicken stock which had been on low bubble all afternoon under Amanda's care. She had also baked. How could he have managed these five months without her? His next thought punctured his growing cheeriness: How could he have that little talk with her that had been building up inside him for nearly a week? No, tonight's the night to say something.

Harold and Wallis bolted into the kitchen from the adjoining dining room, ready to hitch Turk to the cutter and go for a trot *right now*. Frank smiled at them silently. Harold was the first to implore Frank to take them out. Wallis's level voice advocated for the adventure with reasons he'd been marshaling for over an hour: to check on Dr. Ralston; to see that the Tomlinson's un-stabled mule was safe; to make sure the school's windows were all closed; and even more contrived acts of valor. Such rhetoric could not be countered, so Frank said nothing. His eyes spoke as eloquently as his silence. To save face all around, Wallis finally said, "Tomorrow, then?"

Frank rose to his full height, pursed his lips in deliberation, and, after a lengthy pause, said: "Of course!" The boys whooped and galloped away to the upstairs. Frank tried to follow them but his chilled feet had warmed only to a stinging resistance to taking another step.

Later, after cleaning up from a supper of today's soup and leftover fried chicken, Frank took Amanda's hand and tucked her arm under his. He led her to the front parlor. The windows rattled with bursts of the storm's wind. The drawn draperies swayed and billowed, and the candles guttered.

"I'm not sure this is the best night for parlor chat, Frank. Don't you want to go to your bedroom?"

Frank chuckled and said, "I know, Mama, but I want to speak with you about something that's been bothering me for a while. This is as good a time as any to get it off my chest. Bear with me for a bit, all right?"

Amanda curled one foot under her on a green velvet side chair and said, "Of course, Frank. What's on your mind?"

"Well, first and foremost, I cannot think what chaos our home would have fallen into if you hadn't been here all this time. You have been beyond helpful: you've been a pastoring angel as well."

"Come on, Frank, make your point. We all do our duty, and mine's been to help keep your house as best I can."

"Well, Mama, I have to tell you that our life could be even better if you would only help us in a different way. My point is that I'm concerned about you clucking over Harold and Wallis too much, or in ways that do harm." Amanda frowned but said nothing.

"Not intending to, of course. Here's what I mean specifically. A little before Christmas, Wallis brought you a report card with an unsatisfactory grade on it. He wanted you to sign it because he didn't want to face me. You signed it, knowing that Wallis would return it to Miss Dunn without showing it to me."

Amanda started to speak, but Frank held up his hand and continued, "Miss Dunn knew that Wallis was too embarrassed to show it to me, and she told me herself. I hoped you would inform me of it, but you never did. Don't you see? By going along with Wallis on this, my own authority was undermined, both with Wallis and with Miss Dunn." Amanda sank back in the chair.

"In his mind, then, Wallis would have a safe retreat if anything like it happened again. But there are always consequences. You know he's not frightened of what I might do to him. He was simply ashamed. But he was hiding something from me, and perhaps even tricking me. His shame would grow. That would be a crack between us." Frank stood up and began to pace. "I would have signed the report. I would not have punished him, but I would have become more watchful over his schoolwork habits."

Amanda stood and walked to Frank. "You had so much on your mind. This was something I could do without anyone getting out of sorts. Wallis promised to do better, and he has."

"I know he has because I've talked with Miss Dunn. But I've never been too busy to be a papa. To be the right papa, I have to deal with it all, not just what filters through from you."

"I meant no harm."

"Fine."

"I'm sorry. Is there anything else or can we go upstairs now?"

Frank led her back to the side chair and pulled its matching one closer. They sat again.

"One more, and this is a bigger problem. Mama, I have observed that you often make uncomplimentary comments to the boys about Mrs. McCall."

"Frank, that woman insulted me—and you—where your wife lay waiting for the grave."

"You have a right to be upset about that. And resentful. But the things you tell the boys sometimes have been disparaging, and unfounded. The boys can't be expected to assess the merits of your comments. They naturally believe what you say. They naturally believe what I say, and what Mrs. McCall says. You shed disrespect on Mrs. McCall. I know that she hurt you, but she has never hurt the boys. She and her husband talk too much about Allie, or at least more than I'm up to listening to at times. But it's to keep her name and spirit alive with the boys. Maybe she goes overboard at times about it. Still, she has not put bad thoughts in their minds about you. You act like you don't want them visiting her."

"I've never said that . . ."

"No, but it shows in how you act. It is not fair, and our family would do better without it."

"Do you want me to go back to Holton? I can be packed and ready in the blink of an eye." Amanda twisted herself so she could get a better look at the wall.

Frank was calm when he said, "No, no, Mama. This is something you can do without any effort at all. The only reason I'm here talking this way to you, is for you to just think about it. Look, I am determined to keep family peace for everyone's sake. Think about the bitterness between you and Papa. Think about the profound sadness and hardship that hit this family when Allie died. My friend Irene Webb is going through pain over her father's last sickness and death. Those painful experiences are in our destiny. Please don't plant ill will in the minds of my boys toward their other grandmother. It's easy for you to stop it.

"If I lose their trust and respect, then shame on me. But, Mama, I have to insist that you not undermine my position with their teacher and their grandmother."

Amanda sat very still. She could not move because of the cold and because of the chilling honesty in Frank's quiet voice. There was no sound in the room except the steady ticks of the Seth Thomas clock on the bookcase in the next room, and the shrill bursts of Arctic air swirling across the front porch. Then she stood up and faced Frank.

"You would have made a good lawyer, Frank. Better than the ones I know because you do not destroy when you argue. Of course, I can make simple changes that will make a difference. You did not tear me down to make me see. I thank you for that."

"Good night, dear Mama. Thank you, for everything."

January 21, 1897

My dearest Friend,

I am very glad to tell you that my Father is a little better than when I sent my note last Friday. For twenty-four hours after the operation three Drs. worked over him to save his life. They despaired of being able to do so and wanted to go home. We would not let them go and toward evening Father began to rally a little. At five o'clock we thought he was dying and he thought, too, that he was passing away. He talked to us so beautifully and seemed to be preparing rather for a short trip to town or to the neighbors than to the Country which seems so far away.

His mind was and has been perfectly clear all through his illness. He has never been heard to complain even when the pain is most severe. Until this week he has suffered no very severe pain, but Monday and yesterday it was terrible. I can stand anything but to see him suffer; that nearly breaks my heart. If he can be spared to us and not suffer I shall be so rejoiced but if he has to pass days like Monday and Tuesday I feel that I cannot bear it. My brothers are all at home now. Ed came Sunday from Albany, N.Y. at which place he was when my message reached him. My sisters are here and have been for several days past. Thank you for your kind word of cheer and encouragement. I only hope we may be able to keep Father till Spring anyway. His death will be the first great sorrow of my life; I shall bear it as bravely as I can for sake of the others and especially for Mama. She has hardly left my Father's side since he was taken worse. He loves all of us, but Mama comes first always with him. There is nothing sad or gloomy about his sick room—he is cheerful and hopeful and interested in everything when he is free from pain.

I am glad that you felt free to talk to me about the matter of which you told me at Mrs. Alton's. Be assured that any confidence you may see fit to repose in me shall be sacredly guarded. This is a matter that I feel I can neither suggest or advise on. I think that a woman is usually quicker at discerning the source of such things than a man is, but of course I have not had any opportunity for such observation and even if I had, I should not consider that it was right or womanly for me to suggest.

I know Mrs. McCall only as I met her at your house. I did not have occasion to think much about her or any of her family. Miss Pearl I met at your house and occasionally I met her in a social way elsewhere. I think you are very wise not to feel worried over what they might have said at her death. I am sure what unkind things they may have said were only the strange outbursts of their violent grief; I am so glad you do not feel hard toward them. I am sure they are sorry for what they said. If you are ready to forgive you are happier than they. Your Mother I have never met, therefore I have no way of judging for or against. I am sorry, sorrier than I can tell you, that such a condition of affairs exists. It is not a good thing for the children. As I said before while you have my sympathy in everything that comes to your life, I feel that I cannot do anything or say anything in this matter. Do what you believe to be right. I do not think it right to teach children disrespect for anything or anybody—All goodness and love is based on profound respect.

It is very late and I must go to sleep if I can. Papa is resting fairly easy now.

> *Good Night, dearheart.*
> *Lovingly,*
> *Irene*

FRANK BROUGHT HIS VALISE downstairs. Wallis's bag was already there. In fact, Wallis had his coat and hat on even though they wouldn't be going to the station for another hour. Frank said,

"Wallis, take your coat off or you'll be colder when you do go out."

"Why can't we go now?"

"It wouldn't do any good, the train doesn't leave till ten."

Wallis muttered something and threw his hat against the door.

"Say that again, Wallis, slower and louder."

"Nothing. Didn't say nothing."

"Anything, and yes you did. Was it an oath?"

"You didn't hear it so it must not have been."

"Don't talk back to me. We don't have to go to Kansas City today."

"You promised. The magic show. For Christmas. For my birthday."

"Act your age. Anyway, your birthday's a week away."

Amanda, halfway down the stairs, said, "Frank, you better come look at this."

Frank pointed a finger at Wallis and then hurried up the stairs.

"Come take a look at Harold. He's got a fever. And a dry cough." Harold was in bed with his new memory quilt pulled up to his chin. He was pale and blotchy. He looked at Frank. He knew there was slim hope he'd be going to the city.

Amanda said, "Frank, you take Wallis. He has his heart set on it. I'll stay with Harold. I'll get Doc Ralston if I think I need to."

Frank said, "No one is going anywhere for at least another hour. I don't like what I see. Your throat sore, son?"

"No, Papa. It's my tummy. Feels awful."

Frank went to the head of the stairs and called, "Wallis, get up here, please."

Wallis came upstairs and looked at Frank sullenly. "Go in and have a look at Harold."

Wallis exhaled dramatically and went to Harold's bed. The boys glowered at each other. Harold made a rude sound with his lips and tongue. Wallis carefully placed the palm of his hand on Harold's forehead. He looked over at Amanda and then to Frank. He put his fist on Harold's shoulder and shoved it lightly. Harold looked away.

Then Wallis stood and walked to the door, where he turned and said, "Papa, can we talk in the hall?"

When they reached the top of the stairs, Wallis said, "Is he going to die?"

"Oh, Wallis, this is probably only going to last two or three days. A week at most. You mustn't jump to conclusions. Gramma says you and I can go on and she'll tend to Harold."

Wallis went down the stairs, picked up his bag, and came back up slowly. His face was calm. He put his bag down on the landing and said, "Papa, we better not go. Anything can happen, right?"

Frank shook his head and said, "Wallis, don't get yourself worked up. This is probably nothing, really."

"But you're not absolutely, positively sure?"

"No, but . . ."

"Then anything can happen."

Miss Irene Webb, Nortonville, Kansas
Wednesday Evening—or I presume it is Thursday Morning now.

My Dear Sweetheart,

It is now almost 10 o'clock p.m.

Wallis is 12 years old today. We gave him a birthday party last night, entertaining 16 of his young friends, 8 boys and 8 girls. They behaved as well as any children I ever saw and enjoyed the evening very much. His cake contained a ring, which, by right of discovery, became the property of Charley Bernard.

Harold will be 5. in April and is already looking forward to his birthday party. He seems to be having the chicken-pox, a complaint that is going the rounds in our town this winter, but in his case has given us no trouble, though we shall probably keep him indoors for a few days.

I have heard no complaints from my mother recently, concerning the evil effects of permitting the children perfect freedom to go and come, to and from, the McCalls', at their pleasure, and although I have not so informed my mother, I think she has arrived at the conclusion that I do not intend to oppose their visits, and has concluded to make the best of the situation. The more I think of it, the better I am satisfied that non-interference is the proper course for me, and that if my mother will only take the right view of it, that all trouble will disappear, or rather will not re-appear, for it has already disappeared.

I presume that you have had no opportunity for securing photos of yourself since last we met. Your time has been so fully occupied that I presume you have scarcely thought of it, much less had it done. I shall be glad indeed to receive one of them when you feel that you have an opportunity to secure it for me. My last thoughts at night, and my first in the morning are of you. Scarcely an hour passes that I do not think of you.

Had I the wings of a bird I would fly to you tonight. My love for you grows stronger, and brighter, with each succeeding day. What a happy state true love is! What a pity that everybody is not constantly in love! What a happy world this would be. True love brings out the good qualities in us. I hope that I may merit only your best and truest love my dear sweetheart, and that for which I can give you full return.

With assurances of my deepest affection I am

Your sincere lover,
Frank

POSTMARKED JAN. 26, 1897, NORTONVILLE TO HORTON, 5 P.M.

Mr. F. M. Wilson

My dearest Friend,

My Father is growing weaker and weaker as the hours go by. Last night a boy whom my Father and Uncle Dan almost raised came. He is a man over forty now. He heard of Father's illness and came all the way from Old Mexico to see him. Father recognized him and drew his head down and kissed him. To all his friends he sends loving messages but he is too weak to see them. Dr. Emory of Topeka came this morning. My Father helped him when he was a young rising minister and their friendship has always been firm and lasting.

I cannot write more. If you can we would like to have you come over for the funeral—He has arranged everything concerning that as well as everything else. Last night he signed checks for his Dr. bills—the only bills he owes. He then signed checks for a portion of his bank account so that we might not need for anything. You never saw anything like the way he does—he says his work is done and he is ready to go. Mama sits by his side day and night. I dread the reaction after it is all over—dear Mother bride—for 48 years she has walked by Father's side.

I shall advise you when he passes away and if you feel like coming I shall be glad to have you.

Lovingly,
Irene

I hope Wallis may live to see many more happy birthdays.

Irene

POSTMARKED JAN. 30, 1897, NORTONVILLE;
RECEIVED 5 P.M., HORTON

Mr. F. M. Wilson

Dearest Friend,
Father has rallied a little since yesterday. He is very drowsy from the effects of morphine and cannot see any one. All of the family numbering eighteen in all are here and the rest of the grand children come today. He wants all is the reason we are sending for them.

Irene

Miss Irene Webb, Nortonville, Kansas

My Darling Irene,

You have been very kind to keep me so well informed of his condition from day to day, and I have been very much interested in all that has taken place. The scene is a most beautiful and impressive one. I have made up my mind to attend the funeral, unless prevented by other engagements. I very much regret that I shall not be permitted to see him again in this life. I had hoped that I would see him often and enjoy his acquaintance and friendship. Little did I think that our first meeting would also be our last. I am very much gratified to know that his impressions of me were not unfavorable. I regret that during his last illness I can do nothing to testify my respect for him. I hope you and your mother will bear up bravely and not give way to your grief. He is passing from death unto life everlasting, and your loss will be his gain. His life has been pure and noble, and he now goes to his reward.

Now my dear girl, fully realizing how little comfort you will receive from my feeble words I shall not detain you longer. Again begging to assure you of my sincere love and sympathy I will bid you good night.

Devotedly Yours,
Frank

Mr. F. M. Wilson, Horton, Kansas
Tuesday (February 2)—10:30 p.m.

My Beloved Friend,

There is no apparent change in my Father's condition since I wrote you on Saturday. This morning he called me to him and after kissing me, he asked me if I wouldn't play for him. At first I thought I couldn't, then as I looked at his dear face, I suddenly felt that I could do anything for him. He lies in the sitting room just across the hall from the parlor. My brother Man opened the doors and I played for ten minutes the old hymns he loves best—I shall never forget the scene. The curtains in his room were raised to let in the sun light—the front door stood wide open. As I glanced up from the piano I could see my brothers and sisters weeping in the room and at the windows outside.

When I ceased playing I went in to him and asked him if he wanted me to play more. "Just a little more, my girlie, then you may rest," he said. When I again ceased he had fallen to sleep. I appreciate your kind words of sympathy, my beloved friend. I know they come from your heart. I know full well that you can realize how we feel now. I think we do not now fully realize how great our loss will be. Now there are so many around and we are and have been in such a nervous strain for such a long time.

Mama continues to bear up wonderfully. We are pleased to know you will come over— but—oh I hope it will not be to Papa's funeral.

Lovingly and Sincerely,
Irene

Miss Irene Webb, Nortonville, Kansas

My Darling Irene,

I rec'd your beautiful letter of last Tuesday, and read it with much interest. I regret that I have not been permitted to be with you occasionally during the past few weeks. The scene has certainly been a pathetic one, and it is indeed remarkable, that for so many days and weeks, you have expected each day would be his last. You have been thus afforded ample time to learn his wishes, concerning all matters affecting the welfare of his family.

How different were the conditions surrounding the departure of my dear wife. Not a member of her family, nor even a near friend present when she became unconscious, and herself not realizing that the end was near. How often have I wished that we might have been apprised of her approaching death, that we might have gathered around her bedside, and ministered to her last wants, and listened to her parting words. During her illness I never realized that her condition was critical, and we never discussed the question of her death. This will always remain a matter of much regret to me. During your father's illness I have often thought of the contrast of the two cases in this respect.

My brother Forest and his wife Nettie, are here now, and will probably remain with us until the last of the coming week. I shall try to keep his wife with me longer if she will consent to remain.

We had a snow storm last Wednesday night, and on Thursday I made a business trip to Hiawatha in a cutter. This was my first sleigh ride of the season, and I thought of you often and wished that you were my company on that trip instead of Bud Sprague.

Whether or not Bud is a mind reader I cannot answer, but at

any rate he took occasion to speak of you during our ride. He seemed to appreciate the fact that you, and Allie, were among the few women in Horton who always treated him well, and seemed to think there were any good traits in him.

I don't know whether Bud knows that I am very much interested in you or not, but I suspected that he does. I think Bud is very much interested in Grace Dunn. I think he shows very good judgment in this matter.

My sweet-heart I would like to know if you have any objection to my showing your letters to my sister-in-law (Forest's wife) while she is here on a visit, in case I shall conclude that I would like to do so. I have not yet made up my mind that I want to do so, but should like to know your pleasure in the matter, assuring you that I have not but a worthy object in view. . . .

I hope you will fully appreciate this letter when I inform you that Harold has been sitting at this table ever since I began this letter. He has been drawing pictures, and learning to print his name, and you can well imagine that about three fourths of my time is required to assist him in his most laudable efforts. Wallis is also sitting at my table reading "Great Events of the Greatest Century" a book which he seems deeply interested in. It is now half past ten o'clock and neither of the children show any signs of giving up, but seem to be determined to stay at it as long as I do. . . .

Now my dear girl I must close, Forest and Nettie who have been spending the evening with Mr. and Mrs. Henderson have just returned and I will have no more time this evening to write.

With much love and sympathy I am

Sincerely and Devotedly,
Frank

FRANK FINISHED THE LETTER and looked at his sons. Their earnestness at the table evoked memories of Allie, writing out Chautauqua-lesson essays about a required reading.

"What are you drawing, Harold?"

"I just draw what I see. What are you writing?"

"I'm writing a letter to a friend who lives in another town. She knows you but you were too young to remember her."

"Is it Miss Webb, Papa?" asked Wallis. "You write to her a lot."

"Yes, it is. You remember her, of course. How is your book?"

"Very difficult, but it's about history so it's pretty interesting in parts. Will she come back here again?"

"Oh, well, she just might. Would you like that?"

"To visit or to stay?"

"Well, to visit. Maybe to stay. How would that be, do you think?"

"I think Gramma McCall would pitch a fit," concluded Wallis.

Frank turned his head as he stifled a laugh, but managed to utter, "Um-hmm, but then again she might not."

"Papa, my drawings don't look like what I see. They're no good."

"Harold, don't say that. Don't even think it. If you draw it as you see it, and it is honest, then who's to judge how good it is? That's why there are so many artists. Draw it and let it tell its own story. Like poetry." He thought of something. "I'll be right back. Let me go get you a poem."

Frank returned carrying a yellowed newspaper clipping at least three years old. He said, "It's called 'When Earth's Last Picture Is Painted,' and it's by Rudyard Kipling."

"You're a better man than I, Gunga Din!" shouted Wallis.

"Good for you, Wallis. Same poet. This one is for Harold. It goes,

When Earth's last picture is painted and the tubes are twisted and dried
When the oldest colors have faded, and the youngest critic has died
We shall rest, and, faith, we shall need it—lie down for an aeon or two
Till the Master of all good workmen shall put us to work anew,

. . . I'm skipping to the end now . . .

And only The Master shall praise us, and only The Master shall blame
And no one shall work for money, and no one shall work for fame
But each for the joy of the working, and each, in his separate star,
Shall draw the Thing as he sees It for the God of Things as They are!"

The boys sat in silence for a long time. Wallis said, "May I see that?"

"What's an aeon?" asked Harold.

"It's like centuries, only longer," said Wallis. "It's what Mama is doing—lying down, waiting for The Master."

"Then I should save my drawings," said Harold.

"Yes, and we should all go to bed now," said Frank. "Off you go, Harold. Come on . . . quick, like a bunny!"

POSTMARKED FEB. 11, 1897

Mr. F. M. Wilson, Nortonville, Kansas

My dearest Friend,

Your letter written on Sunday evening came Tuesday and I was glad to hear from you.

I have often thought of Mrs. Wilson since my Father has been so low. Do you know I think we can never really sympathize with others until we have experienced something of the same sorrow ourselves—not until we stand with our own loved ones at the brink; not until our own hearts have ached at the loss of those we hold dearer than life, can we know the true feelings of others. Therefore, my dearheart, while I have always felt so sorry for you in your loss, I feel that I can now offer you sympathy true and sincere. Whatever of regret you have or whatever you would have different—let it all pass. It is all we can do!

You asked me if I cared to have you show my letters to your sister-in-law. You may do as you like about the matter. I have no objections to her reading them—though I'm sure she will not find them either very instructive or interesting. My letters are all hastily written. I write a great many letters and you must know that I take very little pains to make them sound nice. I remember Mrs. Wilson. I met her at your house on New Year's day four years ago.

Good Night—Sincerely Yours,
Irene

Miss Irene Webb, Nortonville, Kansas
Wednesday Night
Feb. 14, 1897

My Darling Irene,
Your very long and very interesting letter came to hand as usual last Friday morning. I have become accustomed to look for a letter from you in my Friday morning's mail, and thus far I have not been once disappointed. So faithful and prompt have you been in our correspondence even during the past six weeks when you have had so much care and sorrow to occupy your time, that I scarcely know how I could find an excuse sufficient to release me from my usual Sunday evening letter.

I hardly feel equal to the task this evening but shall not ask you to excuse me entirely. If you will accept a short letter this time I will try to make it up at some future date. My brother who has been visiting with me for some days went home last Friday, but his wife is still here and will remain for some time yet. We are enjoying her visit very much. Mrs. Henderson entertained a small company in her honor yesterday evening, commencing with a

6 o'clock tea, and ending about 12 o'clock with a dance. Returning at that hour Nettie & I sat up, talking until about 2 o'clock, so you can well imagine my reason for asking you to accept a short letter this time. I thank you for permission to show your letters to Nettie, and beg to assure you that in my opinion they will bear inspection and criticism.

But my dear girl, these events do not interest you now. Your whole life is now given up to your dear father, whom you love so well. It is sad indeed to know that his pain and suffering is being prolonged, and that nothing can be done for relief. I am very sorry that he must thus suffer, and that you must thus witness it, without being able to give relief.

It has been snowing here all afternoon, and the earth is covered to the depth of 4. or 5. inches now. It has been so calm and still that the trees are loaded down with their coat of flakes. The limbs of trees being covered to the depth of about 2 inches. A more beautiful snow scene I have never witnessed than the one presented to view tonight. It would be a grand night for a sleigh ride.

Now my darling if you will excuse me I will say Good Night.

Lovingly and Sincerely, Frank
Sunday, Feb. 14-97

NETTIE WILSON STRUCK A match to the paper and cobs and kindling she had stuffed into the stove of the cold kitchen while Frank put away Turk, who had had a long night under wraps, blowing cold clouds into the moonlight. Nettie had long been a good companion to Frank, and, of course, Frank and his brother Forest were very close. Nettie was just about Frank's height, wore her sandy-brown hair in a tight coil atop her head, and had a slender, vulnerable frame. Her hazel eyes were always moist. Despite being in perfectly good health she had the appearance of always needing a nap. She soon had a blaze under the iron lid of the stovetop, and was slicing snack bread when Frank stamped snow off his boots on the south porch outside the kitchen door. When he came in at last, she said,

"You and Mr. Henderson do go on about the banking business. You're no better than your brother Forest and your father."

"I'm sorry if we neglected you," said Frank. "Generally Mrs. Henderson is lively in bank discussions, and never shy to contradict her husband when she has good grounds. Scott respects her for that."

"Oh, Cora Henderson and I did fine with our own gossip. Your Horton is about as juicy with it as Holton. Only the names are different."

"That's a comfort to hear. Forest looks good, what are you feeding him?"

"Beef and garden greens and whatever the tornadoes drop on us before they cross into Nebraska."

"He's lucky to have you, Nettie."

"And you're lucky to have yourself that letter writer, Frank Wilson. I read through them all. You can tell a lot from a letter, even the most casual. This woman does not write casual letters. Those letters not only give out information, they give off a very high attitude. You know she's got a school-teacher's bones and orientation just from the way she writes. Mind if I ask you something, Frank? You sort of made it my business when you gave me those letters to look at."

"Ask me anything. Just be kind to me, Nettie. It's getting late and I'm tired and not up to some debate."

"You'll get no debate from me over Miss Webb. I took a liking to her that time I met her when she first arrived here and I like her even more from her letters. She seems like about as fine a woman as you're going to come across and a very prudent choice for you. Tell me, though: How many times have you visited her?"

"Twice."

"In Nortonville?"

"Once. The other was that time with the Altons."

"The agony she's going through with her father. Not to mention hospitality for a feedlot full of Webbs. And you haven't got yourself up there when she's suffering so? What is it, Frank, a day's ride? Thirty miles on a train?"

"It takes two trains. Look, I haven't been able to get away from the bank, Nettie, you know how it is."

"You can get up to Hiawatha. You can get to Atchison. You can get over to St. Joe. And now, as we was sayin' the other night with Forest, you may be getting down to Indian Territory shortly, Frank!"

"To collect on some fool horse trades of Forest and Papa's."

"No more fool trades than some you've made yourself along the way. Anyway, I'm grateful for you taking it on. You truly have a heart of gold, Frank. And I know how much that's going to take you away. But you have partners and people working for you. I'm just saying you can get away when you think it's important. But is a trip like that so much more important in that heart of yours than to visit Miss Webb in Nortonville? This is her *father*, Frank. What sort of attitude and orientation does all that say about you? I don't know what you've been writing in your letters back to her, but actions speak a whole lot louder. I think your actions are telling her you've got a heart of gold all right but not in the right way."

"The bank isn't just about making me busy or making me money, Nettie. People come in when they need something in the worst way. Maybe they have a chance to buy some acreage on higher ground to farm. Or hail dashed the sorghum just before harvest and now they don't have anything for another year. These people need me at those times just like they need Doc Ralston at other times."

"Frank, like you said, neither one of us needs a debate just now. I know where your heart is, and it's a good one. I know what you and Forest did back then when your folks were so miserable. You boys worked it out so you'd do for Amanda, and Forest said he'd do for Joseph. But Miss Webb only knows what you're doing now, or not doing, so what's she supposed to think? She'll never put blame on you, but you just think about how she feels when you're all about Horton and that bank."

"And the boys."

"And with your mother and a housekeeper to tend to them. You wanted me to know what's in those letters she writes you and say what I think. Well, I think that she sounds like the right woman for you and you better not let her get away."

"It's complicated."

There was a long silence. Nettie got up to put away the bread and stir the last embers in the stove. She turned to Frank and said,

"Because of Allie, right?" He nodded. "Well, that's something only you can work out in your own head. No use me going on about it. I just hope for your sake you find a way to make it uncomplicated for yourself. To me it's really simple. But it's got to be simple to you or you'll never have a happy life."

It had already started. He had to get in his bed before the spell gripped him. Before he left the kitchen he said, "Forest's a lucky man."

CHAPTER FOUR

I HAVE JUST RECEIVED A CALL TO GO TO INDIAN TERRITORY

Miss Irene Webb, Nortonville, Kansas
February 15, 1897

My Darling Irene,

I have just rec'd a call to go to Indian Territory and will start this evening, my first stop being at Hayden, a small town off the railroad. I can't tell how long I shall be gone. I may return in 3 or 4 days, and may be gone 2 weeks or more. For this reason perhaps you had better not write me, until you hear from me again, except in case of your father's death. I will advise you of my return.

Hastily but lovingly,
Frank

Miss Irene Webb, Nortonville, Kansas
Viniti Indian Territory, February 19, 1897

My Darling Irene,

You have perhaps wondered what dreadful offence I have committed that would require me to flee from the states, and take up my
abode among the Cherokee Indians, and Negroes, in the territory,
for such an indefinite period of time as I suggested in the note
mailed to you before departing from home. I will proceed to tell
you why I am here.

When the Cherokee strip was opened up for homestead
settlement the U.S. Government purchased the land from the
Cherokee Nation, paying them therefor at the rate of about $1.40
per acre, a sum aggregating between $8,000,000 and $9,000,000.
This vast sum of money when divided among the Cherokee people, gave to each man woman and child about $265. During the
Summer of 1894 payment was made to the Cherokees who were
known and acknowledged to be citizens, and entitled to a share in
the distribution of this fund. But there are about 4,000 or 5,000
Negroes in this Nation, who are descendants of slaves owned by
the Cherokee Indians, and by them freed. They are known as the
Cherokee freedmen.

These Negroes set up a claim for equal rights in the distribution of the strip fund. Pending the settlement of their rights in the
courts the government of the U.S. held back a portion of that fund
equal to the share claimed by the freedmen, and proceeded to pay
the Indians as before stated. The rights of the Negroes were fully
established by the court of claims of the U.S. and they are now
receiving their portion of the fund. There are over 4000 of these
Negroes to be paid. They reside in various parts of the Cherokee
Nation but all will be obliged to come to the town of Hayden

(some times during the past few days called "Hades") to receive their money. The enclosed newspaper report, while not accurate in details, is near enough the truth to give you some idea.

But as I proceed the mystery deepens, in your mind, for by this time you must be wondering whether I am claiming a share in the distribution, as a descendent of one of those old slaves, or as a Cherokee Indian. On account of my complexion and the color of my hair, I fear that my chances would not be very good for either claim.

When it became known that each member of the nation would soon receive in cash $265 from the government, the Yankee begun to figure on securing a good share of it. Merchants and traders sold goods, and live stock, on time at enormous prices, agreeing to wait for payment, until the Cherokees received their per capita settlement. My brother and father who live at Holton, and are engaged in handling cattle & horses, sold considerable stock on time to traders in this country, who in turn retailed them out to the Cherokees at a good profit. When the payment came off during the summer of 1894 collections were made, and the transactions proved quite satisfactory all around. Later on when the rights of the freedmen were established my brother & father sold some stock to a trader here, and now that the payment is to be made I came here to represent their interests and collect the amount due them.

During the payment of 1894 I spent 2 or 3 weeks down here so that I know about what to expect. I rec'd word last Monday, that payment would begin at Hayden on Wednesday. In order to be on hand at the start I left home that evening. Wallis and my sister-in-law Nettie who is visiting me, drove me over to Willis after supper in a cutter. It was a beautiful night and the trip was very pleasant. I came to K.C. over the Mo. Pacific. and remaining there over night, came here on the M.K.&T. arriving at 5:37 P.M. Tuesday afternoon.

On my arrival here I learned that the payment would not begin for several days, and on account of poor accommodations at Hades, or Hayden I should have said, I decided to stop here for the present. I am still here but may leave for Hayden tomorrow. It is still uncertain when the payment will begin. Tomorrow is Saturday, followed by Sunday, and Washington's birthday. This may afford the paymaster an excuse to postpone it until Tuesday. His policy seems to be to delay it, and prolong it as much as possible so that he may reap a harvest for himself from the sale of ground privileges. He of course controls the grounds upon which the payment is conducted and charges good prices for all privileges granted.

Hayden is about 20 miles from here, and is about 12 miles from nearest railroad point. There is a post office, a blacksmith shop, and a small store, but no hotel. Imagine if you can 5,000 to 10,000 people congregated in such a place for 30 to 60 days, at this season of year, and you have a conception of the winter picnic which I came so far to attend. Tents and temporary sheds are there to protect the people from storms. I have no idea how long I shall find it necessary to remain here. I shall not unnecessarily prolong my stay at Hayden.

Viniti is a town of about 1500 population, having two good hotels, and several not so good, a national bank, 2 railroads, 2 colleges, one a Methodist, and the other a Presbyterian. If the payment was to be held here, I should not mind it so much as the accommodations are good enough. Still I don't fancy having to wait here almost, if not quite, a week for it to begin. I have had letters from home since I came here but no word from you. I did not expect any word from you until I informed you of my whereabouts. I presume if you should write me at home, it would not be opened or forwarded to me, as I failed to instruct them concerning such mail when I left home, not knowing how long I should be absent.

I am anxious to know about your father's condition and while I hope that he may be improved, I fear the worst may have happened. How sorry I am for you all. I cannot tell you. These long weary weeks of anxiety and care must be telling on your strength as well as his. How I wish that these long weary days which I am wasting here, might be spent in ministering to his wants, and in relieving you from duty. I wish I might be able to say something to comfort you in this sad hour, but I fully realize that I cannot, and I shrink from the attempt. You already have been assured of my deepest sympathy. I hope to hear from you soon, that I may know his condition. You may address me at Hayden, and if I leave there I will have my mail follow me. The post-office facilities there may not be perfect, and if I do not receive your letters you need not wonder at it. If I remain here long you will hear from me occasionally.

I should have brought Harold with me, had I not known that the accommodations at Hayden would be very poor. I should very much like to have him with me. He is the greatest comfort of my life. He too would enjoy the trip. When he was a little more than 3 yrs. old I brought him to this country with me on a business trip which lasted a week. During the entire trip he never once mentioned home or anyone connected with home except when reminded of it by me, and then only in an indifferent way.

He seems perfectly contented with his lot, wherever cast. He gave me no trouble on that trip, but enjoyed it himself and made it pleasant for me.

Some time next summer, during school vacation, the McCalls are expecting to visit their son in Oklahoma. They want Wallis &

Harold both to go with them. I shall probably let Wallis go, but am not yet decided on Harold.

I should probably have brought Wallis with me on this trip, had it not been an interference with his school work.

My charming sweetheart, how I should love to be with you this evening, to gaze into your gentle loving eyes, and hear your sweet voice again. It seems like months since we parted and I am growing impatient to see you. The next thing to being in your presence, is to receive your beautiful letters which I prize so dearly. I believe in my last letter I begged to be excused with a short one, promising to make up for neglect at a future time. If this will fill the bill you may square the account.

Awaiting anxiously a loving message from you I will bid you Good Night.

Your sincere lover,
Frank

Mr. F. M. Wilson, Hayden
February 21, 1897
Sunday Afternoon

My dearest Friend, It is all over. My beloved Father is now at rest. I wired you at Horton this morning—and at Viniti as soon as I rec'd your letter. Oh, how I wish you could come. He is so beautiful. The end was peaceful, we hardly knew when he breathed the last—

Can't you come dear love?

Irene

Miss Irene Webb, Nortonville, Kansas
Viniti Indian Territory, February 23, 1897

My Darling Irene,

Upon my return here this afternoon, I received your sad message which has evidently been awaiting me here since Sunday evening. While it occasions no surprise, but on the contrary is that which I have been prepared to receive each day for the past 5 or 6 weeks, the announcement is none the less sad and unwelcome. At last he has been called to his final home, a world free from the cares, trials, and afflictions of this life, there to dwell among the angels forever. His was a life filled with good deeds, and good works, and he has gone to his reward. Oh! death where is thy sting; Oh! grave where is thy victory: All that human skill could accomplish to restore his health, and to prolong his life, was tried in vain. All that loving hearts and hands could do to render his last days upon earth peaceful and happy has been cheerfully done. Ample warning, and ample time for farewell messages, and counsel, to loved ones was allotted to him, and then he was called from a bed of affliction to the rest beyond.

All of these, and many more consoling thoughts, can but in part assuage your grief over the loss of your dear father, who has always been so good and so kind to you, and who bore to you a love second only to that of your mother. To you, dear heart, the loss is great indeed, but you are young, and strong, and must help your dear mother to bear up under the grief which overwhelms her.

I extend to her the sympathy of one who has but recently experienced the loss of a faithful, loving, life companion, but who has not yet reached that stage in life's race, where such a blow comes with greatest force.

I have often during the past few weeks tried to imagine her feelings, when she came to realize that her life companion had passed from death unto life eternal. She must at times feel a longing to follow him to that beautiful home prepared for the faithful. But she too has much to live for, and should not take a gloomy view of life. Her large family of loving children, will now seem dearer than ever to her, and will furnish an incentive to a longer life of usefulness here. He has gone, and the world is better for his having lived. What more can be said of any of us? "He acted well his part, therein all the honor his."

Dear friend I wish that I might see you, and tell you how much I sympathise with you in this your first great loss. I am sorry indeed that I was unable to be present either during his last illness or at the final ceremonies.

You have ere this, doubtless rec'd my letter mailed at Hayden last Sunday, and have ceased to wonder why you did not see or hear from me in reply to your message. I expect to return to Hayden tomorrow for an indefinite period. I merely came here today on business. No doubt I will receive a letter from you at Hayden soon, giving me full particulars of the sad events. I am anxious to hear from you. Believe me to be

Sincerely and devotedly

Yours,

Frank

P.S. I enclose letters just rec'd here from Wallis & Harold. Wallis is evidently learning the use of our typewriter under Pearl's instructions. I guess Harold must have had some assistance with all, excepting his signature, and his kisses. They both look to be genuine.

Miss Irene Webb, Nortonville, Kansas
Hayden Indian Territory, February 28, 1897

My Darling Irene,

I don't know that I am indebted to you in correspondence as I have received no letter from you since I left home, excepting the note written last Sunday announcing the death of your father, which I rec'd here upon my return from Viniti Wednesday.

I feel sure however that you have written me, and would not be surprised if your letter is in his office. The postmaster is incompetent to handle the volume of mail now coming here. I am not going to write much of a letter tonight, but could not let the day go by without dropping you a brief note to tell you that I have thought of you every day, and every hour. How sad and lonely you must feel, I think I can fully appreciate. Now that the anxiety and strain is over, I wonder how your mother is holding up under her load of sorrow. I hope and trust that you and she will not grieve too much. You have many consoling thoughts in connection with your loss. I wish that I might have spent this day with you instead of wasting it here in the camp. What a contrast between a day with you and a day here. As great a contrast as I could imagine.

I visited the soldiers' camp today and put in a part of my time there. I also moved my collar box, and took up board with a negro farmer about 1/2 mile from the camp where I hope to find more home like accommodations. The paymaster, his son, and his private secretary are also stopping here. The farmer is very well fixed, and I am satisfied I will be well fed and lodged here.

I have very little of interest to tell you this time, and feeling that I need a good night's rest I shall close, hoping that I shall soon hear from you, and assuring you of my unfaltering love and devotion.

I am , Sincerely,
Frank

F. M. Wilson
Hayden Indian Territory

My dearest Friend,

Your Sunday's letter came last evening and I thought I detected a little tinge of blue in it. I am afraid I have seemed almost selfish in my devotion to my Father and in my grief at his death. Papa never wanted to live when his faculties should become the least impaired. He was so reasonable in his life and just so in his illness and death. He was all gentleness and love and patience.

Mama is feeling better than when I wrote you Sunday. We are taking up life again as best we can. Mr. McVey will have charge of the farm this year. He is so perfectly trustworthy that we shall be relieved of any business cares. Papa never talked business in his family—When we children were small, he kept everything of that nature from Mama as he felt she had enough care and worry in the house. The early part of their married life was a very busy one and the habits formed then were never broken. Therefore Mama is very inexperienced in matters of business and I am as much so. As soon as we get rested a little in mind and nerves, we are going away for a little while. I have an old bachelor uncle living in Houston Texas and I have always had a great desire to visit him. However Mama's wish shall determine. I wish she felt able for a trip to Old Mexico.

I was greatly interested in Wallis and Harold's letters. Harold is very modest in his wants, isn't he? I think the child thinks of his Papa as I always did of mine—that he was able to grant anything I should ask for. I do not care to have you bring me anything but I do join Harold in wanting to know "When you are coming home."

I have not forgotten what you told me about your previous trip down to that country and I think that I shall sleep a little better at night when I learn you are safely back in Horton. If I have anything to say about it, you shall never risk that precious neck of yours among those people again. I'd like to know what good that 5 or 10 dollars will do you when some Great Big Injun has your Auburn scalp. Hoping that you are well and that nothing but good may come to you, I am

Lovingly Yours,

Irene

[*Harold's February 19th letter to his father in Oklahoma—sent to Irene for inspection—requested that he be brought: a Shetland pony, a parrot, a saddle, three sacks of rock candy, two popcorn, a fishing pole, a cork, a wagon, a pair of prairie dogs, an Indian bow and arrow, and a little rifle.*]

ON THE LETTERHEAD OF THE NEW ALBANY HOTEL,
KANSAS CITY, MO.

Mch. 6, 1897

My Darling Irene,

I arrived here yesterday morning on my return from Hayden, having left that memorable mud hole Thursday afternoon. I had about decided to pay you a visit today, reaching home tomorrow night. I was up this morning at half past four o'clock to take Mo. Pacific for Atchison at 5.10 but found the train several hours late, on account of washouts. Upon further reflection I have decided to go direct home this morning, deferring my visit with you until some more convenient time, when I am sure to find you at home. The more I reflected upon it, the more likely it seemed to me that you might be absent from home, with some of your sisters or brothers, for a rest which you and your mother must certainly feel need of now. Having been absent from home almost 3 weeks you can well imagine how anxious I am to return to my boys, and how much my presence is needed at the bank. Notwithstanding all this I am so anxious to see you, that I should certainly stop over, if I were assured that I would find you at home.

When you contemplate my thoughts and feelings, should I learn upon my arrival at your home, that you and your mother were absent, I am sure that you will pardon me for changing my mind. Knowing how much I will find to do at home, and that it will be difficult for me to find time to write you for several days I thought I would spend my time this morning while waiting for my belated train, in writing you.

My departure from Hayden was occasioned by an indefinite postponement of the payment, owing to charges of bribery, fraud, and corruption against the paymaster. The payment may possibly be resumed at any time, but I feared a delay of 10 or 15 days, and concluded to return, and if need be send a substitute. The weather down there for some days past has been very disagreeable. It has rained often enough to keep the roads almost impassable. I left Hayden at 3. P.M. Thursday for Viniti, in a hack drawn by four good horses, and loaded with 6 passengers. It had been raining all day, and the previous night, and creeks were rising fast. About 6. o'clock we reached a stream that seemed dangerous to cross. The driver took one of his horses from the hack, and rode in, and across. He decided we could cross it and we did, but it was a dangerous experiment and might have cost us dearly. The driver mounted one of his lead horses, so that he could better control them, and one of the passengers with whip in hand held the reins on the wheel team. We took our baggage in hand to hold it up out of water, sat upon the backs of the seats and were ready to jump and swim in case of necessity. The hack came near turning over twice, the water rose over my feet on the seat. The horse carrying our driver fell and went under water; he slid off, gained a footing and led the team out safely. We congratulated ourselves, but resolved to not try the next stream which we knew we would reach about 2 miles from Viniti. The ford to this stream happens to be very near a railroad bridge, so we abandoned the hack at this point, and crossing the stream on the railroad bridge, walked to town, a distance of 2 miles, carrying our baggage, in the rain and after dark. Arriving at Viniti about 8 o'clock wet, and muddy, I spent the time until departure of my train at midnight in cleaning up and drying out.

In walking to town that night we overtook a party of 6 or 8 men, women & children, with luggage, who were walking to town, having left their conveyances on the other side of the stream which we crossed as related above. This made for these people a walk of about 5 miles. I could fill many sheets, with reminiscences of my trip, but there would be such a painful sameness to it, that I fear it would not interest you. I spent the day here yesterday very satisfactorily to myself.

For some time I have wanted an opportunity to visit a well kept cemetery, in a large city, for purpose of making observations. After spending an hour or two in the forenoon in obtaining facts and information which would aid me, I spent most of the afternoon at Elmwood Cemetery, which I am informed is the finest one here. I feel amply rewarded for the time thus spent, and think I shall now find it less difficult to decide what to do for our family burying lot. A few days ago I rec'd a letter from Mr. Alton, forwarded to me from home, in which he returned a draft which I had placed in Mrs. Alton's hands more than a month ago, with instructions to secure and forward to you a floral tribute, in case I should learn of your father's death, and be unable to attend the funeral, and would wire her the simple message "Forward tribute."

I thought this would insure more prompt delivery, in case I should find it impossible to attend the funeral. Then when I left home, I wrote Mr. Alton announcing my departure, and asking him to forward the tribute without further notice from me, in case he learned of his death during my absence, in time to send it. In his letter he informs me that he did not learn of his death until too late. I was very sorry indeed that Mrs. Alton did not learn of his death in time to send my tribute to his memory, and more sorry that I was unable to be present. I rec'd your beautiful letter of last Sunday, before leaving Hayden, and was much interested in the account of his last hours. Indeed you have kept me so fully informed of the many incidents, and changes, connected with his illness, all related in a manner so impressive, that I can imagine that I have been present at his bedside many times during his last days. A noble life, a peaceful end, Rest at last.

My dear, I find I have used up my time and must hastily close. With much love I am

Sincerely,
Frank

IF HAYDEN IS WHAT Hades feels and smells like, Frank thought, the Horton railroad shops is what it sounds like.

The day shift had just started in the saw mill and the machine shops. In their clamor Frank stood on the platform, gazing westward at the train that had just carried him home as it chuffed up the grade westward to Manifest Destiny, carrying with it his box of six starched collars beneath a cane-covered horsehair seat, the seventh one chaffing his neck. The rest of him was considerably less than starched. His wadded-up, tweed trouser legs were caked in mud riled by four struggling horses in a fording that had nearly failed. His brown shoes from Chicago were soaked beyond any hope of recovery and his feet were very nearly the same. His shirt had not left his back in four days.

He was too stubborn to laugh. Instead he yielded to vanity and reflected on a successful life thus far. He was president of one of two banks in this town and had considerable influence in the affairs of men, at least those within a day's ride. Customers and employees depended on him. Townspeople depended on his vision for libraries, waterworks, and the business boom that would surely emerge from the current doldrums. Horton was the future and Hayden was the sorry remnant of an ugly episode of the Nation's past. The sun began to warm him nearly as much as his pride. He was home again, eager to fill the void his three-week absence had left in the town's vibrant life.

Stationmaster Dixon strolled along the platform, then stopped.

"Morning, Frank. Going somewhere? Just kidding, welcome home. There's a carriage with your womenfolk waiting on the road for you."

Frank managed an affable smile when he reached the carriage and thanked his mother and Mrs. McCall for getting up at dawn to collect him.

"It's the least we could do," said Mrs. Wilson.

"And doing less than we've had to during that jaunt of yours will be a welcome thing," said Mrs. McCall.

"Don't start in on him, I haven't noticed you being so put out," said Mrs. Wilson.

"And noticing things is not exactly your greatest strength," said Mrs. McCall. "For example, there's limbs and sticks still down on your yard from the storm ten days ago. Frank, that means you'll have to pick up, and today is none too soon."

"Actually, I have to get to the bank."

"Oh, no you don't," said Mrs. McCall. "Besides the yard, the chicken coop collapsed in the wet snow from that storm. The boys and I managed to prop it up but it needs proper fixing or those birds will be brooding in the next county."

"Mother, you could just get Mr. Edwards in for that."

"You people have that man practically full-time as it is. I hope you're not paying him out of McCall family deposits down there. You look a fright, anyway. You've no business going to the bank looking like you do."

"It *is* his bank, after all, Mrs. McCall."

"May we just get Turk moving so we can go somewhere today?" said Frank.

Amanda Wilson got Turk and the carriage turned around and up the soft road to Main Street. Frank did, in fact, prevail on them to wait the carriage outside the bank while he went in to look over accumulated mail and to bring home for attention anything requiring urgency for the day. The news was not good. An important foreclosure had been nonsuited because of faulty notice. A man from the Comptroller of the Currency would be paying a "courtesy call" the next Monday. Phillip Latham left a note saying the daily accounts wouldn't foot this week. How could that be? You don't go home till they foot!

He concluded that his desk held all troubles and no opportunities, and went back to the carriage. On the way home, he took the reins and made a deliberate detour over to Edwards's place to wake him and engage him for the day, picking up windfall and repairing the coop.

"Tell me about the boys," Frank said with a grin as they turned for home.

"Well, their names are Wallis and Harold, Mr. Wilson. Can't be faulted for forgetting after such a long absence."

"Spare me your sarcasm, Mrs. McCall. I have just been to hell and gone and back. I'm sore and I'm in no mood for a War of the Roses."

Amanda spoke up brightly, "They are both fine, Frank. They missed you terribly. Wallis stuck up for Harold against a bully and got a bloody nose."

Finally, some cheery news, Frank thought. Outside Mrs. McCall's house he said again how much he appreciated her coming out on a cold morning. As she stood by the carriage, Mrs. McCall said, "You are welcome. Ross, Pearl and I would enjoy it if you could all come for dinner Sunday."

"That is kind of you, but may we make it the following Sunday, please? I just learned that I have the US Government paying me a call on Monday and I have no idea if anyone has prepared for it."

"That'll be fine, Mr. Wilson. I'll make my stewed guinea hen and dumplings."

Amanda and Frank rode in silence to the corner. Amanda declared: "Her stewed guinea hen and dumplings cannot be eaten."

MAILED MARCH 11, 1897.

F. M. Wilson, Horton, Kansas

My Beloved Friend,

Your letter which reached me Monday morning explains in part my feelings Saturday and Sunday. All day Saturday I felt that you were near me. Indeed I do not think I should have been very much surprised to see you, although I did not know you were any place in the country. Sunday I felt the same way. I felt that you were coming. Mama and I went for a little ride Sunday morning. I was so impressed with the thought you would come that, as we left the house I said to Mr. McVey—if anybody comes, tell him I will be back in a little while.

You would have received a hearty welcome had you come. Saturday Mama and I were all alone for the first time since Father left us. Mr. McVey took Mrs. McVey home and spent the day. Sunday was a very lonely day for us.

I do not know when we will go away. I am really uneasy about my Mother's health. She was not well before my Father took down, then the strain and excitement of his long illness and her grief over his death have left her very frail. She does not feel able to go any place now, but I am in hopes she may feel better very soon.

I thank you sincerely my dearheart, for your thoughtful kindness in endeavoring to secure a floral tribute for my beloved Father. I am very sorry you did not mention the matter to me as I could have asked my nephew in St. Joe, to bring it with him. He came to the funeral and had I known he could have brought it or I might have wired the Altons. I knew though that they were not expecting to come and thought a letter written later would be more satisfactory to them than a message sent at the time.

As I said before I am sorry about the flowers, but never mind—it is all right—it was sweet and kind of you to think of it—the spirit is the same.

It is getting late and I must close. This has been such a lonely day—gentle spring is almost here—my first Robins have returned from their southern home. They seemed very glad to see me and I was happy to have them back. I notice little green blades of grass here and there.

Well Good Night—

Lovingly,
Irene

P.S. If you can make it convenient I should be glad to have you come over a week from next Sunday. You can tell me in your next whether or not to expect you. Your time is of necessity so short that I suggest you come on to Nortonville Saturday night—9:54 instead of spending the night in St. Joe.

Irene Webb, Nortonville, Kansas
Sunday, March 14, 1897

My Darling Irene,

It is Sunday evening. Mother and Wallis have gone out to the M.E. Church to hear a temperance lecture. I have put Harold to sleep and will devote the remainder of the evening to my sweetheart.

I am very sorry now, that I did not venture to call on you on my return home from K.C. a week ago yesterday. It was only the fear that you might be absent that kept me from it. I think it strange indeed that you should have such a feeling that I was not far away on that day.

If there is no preventing providence, I shall avail myself of your kind hospitality next Saturday night, and be present in person as well as in spirit. I shall act upon your suggestion and may go from Pierce Junction to Atchison, thence to Nortonville on the night train.

I can leave here at half-past-five, and be waiting at Pierce about 2 hours, get to Atchison in time for the Santa Fe. If I am unable to get away I will advise you by letter or by wire. I trust I shall not be prevented from making the trip as I am very anxious to see you. It seems an age since we parted, and you must remember that I haven't even a photo to look at. Don't you think I have waited about long enough for that Photo? I know you have had no opportunity to secure once since I saw you but perhaps now you can have one taken for my especial benefit. Please let me have one as soon as you feel disposed to sit for it.

You have probably heard that the N.E. Kansas Teachers Association convenes in Horton April 15th, 16th and 17th. This includes you, and even though you may not have been in the habit of attending these conventions I can think of many good reasons for your attending this one, and I have constituted myself a committee of one to extend a special invitation to you, and to see that you accept it. The committee on entertainment are trying to secure a list of those who are willing to entertain the teachers while here, and have left slips similar to the one enclosed, with those who might do so, asking them to fill up and hand to the committee. I enclose my slip, which I will permit you to examine before I hand it to the committee.

Mr. Dixon tells me that Robert McIntyre has been secured for one lecture, and they will secure some distinguished speaker for an educational lecture, during the convention. The musical program has not yet been completed. I have not yet given the committee my consent to render a vocal selection. The greatest objection upon my part comes from the feeling that if I consent to furnish music for this occasion, it would be difficult to excuse myself from the numerous invitations which are sure to follow. I find I must be very careful to avoid giving offence. Whatever may be your conclusion as to the remainder of the foregoing remarks, I don't want you to get the idea that my invitation is a joke. I am extremely anxious to have you visit us, and it seems to me that the teacher's convention is an intervention of providence. Had I started out to devise a scheme I couldn't have beaten it. You will enjoy the convention, you have many friends in Horton whom you will be glad to see, and I can speak for one of them, who I am sure will be delighted to see you. Now I can think of no excuse which you can offer, for declining this invitation, which will be accepted unless it should happen that you and your mother should be absent upon your proposed trip at that time, and I hope this will not occur. I don't mean that I wish you to miss your proposed trip, but I trust it will not conflict with the convention.

Your letter of 4th inst. addressed to me at Hayden was returned and reached me in due time. Yours of last Wednesday was rec'd Friday morning as usual. I should be very much disappointed should a Friday pass by without a letter from you. I have come to look for them on Friday morning with the same regularity that I look for my meals.

Well I have used up the last drop of ink in the house and must resort to pencil or quit.

Dear sweet heart, I cheerfully forgive you for what you term your neglect of me and my doings of late. Although I crave your constant attention, I had no right to expect it during the illness of your father. I have often wondered how you found time to write me at such length during those long weeks of anxiety.

It seems to me you are very fortunate in having Mr. McVey to take charge of the farm, and help you manage affairs. My observation has been that most women, who thus have the full responsibility of business cares suddenly thrown upon them, are quick to acquire a faculty for the discharge of this duty, equal to that of the average man. I am sure that you and your mother will meet with no difficulties along that line.

I think a trip to Mexico would be the finest trip you could imagine. I believe your mother would receive much benefit from such a trip, and that she would grow stronger from the time she started. I don't think there is the slightest danger that she would not be able to stand such a trip.

I am not yet decided whether I shall return to Hayden or not. You know I left rather suddenly because the payment was postponed a few days & I felt that I was needed at home. I have found much to do since my return. Have worked almost every night. Have been quite busy in the bank for several weeks. I hope to catch up with my work during the coming week and it is barely possible that I may conclude that I ought to return to Hayden to complete the work which I left unfinished.

I hoped that my brother could go if we concluded that it was advisable for one of us to do so. But he seems to have so much on hands that he cannot be spared, and perhaps I can arrange my affairs so I can be spared again. The three weeks already spent there afforded me a good rest and another term of 2 or 3 weeks would fatten me up considerably I think. If I do go I will stop and see you on my way to K.C.

I think I must now ask you to excuse me. It is growing late and fires are getting low. I will think of you every day, love, and every hour, and long to see you until we meet again, anxiously counting the hours and days as they pass by, and looking forward for your beautiful letter which I am sure to receive and in pleasant anticipation of my visit next Saturday night.

With much love,
Frank

F. M. Wilson, Horton, Kansas
March 18, 1897, from Nortonville, Kansas
PRIVATE

My dearest Friend,

The days are growing so much longer that I can go for my Monday's letter on Monday evening now instead of waiting till Tuesday for it. I rode up for my—your—no my letter last Monday evening and was well paid for my trip. Thank you, Mr. Committee man for your very kind invitation to attend the Teacher's Association which convenes at Horton in April. I do not know whether or not it will be possible for me to go. I note what you say about your pleasure derived from "entertaining distinguished guests—" Is that the reason you want me to stay at your house?

The terms upon which I am to "board" at your house during the association, should I attend it, are entirely satisfactory. I presume you will give me a reduction, should I happen to receive an invitation to dine out.

Tomorrow I can say to myself day after tomorrow you will be here. It seems to me this week is dreadfully long—I presume Father Time will make up for his slowness about next Sunday. Mr. McVey will meet you Saturday evening. It is much too late for me to go. Mrs. McVey and Maggie Rea will spend Sunday with us. I shall be glad to have you meet them. Maggie Rea is a sweet girl of thirteen—very bright but badly spoiled in as much as she is the only child and has things her own way at home.

We have about decided to go to Texas for a trip. I am glad it is over; perhaps now we shall hear something of the spring styles and Easter bonnets.

Good night dear heart till Saturday night. Can you not bring Harold with you? Or both of the boys for that matter. You ought to get out home by 10:15 if your train is on time. Be careful not to get confused in trains at Pierce Junction.

Lovingly and Sincerely,
Irene (Wednesday, 9:20 p.m.)

MORNING THREE

On the morning of Saturday, March 20, 1897, the two Irenes rearranged the upstairs bedrooms. Frank and Harold were to be put up in the big bedroom upstairs and the two Irenes were to double-up in Tot's room. During the day Irene's mother was chattier than she had been in weeks. She kept up a constant chronicle of anecdotes about Webb pioneers and Webb cattle and Webb babies. Irene had heard the stories before but did not hear a word of today's chatter.

Irene could only think in terms of apocalyptic events meant to doom this visit. Something would. Would it be a tornado? Unlikely in early spring but not impossible. Would the train derail? It happens all the time. Never on this stretch of tracks but that doesn't mean a thing. Would Harold take sick at the last minute? She fought off those thoughts, but new ones stepped from the rear ranks to take their place. She would appear plainer to him than she did three months ago. Too plain, in fact. Not as pretty as the newest schoolteacher in Horton. Maybe the pretty new teacher played dominoes with Harold. And probably she was an actress and performed in light operas— say, *The Mikado*.

Long before the train had even left the Horton station, Mrs. Webb had declared exhaustion and taken herself to bed. The train was late. Indigo turned to black and the outdoors was bathed in the shine of the Milky Way. Oh, they were all true, her misgivings. Not the tornado, maybe, but Harold fell ill and the new schoolteacher was hovering over him and would stay the night and would sing to everyone in the morning. Frank would sing harmony, and make shirred eggs with brown toast for her.

Jerret McVey's shrill, two-fingered whistle pierced the night air. Irene jumped from her chair and ran to the front porch. It was nearly midnight when McVey delivered the Wilsons to the farmhouse.

Irene ran to the carriage and Frank stepped down to catch her in his open arms. She flung her arms around his neck. Frank turned in two complete circles with Irene clinging to him, her legs swinging off the ground.

Harold climbed into Mr. McVey's lap and would have slept the night there had Irene not plucked him away and showered the boy's cheeks with kisses. The two Wilsons stood engulfed in Irene's arms as McVey set the tan leather valise and smaller lacquered straw case inside the doorway. Harold slithered to the ground. Frank held Irene until she stopped for breath. At that point Frank kissed her.

"Finally" and "At last" they said in unison. Frank touched her chin and tilted it up for a lingering kiss. However, Harold squeezed between them and thrust his arms upward for Frank to pick him up. Frank could see only rain-gray eyes in the starlight. Mr. McVey cleared his throat. Irene finally lifted Harold into Frank's arms and tried to hug them both again. Both Harold and Mr. McVey began to squirm with embarrassment.

Frank untangled Harold and carried him upstairs, where he hung up the boy's clothes and slid a nightshirt over him. By the time he returned to the living room, McVey had departed. Irene danced as she set a dish of apple crisp before him.

"Last time a pear, and now it is apple you offer me from your father's garden? Something deep in that."

Irene giggled and twirled twice so that her skirt rose slightly. She moved behind him and pinned his arms in another hug as she pressed her cheek against his. She whispered, "Well, the apples came from the deep root cellar. And it's a deep dish crisp. How much deeper do you want to take it, poet? I assure you the serpent didn't make me bake it. I love you, dearest Frank Wilson."

He stood, turned to her, and whispered back, "I so love you, too, precious Irene Webb."

PERHAPS IT WAS THAT late-night snack—unusual for Frank—that caused him a tormenting headache until first birdsong. More likely, it was the ruminations over his wife's dead face in the night stillness.

BY THE TIME THE Wilson men came downstairs the Webb women had produced a thresher's meal of biscuits, ham, scrambled eggs, and hotcakes. With them were Jerret McVey and Maggie Rea.

Frank said, "I'm afraid we overslept, Mrs. Webb. This is my son, Harold."

"I'm happy to see you again, Mr. Wilson. And glad to meet you, Harold. This is Maggie Rea."

Maggie Rea pumped Harold's hand and said, "Ever see a foal?"

Harold glanced at Frank and then said, "No, I . . ."

"Dropped just last night. New as they get. Hurry up, and we'll go see," said Maggie Rea.

Mrs. Webb said, "Mr. Wilson, you just take your time with breakfast. It's been a real busy night. Irene's out in the stable."

Maggie Rea dispatched breakfast as though she were managing a Fred Harvey House on the Santa Fe line, and then abducted Harold in broad daylight before he could take a second helping.

Mr. McVey had planned the day. He was running the 440-acre Webb farm now along with the adjoining 180-acre McVey farm. First, he led an inspection of the stable, the horses, the foal, the equipment, and seed corn awaiting spring planting. Irene and Frank would have been content to linger holding hands in an empty stall in the stable. That was not to be. McVey organized a carriage ride along the roads that enclosed the fields of the two farms. Geese were feeding in stubble and patches of leftover snow along the creek bed. He and Frank spoke in the argot of grain elevators, cash prices of oats and sorghum, corn futures in Chicago, draft horses, and even harness oil. He stopped the carriage occasionally for the men to walk into a field to get a feel of the soil, or to inspect the underside of a bridge. The two Irenes fidgeted, but they were glad the two men were getting along. Irene did a lot of watching and listening. Next to lingering with Frank in the empty stall, the most important thing for her was whether her mother and Frank were comfortable together. She listened and observed, with sounds of distant hawks, meadowlarks, and quail in the background. All the sounds were music in her ears.

Farm talk soon gave way to talk of money, hailstorms, crop loans, and politics. Irene had heard enough to convince her that everyone was having such a good time that no one, especially the banker next to her, was paying attention to her. That was when Irene drove an elbow into Frank's ribs, causing a yelp that turned heads. Frank excused himself while Irene doubled over in stifled giggles.

Maggie Rea had recruited Harold to spread the butter on the bread she cut, place the ham she'd sliced on the bread he'd buttered, and spread the mustard on the ham. She brought out the yellow cake Aunt Tot had made the day before and had left with sugary quince syrup to soak over the top. She arranged on the good china pickled vegetables from the previous summer's garden. All of this, with pitchers of milk and well water, had been set on the back porch table. Maggie Rea had allowed ample of time for teasing Harold before the grown-ups returned.

When they did return, Irene and McVey tended to the horse and carriage. Mrs. Webb and Frank walked to the back porch and sat down. Frank then scraped his chair to face her and leaned a little closer, his fingers laced in his lap. He said, "I am so very sorry about your loss, Mrs. Webb. Although our one and only meeting was brief, I could see why Hiram was admired by so many. And at least he did have the chance to hear their words at the end. Many do not. My Allie did not."

Mrs. Webb looked away and said nothing for a moment. She turned and smiled briefly. She sat a little straighter and said, "Thank you. You are no stranger to loss, Mr. Wilson. Irene has told me so much about Mrs. Wilson. You must be very lonely without her."

Frank looked carefully in her eyes and gave a quick nod. He pursed his lips, gathering his thoughts, and said, "Let me take a minute while we're alone to be candid with you, Mrs. Webb. Your daughter was a joy to be with three years ago and she seemed to especially enjoy Harold. Of course he can't remember what she said in those days, but I think he does remember how she made him feel. I have fond memories of the six months she was our houseguest. You must know that we have become more than friends over these last six months of correspondence. I have asked your daughter if I may court her. I want you to know from my heart that I have honorable intentions and hope that the courtship might lead to engagement."

She cleared her throat and looked away. So much had happened so fast. All her attention had been on Hiram, and afterward on herself. Just Frank's presence on the porch—and now his words—forced her to think about Irene and her future.

"That is good of you to say, Mr. Wilson. Irene has a good grounding in farm life and in city sophistication, or as much as Lawrence and Emporia can offer. She is smitten with you, Mr. Wilson. A mother knows. And a mother always frets, so your words are welcome. Have you ever worked a farm?"

Frank swallowed, tilted his head slightly from side to side, and said, "No, Mrs. Webb. Not in the way you and your family have lived your lives on this farm. As you know, I'm a banker. I'm connected to farming business but removed from it at the same time. I don't suppose I could change that if that's what you're asking."

Mrs. Webb chuckled and said, "No, Mr. Wilson, I'm not asking you to give up your bank. Somehow this big farm is so much on my mind, I suppose I was trying to see if you could fit yourself into it somewhere. I've lived on this farm but never was the farmer. That's the way Hiram insisted on things. I feel out of my element now even though I'm on my own place. Pay no mind to my babbling."

"It's natural for you to think that way and it is not babbling. Whatever I do know about the money aspects of farming, I am very glad to give advice to you and Irene. I like Mr. McVey very much and I know you are in capable hands there."

"I know, Mr. Wilson. We'll do fine as a family. Always have. I shouldn't give way to my uncertainties. I have adult daughters, sons, daughters-in-law, and Maggie Rea, so I am never without advice. Please ignore my question."

"I'm honored you asked it. I'll always be glad to help if I can."

Mrs. Webb nodded. She looked off to the field beyond the west board fence and saw spring growth. Another season, she thought, the renewal of life—surely a rebirth for me. Then she noticed Irene and McVey closing up the stable. "Look, here they come. I'll call Maggie Rea and Harold. Let's eat!"

Long after nightfall the downstairs eventually emptied save for Irene and Frank. Irene went to the brightly lit coal-oil lamps and turned the wicks as low as possible. Frank began with yet another tribute to Hiram, but Irene interrupted and sat quite close beside him. She said in a low voice, touching the top of his hand,

"It is me you've come to pay a call to, dear Frank, not my father's memory, which you have honored many times already. All that has been written. So much else has been written. Have you feelings which have not yet found their tongue? You certainly gave them voice in St. Joseph."

They shared a companionable kiss. Frank grew clammy within his shirt and his head throbbed. Nonetheless, he decided to press to his main objective in making this trip to Nortonville, which was to build a foundation for a possible marriage proposal another day. First things first, he had thought, and the first thing is a common understanding about married life. For that, he had turned to a source that had stood him in good stead in his first marriage. It set the tone in rational ideas he felt would be the right starting point from which to advance on the emotional front. He had brought a well-worn book, three inches thick, from his bookcase for that very purpose.

Frank held up his palm and said, "So many feelings that I don't know how to start. Excuse me for a moment. I brought you something. It's in my valise."

When Frank returned to the living room, Irene had smoothed her skirt over legs crossed at the ankles. She held her hands together in her lap. She hoped her face did not betray the bewilderment she was beginning to feel. Frank pulled a chair closer to hers and sat down—or rather on the front edge of the seat. It tipped, and Frank had to start again. She noticed tiny beads of perspiration where his mustache had once been. He leaned back and exhaled. Then he patted an ironed linen handkerchief against his upper lip. He coughed. He returned the handkerchief to his trousers pocket. Irene sensed his deliberation—and his struggle.

"Frank, I'm whom you *love*, not dread. Just be yourself."

"I am not well versed in the language our deepening relationship deserves," he said. He looked away. Then he gripped his book and looked back. "Nevertheless, we should be free and open on the topic. Let this book speak what I find difficult to say. It is definitive on the subject. It was written by Fowler, a noted doctor of the science of phrenology and of marriage. Here, I'd like you to tell me what you think after you read it thoroughly." He pushed the book forward.

Irene's shoulders relaxed slightly. A book, she thought to herself. My poet brings a book to be his voice. She reached for it and studied the front cover.

Irene was unprepared for the title: *Creative and Sexual Science*. She regained her mental footing. Well, she thought, it is probably not in verse. It was much more fun than this out in the starlight when everyone was spilling out of the carriage. She was aching for fun with these two unpredictable boys. Must she now be schoolmistress? She wanted to dance. She wanted to kiss this muted banker. That was really all. It would get better from there without the "language of deepening relationships."

She said, "I will study your book with care. May I ask what has prompted you to bring it into my life just now?"

One of the lanterns sputtered and went out, sending a thin pencil line of lampblack into the room. Neither attempted to address it. It was past midnight.

"We have opened our hearts. It's now time for a clear-eyed understanding of certain basic principles and expectations. To me, marriage means equal terms in all respects. Domestic and business alike. And with success in both. Two of my children live of the four born in my marriage. I want more children and to rear them to high standards. I find no better expression of my sentiments than in Fowler's book.

"My closest family has urged me over and over to take your hand and walk together toward our happiness. Nettie, my sister-in-law, in particular has been adamant on the subject. It is good thinking. I suppose we should give it serious consideration. It is a serious matter."

"I have long admired your scholarly ways," she said carefully. "This teacher seems always a student in your school, Frank. I cannot deny that others have counseled me along those lines as well. Good counsel always makes for better informed action. As far as marriage is concerned, it is my belief that if it is based on pure and righteous spirit, it cannot help but succeed. I don't quite understand where science fits in, but I am always open to learning."

While it may have been that Frank's point of departure on marriage was intellectual, and that Irene's was spiritual, her secret hope for this particular visit was for something sentimental—intimate, in fact. She had wanted time alone with him—maybe in that empty stall—for an affectionate hug. Or many. Now she waited, expecting some brio under the stars. However, nothing was forthcoming. She wondered whether to initiate warmth on her own or to let this moment pass until a better moment came.

Frank sat stock-still. Something gripped his mind so much that inaction seemed all he was capable of. Across from him was the woman he hoped to marry and yet he did not feel an ounce of passion in his bones. He steadied his breath. He waited for rescue, making no effort to struggle out of the bog he found himself in.

Finally, she said, "Didn't you sleep last night?"

"No, dear love."

"Do you feel unwell?"

"Actually, yes." Frank sighed. He didn't know how to animate himself. His jaw was tight, his blue eyes pleading. She blinked away thoughts of dancing. Then she tossed her head, laughed brightly and said,

"Come on then, tuck yourself into bed. I hope that tonight will bring you sleep." She winked and added, "And that it is *deep*. We'll all be here in the morning. Mornings on this farm have a certain sparkle that's bound to cheer you up."

But, Irene thought, in bed next to her mother, tomorrow morning will bring departure. And a farm without men. Without dancing. Maybe next visit.

ON THE TUESDAY AFTERNOON following Frank's visit, Maggie Rea came to the Webb farm and found Irene buried in the Fowler book.

"What's that you're reading, Aunt Tot?"

Irene looked up with a frown and said, "Maggie Rea, I'm not in my best of moods right now. This is a book Mr. Wilson wants me to read and give my opinion on. And no, I'm not going to read it out loud or even show it to you. It's my business and it's important. You always want me to drop everything when you come by. I generally do but I can't right now. I don't want to sound mean but I didn't know you were coming."

Maggie Rea stood still, clearly taken aback. She turned to go back to town when Irene said, "No, no, don't leave. I'm glad you're here. We should saddle Bluebelle and the bay and lope over to the stock pond to check on the salt licks. Want to do that?"

Maggie Rea's color returned to her cheeks. She said, "All right. I mean, if you can get away. I never meant to bother you."

"I'm sorry I barked at you. Look, why don't you go upstairs and read to Mama for about an hour. Can you stay for supper? You can ride the bay home and bring her back tomorrow after school."

"I should just go home for supper. I've got studies." Maggie Rea's voice was subdued. She turned and climbed the stairs to Mrs. Webb's bedroom.

At the top of the stairs she turned and said, "It's okay, Aunt Tot, you can't help being mean. You're a schoolteacher, after all. You are still God's creature. I'm enlightened and can love you. Which I do five or six days a week."

Irene said, "I'm smiling. And I'm reading."

She turned again to Fowler. Faded pencil lines down the left-hand margin of the page marked the passages Frank wanted her to read. On other pages of the book she found abbreviated notes in Allie's hand, most of which expressed a form of surprise. Or shock. Frank recently had added, in bolder pencil annotations, the order in which the pages and sections should be read. She was still on the first, entitled "The First Stage of Courtship."

Nature has divided courtship into two stages, each as distinct from the other as seed-time is from harvest, or sunrise from sunset, and bearing a like mutual relation. . . . Two should no more make Love till they have selected, been accepted, and are engaged, than enter a house till they have closed the bargain for it, and obtained its keys. . . . Every courted girl should know whether her beau comes as a matrimonial canvasser, or just for fun, and to have a good time; and if for the latter, dismiss, and rather expel him summarily, as if he were an avowed seducer under the guise of courtship.

The true procedure is this: Before paying his addresses to a young woman, a young man should ask, at the innermost shrine of his being, "Will this one or that make me the best wife?" and let the "light within" first illumine this question. He should next consult his mother then, whom else he pleases. He should next make advances to the girl herself. By letter is undoubtedly the best form; not as a lover, but only mutually to canvass their respective matrimonial qualifications and adaptations.

She should now consider and answer, not whether she will accept his Love, or become his wife, but only whether she will receive him as a suitor, to consider their mutual fitness. Of course she should now consult her father and mother. If she accepts, their next step is to ask the consent of her parents. This fully opens up the whole subject to a frank, intellectual discussion between all the parties interested.

. . . Love confers Conjugal Talent or Knack. Capacity to love and awaken tender passion is as much a gift, a real genius, as any other; and the basis of all conjugal excellence. On it rests the entire super-structure of wedlock. Out of it, like limbs and fruit from their trunk, grow all marital virtues and enjoyments. Its full and perfect action perfectly fulfills them all. Those in whom it is vigorous and normal, cannot make poor husbands or wives, though faulty in other respects; nor those good ones in whom it is deficient however many or great their

other excellences. The former always extra fond, loving, doting, devoted,
and happy in wedlock when fond at all, yet when antagonistic, become
the more so the better it is developed for, like a two-edged sword, it cuts
fearfully, the wrong way when it does not cut the right. . . .

A woman whose love is weak, is cold, spiritless, passive, tame, and
barren in all the feminine attractions and virtues; half dead and alive;
like leather as compared with skin, having the female groundwork, but
lacking its life and soul; may indeed be a great worker and good house-
keeper; the kindest and best of neighbors; refined, proper, and much
besides; but will be barren in womanliness, and therefore lack this "one
thing needful" in conjugality, this very heart's core of female nature,
and the lovable wife. . . . Let the following fact illustrate. A well-sexed
husband on hearing those views said, —

"Prof. F., you really must apply your phrenological skill to
determine why I and my wife disagree thus. I lived in perfect conjugal
happiness with my first wife, and came to my second marriage with the
very best of intentions; planted, built, and did everything just as she
desired, but everything displeases. We live together on tolerance merely.
Say scientifically what and where our trouble lies."

Herein consisted her defect. She was incapable of appreciating
masculine excellence, or manifesting feminine of loving, or awakening
love. . . .

Expect an insipid marriage if it is feeble in yourself or companion;
and that minor differences will alienate you, where hearty love would
harmonize. Yet to those who marry for station, home, money, &c, it is
less important.

"*Men,*" she muttered.

She put the book facedown in a side-table drawer and closed it. She sat looking out the window facing west. The forsythia bush by the fence was starting to bud. She thought, Well, Doctor Professor Fowler, where is God in this book of yours? Or in your phrenological mind? Where is dancing? What about Abelard and Heloise, Professor? Well, Irene, what *about* them? A lifetime of letter writing is not your idea of an ideal marriage, either. So, I suppose he's right to a certain extent. Conjugally speaking. She giggled and tried to say "conjugally" three times fast. Somehow the scientific exposition of romantic love is not as compelling or inspiring as the poetic ones I'm familiar with.

Frank! I know you better than that. *You* know better than that. You're a poet. You're a reasonable, practical, able-bodied man. You are ten times smarter than this charlatan. Why would you put such store in a man obsessed with this *science* of love? Animal husbandry is a science. Entomology is a science.

Do you think this farm girl needs to go to school over baby making? Do you think me "defective," like that "spiritless, tame, insipid, good house-keeper"? Frank, you needn't worry about my part in the conjugal part. Not one iota. Just you wait. Oh. Maybe you harbor some uncertainties about yourself. Hmm. Well, poet-banker, I have no doubts. Or maybe you think I'm one of Fowler's "etceteras" who's after your home, station, and money. I'll set you straight on that right away.

I'm glad you gave me this book. It is the map you are following—the "true procedure" of courtship. That path leads to an engagement proposal, and that leads to marriage to my greatest of known great men. To become Mrs. Frank M. Wilson. Up to now your steps fit the map exactly. And it opens my eyes to you, dear man. Don't you worry about a thing. I'll be Circe to your Odysseus. I'll turn well-sexed Fowler into a pig. She threw back her head and laughed. Her laughter wouldn't subside and she shook from it, tears streaming down her cheeks.

Maggie Rea crept downstairs and hurried to her side. She put her hand on Irene's shoulder and said, "Aunt Tot, are you all right?"

"Of course I am, you darling girl. I'm very all right. Happy, in fact. I have a map and I have a purpose. Let's saddle up and check on those salt licks. And feed the pigs while we're out!"

F. M. Wilson, Horton, Kansas
Wednesday Night, March 23, '97

My Dear Friend of the Family;

I presume you and Harold arrived home safely though I failed to receive a telegram stating that you had. I fear those doughnuts in your pocket were in brick—"hard as rocks" by reason of their having been sat upon all the way to home. Tell Harold the next time he comes he shall have "pancakes" and I shall see to it that he has a nice lunch.

Dear boy, he must have been sleepy Monday night. How manly he was in the morning when he had to get up so early! I am glad you brought him. We enjoyed him very much. Maggie Rea was much disappointed that she did not get to kiss him Good Bye and instructed me to send kisses to him for her. Here they are—"OOOOO." (For original illustration of above quoted kisses see Harold's letter written to you while you were in the Indian Territory).

The book you gave me I have read in part. I never saw any work of this kind before. The author is frequently quoted in text books in Physiology which I have studied and that is all I have ever read from his pen.

I have read the marked passages in your book and I think there is a great deal of sense and some nonsense in what he says.

I shall not attempt to discuss any part of the subject on paper, but sometime if you care to talk about it I shall bicker attentively. I can't talk intelligently. I will say this, however, that I do not think any marriage be it first, second or fifth—should be contracted for convenience or from a sense of duty. I do not think that any two persons who enter such a relationship for these reasons need or have any right to expect happiness.

Marriage to me means something so sacred that I cannot conceive how anyone could contemplate such a step merely for gain.

I know people argue that one must look at such a step from a sensible point of view; I think one should but is not everything pure and holy sensible?

Marriage is indeed a serious matter. I never realized before how serious such a step is and how much depends on a wise decision.

A woman's home is her world and a world where she must either be a wise loving queen and guiding spirit or a creature more than nothing.

We expect to start on our trip next week. I think I shall not write any more tonight. This time last week I was happy in anticipation of your visit. Now I am happy in the knowledge that your visit was a happy visit. I am happy tonight in thinking of you.

May Heaven Bless you and those dear to you, my dear heart, and keep you ever safe and happy.

Believe me always
Sincerely yours,
Irene

P.S. I shall mail you the little booklet you forgot to take. Its value is chiefly in the bright charming way it is written and it will afford you a pleasant evening, I am sure. I haven't the sequel "Aftermath" or I would send it, too.

CHAPTER FIVE

BEWARE OF THE CONDUCTORS AND THE BRAKEMEN. THEY WILL ALL TRY TO FLIRT WITH YOU . . .

MAILED MARCH 29, 1897, FROM HORTON, KANSAS.

Miss Irene Webb, Nortonville, Kansas

My Darling Irene,

What beautiful spring day this has been and how often I have thought of you and wished that I might be at your side. This is the season, when with Adam Moss, I can truly say, "The needle of my nature dips toward the country." I have just finished reading *A Kentucky Cardinal* and quite agree with you that it is a bright and charming little story.

I have already retaliated upon you by mailing to you "The reflections of a married man" which I trust may interest you for an evening. I fancy I hear you remark, as you have finished the book just like him, entirely too practical and commonplace; I shall not wonder at such a conclusion, taking into consideration that it has been less than a week since I placed in your hands Dr. Fowler's scientific work.

However I trust that in this latter work you will find much that is interesting and instructive. Information which is too often withheld from young people on the ground that it is immodest.

You remark that you have read some of the marked passages in the book. Perhaps I should tell you that I have had this work in my possession for some 15 or 20 years, during which time I have made frequent reference to it, and have considered it authority in its line. I placed it in Allie's hands during our courtship. I speak of this by way of explanation as there may be passages that were marked by others than myself.

I confess to having made a great many marks in the book however and some of them were intended for your notice.

I have great respect for the opinions and conclusions of the author, and I believe that if you will take the trouble to again examine the passages which you term nonsense, you will discover that they are not the author's opinions or conclusions.

I heartily agree with the sentiment so beautifully expressed by you upon the subject of marriage for convenience, or from a sense of duty alone. Marriage without true love must be a failure. God deliver us from such a fate. The marriage relation is the most sacred on our earth, and the whole course of at least two lives depend upon a right selection. If I am more cautious, and considerate, than others in this most important of all steps, it is perhaps on account of the example which I have had before me.

You have well said "A woman's home is her world."

The question for me to decide is, can I make your home a truly happy world?

This is the one absorbing question of my mind. I compare you with every girl that I meet. Thus far you have stood the test, and outshine them all in the virtues which I prize most dearly. You are not without fault, but where is the one faultless being on earth? If you were faultless, I would not dare love you, because of the great inequality. Your faults seem solely those which I can best overlook. Darling I love you with all my heart.

Your greatest happiness is my soul's desire. I want you to keep your heart and hand free until all doubts are removed. I want you to have the greatest opportunity for making comparisons between my virtues and vices, and those of others, and if you find one who approaches more nearly to your ideal, please have pity upon me, and release my heart.

If I were called upon to divide a period of say 12 months into two parts, courtship, and engagement, I think I should give about 11 months of it to courtship, leaving just enough time to prepare for the crowning event.

You have other admiring friends, and I am glad of it. I ask for an even start, and a fair race, not wishing to handicap my rivals.

I beg you dear heart to overlook my apparent lack of ardor last Sunday. You could not fail to notice that I was not well. I was suffering somewhat with a vicious headache, but I enjoyed my visit very much, as did Harold also. We made close connection at Atchison, arriving at Willis at 8 o'clock, and found our carriage in waiting. I remained in Willis a half hour and got home at 9 o'clock.

I was glad to have the opportunity to become acquainted with little Maggie Rea McVey, whom I thought was very nice indeed.

Harold wants to return an armful of kisses to her.

He formed quite an attachment for you and Maggie Rea.

I took him with me this morning, and on our way to the depot I asked him if he liked to take a ride on the train. He replied, "Yes I'd like to go to Texas." I didn't know whether you had invited him to go with you on your proposed trip or not until I asked him. He said no, but he seemed to remember that you intended going there.

My brother Charlie will go to Hayden Indian Territory tomorrow to finish the work which I left undone. I do hope that your trip to Texas will prove a great benefit to both you and your mother, and I know it will if you stay long enough.

With kind regards and best wishes to your mother, and my best love for yourself.

I am a sincere
Friend of the Family

MAILED APRIL 1, 1897, FROM NORTONVILLE, KANSAS.

F. M. Wilson, Horton, Kansas

My dearest Friend,

It is now the bewitching hour of nine o'clock and if you are to receive your usual weekly letter I must leave my sewing for this more pleasant work—writing to you.

I have been unusually industrious today. Mrs. Miller is with us this week and today we have been sewing. My work was not completed and I have been at it since supper until I suddenly rethought one of my letters—now the sewing can wait till another day.

Please allow me to thank you for the very pretty copy of "Reflections of a Married Man" which I received Monday from the Family Friend. I have not read it yet although I am very anxious to. I was reading another book aloud to the folks when my new book came and they insist that I shall finish that before commencing the other. I have been so busy this week that I have had no time for reading except in the evening and then it is difficult to oppose the majority in the book to be read. I glanced over the first few pages when I first looked at it and I am sure I shall enjoy it.

It seems to me this "Friend of the Family" is very kind indeed and I must remind him that this isn't Christmas or New Year's or Fourth of July or Easter or my birthday and he must not send people presents on just common days. Seriously, my dear, I think you are too generous and I must beg you not to "retaliate" again.

I do not know what day we will get away. The weather is growing so much warmer (it may be snowing by the time this reaches you) that I am almost in favor of going some other direction than south.

I see by the papers there have been terrific floods in the part of Texas we expect to visit. This is a little bit scary for neither my Mother or I can swim.

I am pleased to know that Maggie Rea and I made a favorable impression on Harold. I have not seen Maggie Rea since she went home.

I was very much surprised last Saturday morning to receive a call from my friend Mr. Murphy. I did not know he was coming. He came to Nortonville Friday night and spent the night then drove out Saturday morning and stayed till the train goes to Kansas City on the North Western at 2:40 p.m. He is spending this week in Lawrence. I think the Horton Schools do not have a spring vacation—they had none the year I was there.

My dear heart, I shall certainly overlook your line "your lack of ardor" if you will forgive my stupidity in not observing that you were not well. I thought you looked badly but attributed it to your over-work after your return from the Ind. Tr. I did not know you were sick. Why it's terrible to think how late you sat up, too. Next time I shall send you to bed at 9 o'clock sharp. Now if you don't want to retire at that hour, there is only one thing that will save you; having your headache at home or better still not having any.

I think I must tell you good night now. It is after ten and I shall be so-o-o sleepy in the morning.

With love and a kiss for Harold and Wallis if he isn't too big for such things. I must leave you. Remember me to you!

Lovingly Yours,

Irene

MAILED APRIL 2, 1897, FROM NORTONVILLE, KANSAS.

F. M. Wilson, Horton, Kansas
At Post office—Friday

My dear Mr. Wilson,

We are off for "Away down South in the land of cotton, Cinnamon seed and sandy bottom" next Monday morning. Our transportation is over the Santa Fe direct from Topeka to Galveston. If you will write your Sunday evening letter Saturday evening it will reach me here Sunday evening or Monday morning and I shall have something interesting and instructive to read while en route. Wish you were going with us.

If I keep on writing notes to you the Gov't debt will be greatly decreased in a short time.

Hastily,

Irene

MAILED APRIL 2, 1897, FROM NORTONVILLE, KANSAS.

F. M. Wilson, Horton, Kansas

Dear heart,

Did you get my letter in time? I have a romantic or some other kind of a notion that I want to mail my letters to you myself—so I didn't send it to the office with the other mail this morning, as I expected to go myself this afternoon. Just as I was about to start the rain came in torrents so I could not go. As a last resort I sent it by a boy who happened to pass the house. I should not be as self sufficient if it remains in his pocket. I never saw the boy before.

If you do not receive it you will lose very much, but I wanted to tell you the reason—

In Haste—
Irene

Thursday, 7 P.M.

If you do not get this note let me know at once.

Irene

FRANK HAD JUST REREAD Irene's short note but could not reconcile its contents. She says, "If you do not get this note let me know at once." I'd write and tell her, of course, that I *did* get the letter—letters—all of them, but if I didn't receive it how on Earth would I be expected to communicate that to her? Let me look again. Her query was mailed April 2. She adds the enigmatic instruction at the end. Wait. She has inserted "Thursday, 7 P.M." That's the First, then. Ha! April Fools'! I owe her for that.

Who the hell is this Murphy? That's not as funny. Not at all. At all. At all. Where did he creep in from? Can't have it. Show restraint. But not indifference. Can't be indifferent.

MAILED APRIL 3, 1897, FROM HORTON, KANSAS.

Miss Irene Webb, Nortonville, Kansas

My Darling Irene,

I received your regular weekly letter promptly at 8:30 A.M. yesterday, but have not rec'd your tracer mailed by you personally last night. I can't imagine why, unless it is possible that you were mistaken about having given the original letter to the boy to mail, but gave him the tracer instead.

No doubt in my mind but that the boy is carrying it yet. His curiosity probably led him to open it on the way to town, and being unable to seal it up so as to avoid detection he is still carrying it, and wondering what to do with it, and what the consequences will be.

As you doubtless keep a letter press, or a clothes press, copy of all important correspondence, I trust you will wire me a duplicate of the last one.

Your constant, sincere lover,
Frank

P.S.

When I read in the letter which I did receive yesterday, of the visit of your other friend last Saturday, I repented of my liberal proposition, and wished that he were in Cuba, or Armenia.

Your somewhat agitated lover,
Frank

P.S. No. 2

Upon third reading of your letter I discover that he is spending the week in Lawrence. I wonder if this means that he will return to visit you again next Sunday. Confound it, this seems to me to be once too often.

Your greatly agitated lover,
Frank

P.S. No. 3

Upon careful examination of the letter which I received from you I find that you did not invite me to call next Sunday. You didn't even say that you expected to pass a lovely day at home. It is all very plain now. My worst fears are to be realized.

Your (jealous) lover,
Frank

P.S. No. 4

I wonder if his recent visit accounts for the lack of cordiality which I thought I discovered in your letter. No, it cannot be. I must be mistaken. I will not believe it.

Your faithful lover,
Frank

P.S. No. 5

I shall not attempt to answer your letter tonight—but will do so
Sunday as usual hoping to be in the proper mood.

Your devoted lover,

Frank

MAILED APRIL 4, 1897, FROM HORTON, KANSAS.

Miss Irene Webb

My Beloved Sweetheart,

It is now almost that bewitching hour referred to by you, in your
late epistle to the heathen, and having scrubbed the babies, and
put them to sleep, I shall undertake my usual weekly discourse,
one day earlier, by special request.

As I sit here musing, my mind wanders back in pleasant recollection, to bye gone days, when the women performed the
domestic duties which I have particularly enumerated above,
while the men whiled away the evening at the lodge or the club.

Alas, those happy days.

How our positions have been reversed.

If the present rate of progress is to continue, I wonder what use
the women will have for us poor male creatures after a while and
how long it will be until we can be dispensed with altogether.

Verily I am glad I was born so soon. I don't exactly mean that
I rejoice because I am growing old, but I can't help thinking how
less fortunate will be the fellows who are born later.

Then casting aside all thoughts of "man's inhumanity to man,"
another unpleasant thought rushes into the vacuum.

While I am seated here quietly performing my pleasant duty of writing a sentimental message for you, I wonder if that other fellow isn't seated at your side, pouring sweet messages of love into your ears and eyes.

I have something of that peculiar feeling which you described, the day I came home from Ks. City and failed to stop to see you, with slight variations. Instead of feeling that you are near me, I can't avoid the feeling that you are much nearer that other fellow tonight.

Now having thus described the state of my mind I am sure you will make due allowance if the following pages shall prove uninteresting.

How can a fellow be real sentimental, when harrowed by the thoughts that his loved one is listening to the soft words of his rival, who may occupy first-place in her heart.

Then there comes another sad thought. Immediately after the departure of the aforesaid rival, as though premeditated, and with malice aforethought, she is to depart for "that land of cotton cinnamon seed and sandy bottom" where the sweet magnolia blooms, and many other advantages along that line, with her latest impressions of the aforesaid rival, not upon her lips perhaps, but stamped in her memory, to be recalled during the many hours of leisure and reflection now to be at her disposal. To think that I have had, and am to have, no opportunity to efface, or obliterate, or even modify those aforesaid impressions, before she leaves upon this journey, the duration of which I am not fully apprised, seems cruel and unjust.

But sad as are all these thoughts I must not disappoint you entirely. You expect something interesting, and instructive, from me. I presume you want a few useful hints on travelling.

I want to caution you particularly of the danger in getting on, and off, trains while in motion. Several people annually sacrifice life and limb to this foolish habit. Understand me, I do not mean that the same individuals sacrifice their lives and limbs each year, but that each year claims new victims.

To avoid this great sacrifice, the most of the great railroads in our land, (thanks to the efforts of Mary Ellen, and other noble women) now cause their trains to stop at all important towns through which they pass.

As you will ride upon a free pass, remember that you are entitled to all the privileges, and accommodations, the roads afford, and should the conductor and brakeman fail to show you the attention and consideration to which you are entitled as the holder of a free pass, do not hesitate to pull the bell rip and put them off.

Passengers who pay their fare are expected to check their baggage, and to occupy but one or two seats, but remember that these rules do not apply to holders of free passes. You are entitled to take all the baggage you desire into the coach and to occupy as many seats as you care to use.

Beware of the conductors and the brakemen. They will all try to flirt with you but most of them have a wife and children at home. Poor fellows, they are away from home so much they can't help it. If you take a sleeper, don't forget the number of your berth. I don't mean the order in which you were born into the family, as for instance 1st, 2nd or 3rd but the number written upon the curtain of your sleeping apartment, commonly called the berth.

A good reason for this precaution exists in my mind which I need not name here. There are many other suggestions which I would like to make if time and space permitted. But I am constrained to close these hints with the suggestion that the newsboy possesses a valuable store of information of use to the unsophisticated traveler, and if you will buy your chewing gum from him, you can draw upon his resources for any information you may require.

I wrote you a short letter last night, and amidst perplexity forgot to date it. If you will return it I will attach the date as a postscript.

Well my dear, in all seriousness, I do hope that you will have a very pleasant trip, entirely free from any unpleasant incidents, and that it will prove of great benefit in restoring your mother and yourself to your usual good health.

Don't be in a hurry to return, I shall be impatient to see you if you remain long, but I feel that a prolonged visit will do you both so much good, that I can quite readily consent to your stay. I would be delighted to have you visit us during the teacher's convention, 15th, 16th and 17th and if it should be possible that you would return in time, I don't think I can excuse you from coming, yet I hope you will not think of cutting your trip short as this.

How I join you in the wish that I were going with you; it would be a pleasure indeed, and yet if confined to a choice I think a more enjoyable trip, would be the Colorado trip next summer.

How easy to plan a nice time. I shall not forget your promise to tell me the story "Aftermath" some time. Since you have made me this promise I shall have no desire to read it, fully realizing how much more I shall enjoy listening to you repeat it.

How fast the time flies when in your presence.

On the occasion of my last visit I spent one day, and two evenings with you, and yet it seemed but a few hours, not half long enough. I wish that I were with you tonight; I would love to have you sing, and talk to me, until the wee small hours. I love to hear your gentle voice both in conversations and in song. I think the refining influence of music in the home, cannot be overestimated. I think I will act upon your suggestion and organize an orchestra in the family and thus makeup for the entire lack of music in the family heretofore.

I shall need a pianist, and will be on the lookout for one.

No long haired man need apply. If Maggie Rea has Huckleberry

Finn, and has not read Tom Sawyer, she can exchange with Wallis when convenient and each will enjoy the treat.

I want to again remind you that I haven't received that photo. You will have plenty of time to sit for one while on your southern trip, and I hope you will not forget it. I am real anxious for it and must insist. I shall look for some real nice, long, sweet, letters during your absence, for no doubt the conditions will be favorable and conducive. Whenever you get homesick, or time hangs heavy on your hands sit down and write me.

Believe me to be your affectionate lover,

Frank

MAILED APRIL 7, 1897, FROM HOUSTON, TEXAS.

F. M. Wilson, Horton, Kansas
Wednesday Morning

My dear Mr. Wilson,

Just a line this morning to advise you of our safe arrival at Houston last evening at 9:25. We had a very enjoyable trip entirely free from any unpleasant incidents. My mother stood the trip splendidly and is already feeling better. We found the acquaintances of the celebrated Buffalo Jones and a party of his friends on the train. They were very nice to us.

I shall write you more at length later today. Until then Good Morning. Your two letters reached me before I left home.

Lovingly,

Irene

Houston, Texas

THE MORE I LEARN, the less I know, Irene thought as she looked out at the tops of palm trees from her uncle's upper balcony. Even though the days were long, the breezes warm, the flowers fragrant, and the fruit sweet, Irene spent much of her time brooding over Frank. When he writes to me, his letters enliven me, she thought. His words are more endearing than those of the Bard. When we are together our minds are either as twins or as strangers. We live nearby but we are far apart. When we are together . . . Glory, even then he can seem so distant. I expect I should have brought the Fowler tome to read. Or should I say tomb. I should say at least something since he puts such store in it. When he speaks to me, his words flow like glue. Oh, if he would just speak as he writes on love. If he does not do that, what does he really think? A romantic pen is lovely. I want a romantic man.

"Penny for your thoughts, Irene," her mother said. "Anything to do with the banking business in northeastern Kansas?"

"You! Mama, I need your wisdom. What do I do about male ardor? A particular one, not that of mankind in general."

"Hmm. That'll run ya two cents for my opinion, which is what it's worth. Well, to begin with, you should try to at least get as close as the same county. Closer, preferably, and oftener than you do now. From there, it's not up to the one or the other, Irene. We are not rutting farm animals. It is something that two people have to feel at the same time or it doesn't happen. But if it doesn't happen at a given time, that doesn't mean the two people don't feel it at other times."

"You don't know either, do you, Mama."

"No. I just know you can drive yourself to distraction over it if you let yourself. Look here, we were given free passes by the railroad on account of Hiram being such a good customer with his cattle and all. We are living in luxury with precious family we never get to see. Don't go spending our time here in a mood. Get up on your hind legs and walk on the tropical sands. Then write to your banker all about this Southern charm and how you are at risk to getting so used to it you might never leave. I'm not saying to tease him."

"Yes, you are, Mama."

"Yes, I am, Irene, but go gentle with him. They spook real easy. That's two cents to your account."

Chapter Six

HOW LIKE OUR LIVES
ARE THESE WAVES

Mailed April 8, 1897, from Houston, Texas.

F. M. Wilson, Horton, Kansas

My dearest Friend,

I sent you a brief note this morning telling you of our safe arrival and promising to write a longer letter later—alliteration unintentional.

I believe you suggested in one of your letters the advisability of a private telephone. I am afraid our conversations would melt the wires so I think the scheme would better be abandoned as an impracticable one.

Monday morning at 9:34 we left Nortonville; Charlie met us at Topeka where we had dinner, leaving there at 12:00 p.m.

At Emporia I went into the car ahead as it was nearer the station and I thought I might see someone whom I knew. You didn't caution me about that in your rules and regulations in travelling so concluded it was permissible. My Mother happened to be looking out of the window at the time and did not observe I had gone till she glanced around and saw my seat vacant. In the car ahead I met a very pleasant girl and had a little chat with her; after awhile

I walked leisurely back into our car to find my Mother and some of the passengers greatly agitated on my sudden exit. The whole scene was so ridiculous that I laughed heartily—my view of the situation seemed to be contagious for immediately the whole car saw the funny side and joined in the laugh. No one seemed to have seen me leave the car and the general impression I think, was that I had escaped through the train or vanished in thin air.

We reached Arkansas City at 7:25 when we had supper or rather the train stopped then for supper. We were supplied with a huge lunch basket and ate earlier in the evening. We went to bed at 8:45 as Mama was tired. We both rested splendidly and arose at 6:30 Tuesday morning very much refreshed. We were very sorry to pass through Oklahoma and the Indian Territory at night. We saw nothing of that country as we retired in S. Western Kansas and arose near Fort Worth Texas.

I wonder if there isn't more truth than you thought for in your remarks about Mr. Murphy. I received a letter from him today. He did not spend last Sunday with us as you imagined.

Lovingly and Sincerely,
Irene

Miss Irene Webb, Houston, Texas
Sunday, April 11, 1897

My Dearest Friend Irene,

I am glad to know that my suspicions as to your whereabouts and your company a week ago last night, while I was writing to you, were not well founded. I confess to a great relief when I received the evidence of it. Now I am anxious to know what portion of my remarks about Mr. Murphy contained "more truth than I supposed." You will have to explain just what you mean, for I am sure you will not want to keep me guessing any longer. If you would rather not explain you might send me his last letter which you mention having rec'd. and perhaps I can figure it out myself. "Not necessarily for publication, but merely as an evidence of good faith," as the editor sometimes remarks. You know that I have discovered that your recent letters are not open to the criticism of "too much sentiment" and you cannot wonder that I am anxious to know why you have thus locked up your sentiments, or if not this, if they flow in other channels.

How are you progressing with the reading I furnished you, and what opinions have you to express about it, now that you have proceeded farther into the subjects treated?

I love to bask in the sunshine of your soul and feast upon the smiles of your sweet face. Of this I would never grow weary. Believe me darling to be your

Ardent Lover,
Frank

F. M. Wilson, Horton, Kansas

My dearest Friend,

Your letter written Sunday has just reached me. It seems to take longer for a letter to come here than to travel across the continent. Then after letters reach Houston it takes another age for them to be delivered.

My uncle whom we are visiting lives just outside the city limits—his mail is left at a house a short distance from here by the carrier. I go each day for the mail and you can imagine how disappointed I have been each day when "there was nothing." We received our first letter from home this morning. It and your letter had been given to the wrong carrier. I do not know when mail reaches the city from the North. I am so glad to have your letter dearheart. Doesn't it seem strange how such a thing as not getting a letter when you expect it can make one feel so unhappy. You will have to write me a bi-weekly missive. I never can wait till Wednesday for my letter. I shall write you on Sunday too, dearest, then our letters will cross. You will receive a letter on Wednesday or Thursday and another Saturday or Sunday. Does this meet your approval? I have abandoned the idea of writing a circular letter that includes you. I can write home and to my sisters all in one but your letter shall be yours exclusively. I am glad Harold likes his book. How did I come to make the mistake in the date, I wonder. Tell him I thank him very much for his kind invitation to his party. I shall send his letter to Maggie Rea. Since I cannot attend the party I should be much pleased to furnish the souvenirs for the occasion, if he will consent. Taking it for granted of that he will, I shall ask you to tell me about the number you expect to entertain.

My idea is to send Cap Jassamine buds tied with some dainty ribbon. I shall send you a basket of Magnolia buds for Easter which I am sure you will enjoy. I hope they may reach you in good season and in good condition.

This is but the advance agent of a letter which I shall write this evening. Don't wait for my other letter but answer this.

Lovingly Thine,
Irene

MAILED APRIL 15, 1897, FROM HOUSTON, TEXAS.

F. M. Wilson, Horton, Kansas

My dearest Friend,

I have just returned from a trip through a very pretty part of Houston. Houston is ablaze with roses; and such beauties! The magnolias are in blossom and their fragrance is delightful. There is a drowsiness about the atmosphere here that is very pleasant. One feels just comfortably lazy all the time. My uncle whom we are visiting lives just outside the city limits in a very pretty place. The house stands in a grove of natural pine trees and back of the house not very far distant is a large forest of these trees. I have explored a portion of this forest and shall make another expedition soon. My uncle is a widower with no children and at present (or until we came) is living alone. The family he had left about a month ago. He has very fine fruit and raises garden stuff—so you see we are supplied with the best the market affords.

We are going to Galveston to spend Sunday. The bathing season has already commenced there and I am sure I shall enjoy that feature of our visit. We will probably go down on the boat.

I want to go to San Antonio before we return home. The Battle of Flowers is there thru 21st. How I wish you were here to enjoy everything. One could not ask for more romantic spots than some of the shady nooks I have discovered, but it isn't an easy matter to grow romantic when one is alone. You must know that I am left much to my own resources for the good time I am having here. My mother and Uncle sit and visit by the hour talking of things that happened fifty years ago. My mind is naturally somewhat dull on those subjects and when they begin I take me to the woods there to dream dreams of the future and to enjoy the present and best to live over again my careless happy girlhood days. . . .

My dearheart, I have not meant to be unsentimental in my letters. How I wish I could see you and talk freely with you. There are many things I want to tell you. I think of many things after you are gone each time that I intended speaking of and I presume it is the same with you. Let me assure you of this. I have been true in thought, word and act to you always and I shall be. I have no reason to doubt your affection for me. I have all faith in you and no one but you, yourself, can shake that faith. I would rather not tell you more about Mr. Murphy now and I would rather not send his letter to you. I do not think it is right to interchange letters of that nature. No one to my knowledge has ever read a letter you have written me. I have read portions of them to members of the family. Do not think I mean to criticize you showing my letters to your sister in law. You did it with my permission. People feel differently about such things and I do not question any act of yours that you deem right.

If "my sentiments have been locked up" you know, I think, who holds the magic key that unlocks them.

The scientific work you placed in my hand on the occasion of your last visit, I could not well bring with me as it is such a ponderous volume. I too, think every person should read such a book and I am glad you gave me the work, though I confess to a rather peculiar feeling when I first opened it.

Now, my dear, asking you to please excuse "haste and a bad pun" I shall leave you.

Lovingly,
Irene

FRANK PUT THE LETTER down. He thought, Well, if she didn't take the book with her I wish I had it here. Ralston was no help at all on the Thornton question. And he doesn't have a copy of Fowler. Says he threw it away. Odd for a man of science. Probably a sign of old age.

Frank had never been to the Gulf Coast and found it hard to imagine tropics in America. A honeymoon there crossed his mind. Daydreamer, he thought. Then he thought about engagement. He knew that Fowler was adamant about it. Somehow it seemed too soon and too late at the same time for it. Everything is going well as it is. If courtship for one year is my guide, it's too soon to get engaged. But it's not too soon to think about it. Have to give her time to accept. Can't put her under pressure. Spring's coming on and spring is a tonic. I should start taking more short trips to Nortonville when she gets back. Longer days. And there's no reason, really, not to bring her here. She could stay at the Hendersons' for a couple of nights. Nothing out of line in that.

She has a way of touching my hand. And one thing that's missing is getting to know each other's mind just by a look, or a silence. That takes being together more than we are now. This spring would be a good time for that. McVey's running the farm so there's no reason she can't get away to here or to the Altons'. Maybe even meet in Topeka. Lawrence and the university are spectacular in the spring. We could take separate rooms at the Eldridge Hotel and meet her friends from there. Not Murphy, of course. Topeka would be better. She has that uncle and cousin there.

So, that's the plan for spring. She'll have time on her hands after they get back. I'll simply have to make the time. Latham has to pull his weight. What's the point of working ten years to get a bank running if I can't take time for myself? Too many money worries. He chuckled as he remembered Thornton leaning on the hitching rail, helpless with laughter.

Right, so this spring is the time to pick up the pace here. Get to those knowing glances. Get to the point I can practically read her mind. Everything is two-dimensional now, even with the long letters. Too much trying to read between the lines. Good plan.

MAILED APRIL 18, 1897, FROM HORTON, KANSAS.

Miss Irene Webb, Houston, Texas
Easter Sunday
April 18, '97

My Darling Irene,
Saturday morning I rec'd your letter of 14th and this morning I rec'd the one mailed on 15th. The precious basket of magnolia buds were delivered to me yesterday evening in excellent condition.

Only one of them had begun to open. I placed them in a vase last night and this bud opened up, and sent forth its rich perfume filling my bed room.

Allie used to talk so much of the Magnolia and she loved it so much, that I could not resist the desire to place a few of these buds upon her grave today. So taking three of the buds to the greenhouse, I placed them in the center of a bouquet of yellow roses and smilax, and carried them to her grave in a vase, which I filled with water, and hope they will open out perfectly.

The remainder of the buds are sending forth their fragrance from a vase resting upon the table upon which I am now writing. I have often regretted that I did not accompany Allie on her visit to her old Georgia home some 7 yrs. ago. I then thought to postpone my trip to some more convenient time supposing of course that Allie would repeat her visit—to that sunny land many times.

Alas, how little do we know what is in store for us, and how seldom do we think of the uncertainty of this life.

We go on making plans for the future, expecting after a while when we have reached a certain position in life to spend a greater portion of our time and money in travel, and the pursuit of happiness, and pleasure. How many times during the past 8 months have I regretted that we did not live more in the present and less in the future.

I presume all of us would do differently, had we an opportunity to again live over the past.

I feel sure that in this respect I would do differently.

I would not think less of the future, but more of the present. We seem to be living in an age when wealth is made the end sought, rather than the means.

Well my dear, aside from a strong south wind, with its clouds of dust, this has been an ideal Easter day. The wind and dust did not prevent the annual bonnet parade, which came off at the usual hour and far exceeded any former event of its character.

I took the boys to the Catholic Church this morning. The music was grand. Not more than 1/4 of those present were Catholics.

I regret that I neglected to send you an Easter greeting. It was neither indifference or thoughtlessness upon my part for I very much wanted to do so but it seemed to me like mockery to send flowers from this country to you in the land of sunshine and roses.

I could not think that you would appreciate anything of that sort at this time.

I trust that you will take the will for the deed this time. If you knew how much I enjoy the fragrance of these buds before me this afternoon I believe you would feel repaid for the expense and trouble they cost you.

I am now going to inflict upon you another book to be read in the quiet and solitude of these shady and romantic spots of which you speak. "Reveries of a Bachelor" may in some degree supply the absence of a congenial companion. Perhaps you wonder that I did not reverse the order of presentation of my literature, and commence with "Reveries of a Bachelor" ending with the words of Dr. Fowler.

No doubt it would have been a more appropriate program but I trust they will lose none of their merit by this blunder upon my part.

With assurances of my highest esteem and love, believe me.

Sincerely Yours,

Frank

MAILED APRIL 22, 1897, FROM HOUSTON, TEXAS.

F. M. Wilson, Horton, Kansas

My dearest Friend,

This is a most lovely morning. I started out for a walk soon after breakfast and came to one of my favorite nooks. Seated on the grass by a large pine tree I have been reveling in this delightful balmy breeze and drinking in the fragrance of the sweet wild flowers. I brought "Reveries of a Bachelor" with me and have been enjoying it very much. I read the book two years ago—but that takes away none of the pleasure it affords me now. I am enjoying re-reading it more than I can tell you. Some books are well worth a second reading and this is one of them. The marked passages I am paying special attention to. You have a very clever way of calling my attention to beauties you admire by marking analogous descriptions in the books you place in my hands. I might say with Priscilla, "Why don't you speak for yourself, John . . .?" Your method reminds me of the man who one day found a prayer that suited him very well. He pinned this prayer on the head of his bed and each night before retiring he would glance at it and say "Lord, them's my sentiments." I suppose I am to infer that "Them's your sentiments" you marked in Dr. Fowler's and in Donald G. Nichol's books. Well, they're very good sentiments and will stand the test of time I am sure.

I received your letter and the book you so kindly sent yesterday morning—Wednesday. I am glad to know you were pleased with the Magnolia buds and that they reached you in good condition. The buds were not as large as some I have seen but the man at the green house assured me they would be the best kind to ship.

My dearest Friend, I am glad you placed some of the buds I sent you on Allie's grave; it was sweet and tender of you. You say you placed three there. May not the smallest one of the three be my token of love to her memory? No, I will not ask that—but when I go home I shall take a basket of Jassamine buds which I shall forward to you and ask you to place on her grave for me. The Magnolias shall be yours and Wallis' and Harold's. If she loved the Magnolias I know she loved the sweet scented Jassamines.

How fondly you treasure the memory of your loving Allie! As I sit here this morning I can see her bright, happy face in her pleasant home. She loved you and she loved her children so devotedly. No wonder "your eyes, full of tears, climb with quick vision upon the angel's ladder and open upon the futurity—where she has entered and upon the country which she enjoys."

She was everything to you! She proved by her loving devotion thro' sunshine and shadow how worthy she was of your best and purest love. It seems so strange when I recall the winter I spent in Horton. While at your house Allie and I had many heart to heart talks. I shall never forget them.

My friendship with her I value as one of the finest of my life. How true and good she was! I wish she and Papa had known each other here. Who knows but that they do know each other now in that Beautiful Home where they are happy and at rest? But what floodgates of memory I am opening for you and for myself!

I wrote you a short note Sunday afternoon in Galveston. We all enjoyed the day very much indeed. How I did enjoy the water! It was a grand sight! Grand old ocean! I could gaze for hours in silent wonder and appreciation out over the boundless waves. I thought as I watched the great white caps away in the distance how like our lives are these waves. Sometimes gliding along smoothly, then rising and swelling and plunging, then after awhile receding again and flowing quietly and peacefully till at last they reach the shore. Each incoming wave striving to reach a little farther on the beach than the one before it. How like human ambitions!

We think soon of returning home next week but haven't fully decided. Uncle insists upon our remaining but we are growing eager to get home.

Now good morning to you dearheart.

Lovingly Yours,
Irene
Thursday morning, Apr 22-97

Miss Irene Webb, Nortonville, Kansas
Wednesday Eve, Apr. 28, '97

My Dearest Friend,

Your Sunday letter reached me today, and I presume you are now once more at home, or at least will be ere this reaches your home. I presume that you haven't rec'd my Sunday letter yet as you doubtless left Houston before its arrival.

I have somehow or other, formed the opinion, that to you, correspondence is a pleasant and easy task, and that a daily letter, would not be a severe tax upon your resources.

If this letter should be brought to a sudden and early close, I will try to make amends by mailing under separate cover two pieces of music, which I hastily selected for you while in Kansas City last week. I say hastily, because I had but a few moments to reach my train, and I permitted a clerk to select the latest popular song for me. I hope you will like them both.

After a three weeks absence I am quite sure that home will seem sweet to you and you will take a new and deeper interest in all its surroundings. There is nothing like an extended absence from home to make one fully appreciate its beauties and comforts.

I thank you for the Jassamine bud and leaves, sent in your letter. It is indeed sweet scented. How you must miss the beautiful and fragrant flowers since your departure from Houston. You will doubtless be surprised at the backwardness of our season. I had our florist set out some bulbs, and plants, both at the house, and cemetery, this week, holding back some of them until the weather gets warmer.

It is almost cold enough for frost tonight if it should clear off. I shall endeavor to keep up the flowers and plants as near like

Allie designed it as I can. The plants in our lawn were very much admired last summer and resulted in furnishing much work for our florist this spring from people who saw and admired. I observe also that in our cemetery greater interest than ever before is being taken this spring, and the work done there by Allie last year seems to have proven an example for others to follow.

In my Sunday letter I think I told you that Harold seemed to be taking the measles. Well this proved to be a correct diagnosis, and he has got them. Not all of them, but all that his little body is capable of holding. There seems to be an unlimited number of them here. I presume there are 50 cases in town, possibly double that number, and they have been going the rounds for several months. It is so general as to interfere with school work though no attempt has been made to keep the children out of school who have been exposed to them. Many pupils will be unable to pass their grades this year unless they make up for lost time during vacation. Harold is having an easy time. Monday morning I tried to keep him in bed but by 11 o'clock he was downstairs and dressed and since that time has not been in bed except during the nights. He has no fever, and gives us no trouble.

I have not yet decided on my trip to Fort Gibson, but may go upon a moment's notice any day, though I hope Harold will be able to go with me when I do go. I am sure that I will enjoy having him with me, and that he also will very much enjoy the trip.

Now dear sweetheart I must bid you all affectionate good night hoping to hear from you Friday.

Lovingly thine,
Frank

MAILED APRIL 29, 1897.

F. M. Wilson, Horton, Kansas, from Purcell, I.T.

My dearest Friend,

We are delayed here by the washout near Guthrie. Arrived here at 3:15 this morning and I do not know how long we will have to remain. We can get no definite reports—the last is there will be no train until day after tomorrow. I trust the reports from Guthrie are exaggerated and that so many lives have not been lost. We are very thankful indeed not to have been nearer the storm and consider ourselves very fortunate.

This hotel is filled with passengers for the North. No trains have gone North since Tuesday. I would wire you that we are safe, but all lines are down. I do not know when this will reach you. My mother is not feeling very well and this entire excitement is a little hard on her. I shall advise you of our arrival home which I most sincerely hope will be very soon.

Lovingly yours,
Irene

IRENE COULD WALK BLUEBELLE and the carriage to town faster than this train's glacial passage through splintered trees, rail ties and twisted track uprooted in the catastrophic Guthrie flood. She stared out the window of the car being cautiously towed in short jerks over makeshift tracks. The windows were closed in a vain defiance of sand gnats swarming over the receding river's pools and bogs. The sun was fierce.

A track-laying gang of about twenty men stood staring at her train as it creak-crept the working track toward redemption. It was a hasty conscription of regular crews and townspeople who could earn good day wages for agonizing labor on a sun-glazed riverbank. Irene noticed a young man no older than sixteen. He had short-cropped reddish hair, gray work pants, and bloused long-sleeved shirt and was fanning his sunny face with a straw farm hat. He reminded Irene of Frank and how he might have looked at that age. He looked at her gazing at him. For a long moment they were not strangers.

It was the third day after the disaster that had claimed scores of lives, swallowed entire timothy fields, and entrapped northbound train passengers at Purcell, in Indian Territory. Dozens of stranded travelers had filled Purcell's one hotel and overwhelmed its dining room and kitchen. The hotel had been ordered to boil all water and had organized three dinner sittings; the Webb women's was at 5 p.m. The rainfall on Purcell had been unrelenting. The air steamed above the muddy road outside the hotel. A sense of awe and quiet respect had settled over those in the hotel parlor as more people drifted in, murmuring horrific stories of the Guthrie disaster sixty-five miles to the north. Just eight years earlier, the resident population of Guthrie at noon on April 22, 1889, was zero at the starting gunshot for the Oklahoma land rush. Before sundown it was at least ten thousand, streets laid out, town lots staked, and municipal governance in motion. Now, in as many hours, the town had been devastated by the Cottonwood River flood.

"Will we never see home again?" her mother had asked on their second day at the hotel.

"Of course we will, Mama. I've been to the station. We will be put on our same Pullman car and a switcher will pull us up past Norman to Oklahoma Station, which is only thirty miles, and then west to high ground where there's a junction to a railroad bridge, and then join onto a cattle train north, and eventually to Topeka. And all will be under the original free pass except for the sections when we are with the cattle, but I have already paid the fare for that."

At Norman, bundles of the *Norman Transcript*'s special edition had been hurled into the vestibule car, and the Webbs now pored over its account of the flood. The newspaper confirmed thirty dead and reported rumors of more than two hundred victims. Irene sat close to her mother and held her hand as she read in a low, flat voice:

GUTHRIE, I.T., April 28.—For miles tonight the Canadian valley is a dreary waste and the people are overcast with gloom. At sunrise this morning a mighty wall of water, from six to eight feet high and a

mile wide, broke upon West Guthrie without warning, crushing houses,
sweeping away property and drowning people by the score. Every mov-
able thing was swept before the wave, which passed on into the valley
with resistless force, wreaking terrible destruction to life and property
wherever it reached. Dozens of lives are known to have been sacrificed,
how many may not be known for weeks. Hundreds of houses were
wrecked; for miles farms were completely ruined; bridges and tracks
washed out and railway traffic in every direction is at a standstill. The
most complete chaos has prevailed all day. The efforts of rescuing
parties have in many cases proved in vain. Many people floated down
stream before they could be reached and their fate is unknown; others
will pass the night in trees in mid-stream or perched on house tops. It is
impossible to estimate the number of dead. The property loss is placed
at something near a million dollars. Fully two-thirds of the victims
were colored people.

Business has been suspended all day in Guthrie, the stores and
banks being closed. As thorough an organization for relief as is pos-
sible has been made, but all aid has been necessarily retarded by the
confused condition of things. It will be impossible to explore the houses
until the water subsides, as many of them are submerged. As darkness
gathered over the scene many overturned houses could be seen far
out in the flood, but it could not be learned whether their occupants
escaped. The river is thirty feet above its ordinary level.

Irene paused as her mother uttered a moan of pain that was both empa-
thetic and real from the fever that had started ten days before. Finally, her
mother said,

"I will suffer some with the cattle, Tot."

"No, no, dear Mama, we don't go on the cattle car; our own Pullman car
gets pulled along in a cattle train for a bit."

"You are resourceful, Tot. I couldn't make this trip alone. I was so happy
there by the sea. Now I'm not so sure it was a good idea to go. I'm very much
afraid of how sick I feel."

Irene began to tear up. She hadn't slept the night before and she knew
that her mother had only slept in a fevered unconsciousness. The hotel air

had been hot and smelled of mold. "You will get better, Mama. Uncle Doctor will make you better. I have to have you better."

"Tot, dry your face and face up to where we are and what's ahead. People's lives were snuffed out in their homes with their families just ten days after Easter Sunday. Look at that paper—it says five children drowned with their parents. No warning. Something like that can strike anyone at any time. You are going to have to find the strength of your pioneer Webbs, Tot, because the future is uncertain in any case and you will eventually face it alone. My own future is beginning to take shape in my mind, and that picture is dark. I want you to act on Webb strength. If Mr. Wilson is right for you, you have to go in that direction. I don't know why he wouldn't be right for you unless there is something I don't know about, maybe something over the Mrs. Wilson that died last year. That's none of my business. If he is not right for some reason, you have to find a school."

Irene looked out the window again. She remembered the heart-to-heart talks with Allie. They were genuine. Then she remembered Frank's letter hinting of jealousy and his statement that Allie and her mother closed the door to future teacher-boarders. Irene could not reconcile these aspects of Allie, but she never doubted the bond between them. She looked at her mother, pressed closer and said,

"Mother, Allie Wilson and I were good and loving friends. There is nothing about my time in that house I have any second thoughts about."

"Fine, Tot, I trust you on it just as you say. In any case, nothing seems to be going on except correspondence." After a pause, she looked back at Irene and said, "You have to be prepared for what happens next and prepare yourself for what to do, not just write letters. That's all I'm saying. Your father has provided for you, but of course the property is in probate, and who knows about me."

"Mother, you and Papa have taught me about faith and family and trust. Not a whole lot about farming, but I'm a quick learner. Mr. Wilson and I are a private matter. I have hopes that he will recover from his loss and that we might maybe make a future together, but there is no rushing that."

"You've aged considerably from a year ago. So much has happened. So much lies ahead that I can't even think about it for very long." She coughed and looked down. "But no matter what, you keep your feet on the ground and do whatever you have to do that is in your own best interest. Not dreams and fairy tales, but hard practical choices. We are Webbs, and the Webbs we came from are your angels. They are dressed for plowing and hard work, not in white silk. Heed me on this. If your own best interest is in Horton, go with my blessing. Don't feel you are tied by nostalgia to the old homestead. Find your own frontier. I didn't tell you this before, but I sent a letter to your cousin Frank Stiles in Belleville to see if he and Nora have some influence in the new high school going up there next year. If your future is Belleville or anywhere else, go with the same blessing and that of Hiram."

Irene wrinkled her nose. "Mother. Belleville? Belleville, Kansas, is smaller than Nortonville and is at the very edge of civilization. Where would I go to see a Shakespeare play anywhere near Belleville?"

Mrs. Webb snorted and set her lips in a tight smile. She tilted her head and said, very slowly, "Tot, Frank Stiles tells me they will be looking for a *principal* at that new high school."

Irene brought her hands to her cheeks. "Ohhh." They looked at each other and burst into giggles.

MAILED APR. 29, 1897, FROM HORTON, KANSAS.

Miss Irene Webb, Nortonville, Kansas

My Dearest Friend,

I just rec'd a telegram from my brother asking me to meet him in Ks. City tomorrow morning. I start tonight, and shall doubtless go to Fort Gibson Ind. Ter. at once where my stay is indefinite. If you have written me your letter will be forwarded to me at Ft. Gibson. I will probably write you from there next Sunday.

Hastily but Lovingly,
Frank

Postcard to Miss Irene Webb, Nortonville, Kansas

Started to Ft. Gibson from Willis this evening, but was overtaken by telegram at Everest asking me to wait for further advice. Stopped off here and will return on C.R.I.&P. train in 30 minutes.

F. M. Wilson, Horton, Kansas

My Dearest Friend,

We arrived home safely last evening at 5:57 and very glad we were to get here, too. My mother is very much worn out from the trip. We were four days en route. She looks worn and weary but I trust a good rest may restore her to her usual health. She has Malaria and Uncle Dr. fears she may get down. I never felt better. I never could keep secrets or surprises and the one I have for you is that I have gained almost nine pounds in weight and actually have rosy cheeks—are you pleased? Your note to Maggie Rea I shall forward to her. She will be greatly pleased. I do hope Harold is better. Your letter addressed to Houston came with me. That is it rode in the mail sack. We were silent companions. We have not yet been out home. Mama was so tired we remained in town last night. I am going out this morning. I am so glad to see everybody I know and home and friends never seemed dearer. With love and best wishes for Harold's speedy recovery.

I am Sincerely yours,

Irene

Chapter Seven

TYPHOID IS
SO SLOW

Mailed May 2, 1897, from Kansas City.

Miss Irene Webb, Nortonville, Kansas
Sunday, May 2, 1897, 11 a.m.

Dearest Friend,

I am starting to Ft. Gibson this morning via Holton and Kansas City. Leave K.C. 9.05 tonight. Will write you on my arrival at Ft. Gibson.

I rec'd your note announcing your arrival at home. I congratulate you on your improved weight; health, and rosy cheeks, which are all desirable but I am sorry your mother is not feeling better.

Train in and I must close.

Lovingly,
Frank

MAILED MAY 3, 1897, FROM FT. GIBSON.

Miss Irene Webb, Nortonville, Kansas
Fort Gibson, Indian Territory
Monday, May 3, '97

My Darling Irene,

I arrived here at 10 o'clock this morning, and finding that I can do no business today on account of the absence of the man I came here to see, I shall take this opportunity to write to you, "from the sunny south."

How suddenly our positions have been reversed. For the past three weeks you have been basking in the sunshine, and drinking the sweet perfumes of the wild flowers of the south and you no sooner announce your return, until I am off for an indefinite time to the clime from which you return.

How much more pleasant for both of us, could we have spent this time together. My landlady gave me two drops of ink and I have used them both. Fortunately I have a short lead pencil which I hope will hold out until this letter is completed.

I arrived here at 10 o'clock this morning. It is now 3 p.m. and I shall try to get this off on the first mail for the north this afternoon. I located myself, since dinner, in the home of a family who occupy a large, commodious house, well finished and furnished, situated in the suburbs of the town in a very picturesque spot. I dropped in, attracted by the surroundings, enjoyed board from the lady who met me at the door, and have not yet seen any of the other members of the family, except a little girl about 4 yrs. old. I don't know whether I am stopping with a widow, or the wife of a prosperous farmer, or business man, as I haven't had time to either take observations, or make inquiries yet. The lady incidentally informed me that she had a lady boarder in the house, but she has not yet been in evidence. The house is approached by a broad gravel walk leading from the gate, distant about 200 feet. Large elm and locust trees, the latter now in full bloom, shade the whole lawn which is broad and expansive, and contains beds of roses, and other flowers which I have not yet had time to examine and probably couldn't name if I did. Judging from appearances only, I think I am fortunately located, for this is a sleepy, forsaken old town and I am homesick already. I spent about 10 days in this town during the Cherokee payment of 1894. At that time the country, the people, their ways and customs, were matters of interest to me, but I have seen quite enough of them all and shall be glad indeed when I can bid a final adieu to the Cherokee Nation.

Now if you move here with me I am sure that the time would pass only too quickly, and I should be well contented to stay for an indefinite period. We could spend most of the time in strolling, lounging and fishing and general recreation and rest as my business here requires but a small portion of my time. I wanted to bring Harold very much but at the last moment gave it up, fearing that I might not find it convenient and comfortable for the little fellow here. He had about recovered from the measles before I left home, and is I presume at Kindergarten school today. I rec'd your letter written at Purcell I.T. and also your note announcing your arrival at home. I presume you received my several letters and brief announcements of departure and return, and second departure from home. If you addressed me at home after your Saturday morning note, it will follow me here.

I was much surprised and disappointed, that your mother did not receive greater benefit from her trip. From your last note I gather the idea that she is far from well. The loss of her dear life companion no doubt seems greater than she can bear. There is no escape from her sorrow, which is almost overwhelming.

You who have never experienced such a loss, cannot fully understand and appreciate the depths of her grief. To her the world seems dark and dreary and life not worth living. I do sincerely understand and hope that she will not break down under her great burden of sorrow, but that she may be given strength sufficient to overcome the effects of it, and that she may be spared for many years to be comforted by her children who seem to love her so dearly.

The little girl of this household has just dropped in to see me, and I find she is 6 yrs. old though she doesn't look or act to be over 4. I presume Harold would find it very pleasant here if I had brought him along. Given this little girl for a playmate, and this lovely lawn and surrounding woods for a playground, I am sure he would have been satisfied and proven to be no burden to me.

In my last note I congratulated you upon increased weight, and rosy cheeks. I presume you have regained what you lost during the long and tedious illness of your dear father. How I would love to see you, and to kiss those rosy cheeks, and ruby lips about 1,000,000,000,000 times or more.

It seems about 3 mos. since I last saw you and I don't think I can wait much longer. I hope that my return trip will be made at a time convenient for me to stop and see you and spend Sunday with you but at present I have no idea when I shall return. How swiftly the hours do pass when in your presence. A day seems but an hour of unalloyed bliss.

Dear sweetheart I must now close and mail this letter else you will be disappointed for I am sure you will be looking for it when it arrives.

Until I see you, believe me solely your

Sincere lover,
Frank

Irene's high-topped shoes were glisten-muddy from an impulsive stop on the road to gather an armload of wild irises and spring-green, spiky cattail fronds. Before her mother could get the words out, Irene had dropped to her rump to shed the shoes for scrub and rub. She stood up in cotton-stockinged feet, face flushed with excitement, and danced over to where her mother was sitting encased in an afghan shawl. Irene held out the bog flowers in one hand and several pieces of mail in the other.

"Postmaster must be glad to see you coming, Tot. You've educated his twins with your postage. What's that in your hand, another invitation to open an account in the Homestead Bank?"

"You! Well, yes, I have some correspondence from Horton, but look at this," she said, wiggling an envelope that she had hastily torn open already. "This one is from a little-known hamlet in Republic County. Called Belleville."

"Glory! Read it to me, child."

"No, Mama, you have to read it yourself."

"You are cruel. Where are my specs?"

"In your hair."

Irene's mother made a ceremony of retrieving her glasses, adjusting them, examining the jagged tear in the envelope with dramatic distaste, and finally reading the contents.

"Oh, Irene, my soft baby, they want you. They want you as principal. When did you apply?"

Irene widened her eyes. "That's just it, I never did. This just dropped out of the sky. Obviously because of Frank and Nora Stiles. I don't know what to tell them."

Mrs. Webb thought, Finally there is some brightness on the horizon for Tot. Maybe it's not as good as a gold ring but it is better than anything else. She looked at Irene and said, "I believe the phrase you are groping for is 'Thank you.' After you say that, you say what comes from your heart. My own heart is much improved from reading this, Irene. How's the view up there in the catbird seat? You've got your decoy duck now. Just give that banker-drake a squawk to lure him out of the clouds."

Irene set her lips. Her mother had not lost her knack. She softened her expression and said, "And you call this Belleview offer a duck decoy. Trick the man, Mama? Is that what you are saying?"

Mrs. Webb squirmed. "No, I didn't say that, Irene."

"'Lure him out of the clouds' were your exact words."

"It's just a figure of speech. Use it as you will, or not."

It was not easy for Irene to resolve this. Frank, I could use a little decisive action from you right now. No, can't blame him. He has his tedious "courtship procedure." The Belleville position is good but the engagement is better. Achieve the good? Or pursue the better?

After several attempts at responding to Frank Stiles, each beginning with profuse thanks, Irene wrote that her mind was filled to overflowing with the needs of her mother and of the farm, especially with the spring planting under way, and that because of the uncertainties attending her mother's condition she could not in good faith commit to the opportunity presented, and that the school board should continue with their search unfettered by delays created by herself. It took her a full day to affix a stamp to the envelope and two more full days to actually relinquish it to the postmaster. To pursue the better.

MAILED MAY 8, 1897, FROM NORTONVILLE, KANSAS.

F. M. Wilson, Fort Gibson, Indian Territory
Wednesday, May 5th, '97

My dearest Friend,

It is now a few minutes past eight o'clock. Mama is lying down and I shall talk with you a little while.

Your letter from Ft. Gibson reached me last evening and I was pleased to know you reached your destination safely. I see by the papers that trains are running regularly now over all roads.

After writing my note to you Saturday morning I came out home when I found a budget of mail from you—two letters, a card, and the music. Your letter addressed to Houston I received on Friday morning so you see I was well supplied with literature from your pen.

Monday I received your note written just before your departure to Ft. G. and yesterday your letter from there came. It must have made the trip in a hurry. I believe I have acknowledged receipt of all documents up to present writing. I am glad to get your letters so soon after they leave your hand. When we were in Texas I did not receive your Sunday letters until Wednesday or Thursday—they were none the less appreciated when they did reach me, but I'd rather not wait so long. Please do accept my thanks for the pretty songs; music is always acceptable and these two selections are new to me. I like your selection better than the other. "Old Love Letters" is very sweet I think. I had heard you speak of it and tried to get it in Houston, but the music dealer had sold the last copy. I intended to play it as a surprise for you, but you have stolen a march or in this case a waltz on me this time.

The other song is pretty but I do not like the sentiment it expresses. In music and in poetry I like something sweet and tender and something inspiring as well. I do not like such songs as "Fallen by the Way side" and never sing them. I never could understand why a song writer should select such a theme as the above and put it before the public in form of a waltz song. You were very kind and thoughtful to secure the music for me and I appreciate it very much.

We found things in good order at home and we are very glad to be here. There was the sad part to our homecoming and it is lonely indeed without my loved Father. He used to love the spring time so much. It is only the assurance that he is now enjoying a far more beautiful home than his earthly one and that eternal spring time and happiness is his, that we feel in a measure resigned to the change. I think my mother is a little better tho she is far from being well. The first part of our visit she seemed to improve in health, but the last week she was very miserable. She looks dreadfully—she contracted Malaria in the South and she is just as yellow as she can be. I am very thankful indeed to have her at home under Uncle Dr.'s care.

He thinks she will not get down in bed but I am not so hopeful. She sits up only a little now altho' she dresses each morning and lies on the lounge. Poor dear Mother, she has seemed only half alive since we laid dear Father to rest. Sometimes as I look at her I think it may not be long until she joins him. At night I often hear her sigh and repeat his name. My heart seems to almost break at the thought of her leaving us, too. I hope and pray she may be spared to us for a while at least.

No I have never experienced such a loss, as you say, but I have scarcely been away from my Mother an hour since Father left us and I think I know something of her grief. I have read with care and interest the article you enclosed in one of your letters in "The Power of Music" and it is a subject the last part of it that I have been wanting to discuss with you for a long time, but I wanted you to introduce the subject yourself. I shall not enter into the discussion this morning as there is something else I want to tell you.

I had a letter from my cousin in Belleville saying the Board of Ed. of that place wished to tender me the position of High School Principal for next year. I wrote him that I was not an applicant.

The party of friends with whom I went camping last year is arranging to spend the month of August camping in Colorado and want me to join them. Not all of the party of last year can go but they hope to find others to take their places. I should enjoy going very, very much. I had such a good time last year. Unless Mama gets much better and some arrangements can be made for her comfort, I will not think of going.

I hope that your stay in Ft. Gibson may be very pleasant and very short. If your transportation home is by K.C. and Horton

I can meet you at Dunavant, a little station six miles from here on the North Western R.R. The train arrives there from K.C. at 10:16 a.m. or used to last summer.

Good Bye for this time—Believe me, dear heart.

Sincerely yours,
Irene

MAILED MAY 10, 1897, FROM TAHLEQUAH, INDIAN TERRITORY.

Miss Irene Webb, Nortonville, Kansas
Sunday, May 9-97

My Darling Irene,

I came here from Fort Gibson last Thursday, a distance of 25 miles by stage. I have not heard from you since I left home, and am growing very anxious for another letter. I wrote you last Monday from Ft. Gibson and was greatly disappointed in not hearing from you before leaving there.

I now expect to return to Ft. Gibson on my return trip home about Tuesday next when I trust I will receive one or more letters from you.

Owing to much dissatisfaction and numerous complaints to the Secretary of the Interior, the paymaster was removed last Wednesday and the payment indefinitely postponed. I then came here to meet the party in whom I am interested in order, if possible, to settle up our business matter so that my further attendance would not be required. Friday and Saturday I spent in company with an attorney here, driving over the flint hills, a distance of about 35 miles, and returned over the worst roads that it has ever been my misfortune to travel. We started to drive yesterday morning at 6 o'clock, and reached this place at 9 o'clock last night stopping once only for driver and horse feed. You can well imagine that we were tired out. After a good night's rest I now feel first rate.

The road over which we travelled was new to both of us and being through a timbered and mountainous country, sparsely settled with no guide posts, and few fences, but many roads leading in all directions. We lost our way many times and probably travelled 25 miles out of our way upon the trip. The district through which we travelled is named Flint, because of the hills and mountains covered with flint rock which compose the greater part of its area of some 50 miles square. Through this country there are many streams of clear, cool, swift running water fed by springs, and with beds of sand gravel and flint. They are the most beautiful and refreshing streams that I have ever seen. The flint rock which covers the hill tops and sides, seems to be constantly crumbling and breaking up into pebbles in size from marbles to goose eggs, then to be washed by the rains into the streams, which run with force sufficient to carry and pile it up in drifts and bars all along the shore.

I have seen these drifts 10 to 15 feet deep, and wondered how the water could carry such an accumulation of rock from the hills and mountains and pile up in such vast bars as though it were sand. I wish that you could be with me for a few days here. We would enjoy an exploring and fishing expedition, in the region just described.

This is the Capital of the Cherokee Nation, but being 25 miles from railroad is a town of not exceeding 2800 to 3000 population. There are two seminaries here. One for the boys, the other for the girls of the Nation, and they are doing good work and have a large attendance.

Last Friday was a National May Day Holiday here and there was a May party at the male seminary grounds about a mile from town, which was generally attended by the girls from the female seminary, and the town folks.

It is customary to suspend business upon that day, a custom which might well be copied in the states for a similar purpose. I don't think we are in danger of having too many holidays in this hustling age of unrest.

I saw the Dawes Commission at Ft. Gibson. They will be here next Tuesday to treat with a Commission from this Nation, concerning the allotment of their lands and dissolution of the Cherokee government. The Choctaw and Chickasaw Indians have already reached an understanding with the Dawes Commission, and I think there is no doubt but that the five civilized tribes will all very soon allot their lands, and come into statehood. When this takes place there will be a great rush of immigration to this country.

The families down here are unusually large. 10 or 12 children is not uncommon for a family. Large families, instead of being a hindrance and expense, are just the reverse, as each child is entitled to an equal share in the distribution of all the lands and moneys of the Nation, and thus great inducement is offered to increase the family roll.

When the allotment of lands and final distribution of moneys are made we may observe a change in the custom, and small families may become more fashionable.

Now my dear sweet heart I think I shall close and take a walk. It is almost 5 o'clock and I have been about the Hotel all day. I brought plenty of reading matter with me. I want to assure you that in all my travels and observations I have not yet found one to compare with my beloved sweet heart. How I would love to be with you today darling. This is an ideal lover's day here. I hope it will not be long until I can see you again. You need not address me again after you get this, until further notice, as I hope to start home before I could receive your letter. When I start home I will advise you, so that you can address me there in case I do not stop on way home to see you.

With unfaltering love I am

Sincerely Yours,
Frank
I don't know whether you can read above or not.
The pen is to blame for faulty work.

MAILED MAY 11, 1897, FROM NORTONVILLE, KANSAS.

F. M. Wilson, Fort Gibson, Indian Territory

My dearest Friend,

I think I do not owe you a letter, but I know letters are always doubly appreciated when one is away from home and loved ones dear. So I shall send a short message with Maggie Rea's letter to Harold. She came out Friday evening on the train and her Papa has gone to take her home this morning. We were very glad to see her again. She is a sweet girl and we think she is improving every day in her manners. She was much disappointed to think she did not bring "her own note paper along"—she does not like the kind I use and has generously offered me some of hers. I happened to have some small envelopes and that helped her some. I suggested that she wait until she got home to write but she wanted to send her letter with mine and decided to use "my ugly old paper without any lines" rather than wait.

This is a lovely morning. I presume you are attending church at Ft. Gibson at this hour. Today is our quarterly meeting service but I could not leave my Mother to attend. The church re-elected me Church organist while I was away. I am sorry they did, for I attend so irregularly that I am sure it would be much better to have some-one else. My mother is just about as she was when I last wrote you. She does not seem to gain strength but she has not given up to go to bed. I am greatly in hopes that she may get better soon.

What lovely moon light nights we are having! The trees are so pretty now all dressed in green. I am late with my flowers this year and shall not attempt to have many. By the way—the Jassamines that I mentioned sending you on my return were all spoiled when we reached home. Not one of the buds opened. I had a basket of beautiful flowers but we were so long on the way that they were spoiled. . . .

Well dearheart my note is lengthening into a letter and I must close. If you were here I should not let you off so easily, for I can cook and talk too. But I can't cook and write very well. It is time to prepare dinner. I wish you were here to dine with us. Our menu isn't very elaborate but you would be very welcome to what we have. I want to spend a day in Atchison this week if I can leave my Mother.

Good morning
Lovingly Yours, Irene
Sunday, May '97

THIS IS INTOLERABLE, FRANK thought as he stood in the Eudora, Kansas, station and stared at the two timetables that simply did not produce enough time. I cannot give up an entire day, not now, not with the Rock Island payday coming up day after tomorrow on top of everything else, and not after that ridiculous odyssey to Fort Gibson. Never again! Let Forest clean up his own mess. This is intolerable.

She doesn't deserve this. I must go to her and I must go to the bank, and I must do so at exactly the same time, but I can't do both at the same time, and if I do either the one or the other, *people suffer.* Intolerable. There will be hell to pay. Damned if I do, damned if I don't. Irene is more reasonable than my bank people. She doesn't deserve it but she's the one I have to hurt. It can't be helped, I have to skip Nortonville.

MAILED MAY 13, 1897, FROM TOPEKA, KANSAS.

Miss Irene Webb, Nortonville, Kansas
May 12, 1897, 9 p.m.

My Darling Irene,
I arrived here at 7 p.m. upon my return home, having stopped a few hours with my brother at Eudora.

I very much desired to call upon you tonight, reaching home via Atchison & Willis tomorrow morning but can get no train to Nortonville until morning. This would lose me another day, and having been absent so long I feel it my duty to report at home tomorrow morning which I have decided to do.

Upon my return to Ft. Gibson I received the letter which awaited me and for which I was growing impatient.

I shall not attempt to write you tonight in reply, but will expect you to address me at home as soon as convenient.

I want to see you and shall try to do so soon. I am very sorry indeed to learn that your mother is no better. Give her my kindest regards and best wishes for speedy recovery.

For you to thus confide to me this family secret, serves to increase the confidence and love which I bear to you. It is in keeping with your noble character, as it has been constantly revealed to me since I have known you.

Dear heart, I will sacredly guard your secret and speak more at length of it at another time.

Lovingly,
Frank

MAILED MAY 13, 1897, FROM NORTONVILLE, KANSAS.

F. M. Wilson, Horton, Kansas

My dearest Friend,

Your letter from Topeka came today. I too am sorry that you could not have spent last evening with me but I could hardly expect you to sacrifice a whole day from business just to see me. Has that last sentence a tinge of sarcasm in it? Pardon me if it has but I was greatly disappointed to have you go home without stopping.

My Mother has the fever. The Dr. says it will be two days or three about before there is any change in her present condition. My hands have been full since I came home attending to the house and caring for her. My brother came up from Topeka Wednesday and he is a great help. If Mama gets worse my sisters will come home but she wants to be absolutely quiet and for that reason it is better not to have too many caring for her. We have a neighbor woman who is very good however so I can manage fairly well. No doubt you are glad to be at home again and the children are delighted. Your letter written Sunday came the first of the week. It was sweetly scented with the honeysuckle. I haven't gotten to do anything with my flowers yet.

I am tired and sleepy tonight so will ask you to excuse a very brief letter and tell me Good Night.

Lovingly Yours,
Irene
Thursday, 10 p.m.
May 13-97

∽ ⊃ ᵚᵚᵚ

MAILED MAY 16, 1897, FROM HORTON, KANSAS.

Miss Irene Webb, Nortonville, Kansas
Sunday, May 16-97

My Darling Irene,

Your letter of last Sunday, addressed to Ft. Gibson followed me home and reached me here Thursday evening. Friday evening I rec'd yours of Thursday, containing the sad news that your mother grows worse instead of better. This is both a surprise and a disappointment to me as I felt sure that she would return from her trip south very much improved in health and spirits. I still hope and trust that no serious consequences may result and that she may speedily recover when the fever has run its course. Perhaps it were best for her condition that I did not stop to see you on my return trip.

If you were somewhat disappointed at my failure to call, I beg to assure you that my disappointment was greater, because I am very anxious to see you, and had counted on doing so ere this. I would gladly sacrifice a whole day to see you, most any time, but as an officer of an institution where others are interested, and have a claim upon my services, I felt it my duty to hasten home and report after a 10 days absence, deferring my pleasure trip until a more convenient date, which I felt sure could be formed very soon.

My apology for stopping a few hours with my brother, instead of going to see you direct from K.C., is that I had not visited him for 4 or 5 years, and it is very seldom that I find it convenient to stop with him, as I did in this case.

I am sure you will excuse me under the circumstances. I would like to visit you next Sunday, but on account of your mother's condition, think best to defer it until she recovers. I wish I could send you someone to help you with your work but I wouldn't know where to look. You surely have your hands full and I am afraid you will soon lose the weight and color lately acquired.

Yes indeed I am glad to be at home again for tho' "it's not what it used to be" still "there's no place like home.". . .

School is out here, and Wallis spends most of this time fishing. He is again without a music teacher. The lady from Topeka ceased her weekly visits without an explanation or notice. I presume it was because she found it unprofitable. I am very sorry that Wallis has no teacher, he was getting along so nicely and had become interested in the work. . . .

I regretted that I did not take Harold with me to Indian Territory. It would have been a very pleasant trip for him. The weather was very pleasant and my lot was cast in pleasant places, so that he would have enjoyed every feature of the trip from start to finish.

He was pleased with Maggie Rae's letter, which is certainly a very creditable one, for one of her age, as regards subject matter as well as form. . . .

Your taste in the selection of music coincides with mine exactly. I am glad to have you express your sentiments so plainly concerning the music I sent you. When I got home from K.C. and found out what I had purchased upon the recommendation of a clerk, without examination (for I had no time to examine it) I felt inclined to burn it, and shall not be surprised or disappointed if you have done so. I shall hope to hear you sing "Old Love Letters" when I visit you again.

Now dear sweet heart I think I must say good bye for Harold begins to think that I am neglecting him.

Lovingly Yours,
Frank

MAILED MAY 20, 1897, FROM NORTONVILLE, KANSAS.

F. M. Wilson, Horton, Kansas

My dear Mr. Wilson,

I have now a few minutes to myself and shall improve them talking to you. Your Sunday letter reached me Monday evening. Sunday was a most lovely day here. I thought I never saw a more perfect day and evening. I spent the day at home as usual. Indeed I am becoming completely ostracized from society life of any kind. The last social gathering I attended was New Year's eve. It seems very strange to me to be so confined. All my life I have been so perfectly free from responsibility of any kind and have always given so much. I could never realize that the experience I have undergone and am now having should come to me. I shall do my best and that's all I can do.

My mother is real sick. I do not think she is dangerously ill yet, but we have not been successful in checking the fever entirely. Typhoid is so slow. Sometimes she seems to have no fever at all, then perhaps in an hour her temperature will be up to 103.

My brother is still at home and my sister came out a few days ago. Yes, indeed, my hands are full altho' I am greatly relieved since my sister came. I know nothing about taking care of sick people. We have had so very little sickness in the family and I have never been seriously ill in my life. Until Papa was ill so long I had scarcely been near any one suffering.

I must close now. We have company for dinner and if I don't hurry up we won't have much to eat. If Mama gets no worse I can do pretty well. It's pretty hard on the people I cook for, I expect, but the experience is a valuable one for me.

Very Sincerely Yours,
Irene

MAILED MAY 22, 1897, FROM NORTONVILLE, KANSAS.

F. M. Wilson, Horton, Kansas
Thursday, May 20-97
Saturday Morning

My Dearest Friend,
My mother is very ill. The fever has increased rapidly the past two days. We are greatly alarmed about her but we are doing our utmost to check the fever.

She is very restless and nervous. Both of my sisters are with us and our friends are so very kind.

Lovingly, Irene

MAILED MAY 23, 1897, FROM HORTON, KANSAS.

Miss Irene Webb, Nortonville, Kansas
Sunday, May 23d, '97

My Darling Irene,

Your Thursday letter reached me Friday evening and today I rec'd your note announcing a serious change in your mother's condition.

Is it possible that our worst fears are to be realized and that she is soon to follow her dear companion to that brighter and better home where sorrow and separation are no more!

I don't know why, but it is a fact, that I have had a feeling ever since your father's death that your mother would not linger long behind him. Poor soul, her burden of sorrow is greater than she can bear, need I fear that human skill can do but little to comfort her, or restore her to health. I enter into profound sympathy with you, in this hour of great anxiety, and pray that you may not be called upon to mourn her loss. How I wish that I might be able to render some assistance to you, or in some manner lighten your burden of care. Yes dear heart, the past six months, to you, has been in strange contrast to your previous experience. In your case it may be truly said, that misfortunes do not come singly. . . .

When Harold had the measles he got pretty thin, but is now looking hearty and rugged as ever. We are getting along very nicely, and it seems to me that the boys never were better, and never gave me so little trouble or cause for anxiety. Now that school is out, and there is no necessity for early rising, we never call him in the morning, but let him sleep. We insist however that he get up at noon.

I wish you could visit us this summer. I would like for you to see us all in our home, and I would also like for you to see our

town at this season of the year. The improvement in its appearance, due to growth of trees, and other internal improvements
being made is quite noticeable. After 2 or 3 years of growth, it
would be hard for one unacquainted with the facts to realize
that the town is so young. Sometime this summer I hope you
and Maggie Rea can make us a visit, and your mother also if she
recovers from her illness.

Now dear sweet heart I must close and say good bye, hoping to
hear from you soon and to be kept fully advised of changes in your
mother's condition. Remember me kindly to her.

Lovingly thine,
Frank

MAILED MAY 23, 1897, FROM NORTONVILLE, KANSAS.

F. M. Wilson, Horton, Kansas
Sunday, 2:30 P.M.

My dearest Friend,
Dr. Webb sent for Dr. Gephart of Valley Falls last night and they
held a consultation this morning.

They have told us that they do not think my Mother can
recover and that unless there is a decided change the end cannot
be far distant.

I cannot and will not believe that she is to be taken from us.

Irene Webb

MAILED MAY 27, 1897, FROM NORTONVILLE, KANSAS.

F. M. Wilson, Horton, Kansas
Thursday Noon

My dearest Friend,

My mother has rallied a little today. Since Monday night we have been expecting hourly for her to pass away. Her Drs. give us no definite grounds for hope and state that her present condition is due to stimulants above.

My brothers are all here. Edd arrived last night. Mama's mind is perfectly clear and she knew the boys as quickly as she saw them.

Lovingly,
Irene

MAILED MAY 30, 1897, FROM NORTONVILLE, KANSAS.

F. M. Wilson, Horton, Kansas
Saturday Afternoon

My darling mother is almost gone. The Drs. tell us it is a question of only a few hours. Will you kindly tell Mr. Alton of St. Joseph and the Dunn girls at Horton.

In sorrow Yours,
Irene
May 30

Miss Irene Webb, Nortonville, Kansas

My Darling Irene,

At noon today I rec'd your note written yesterday afternoon. A few moments later I met the Dunn girls and informed them of its contents, and I have just written to Mr. Alton. I have received your several almost daily reports the past week and have expected each succeeding mail to bring the sad intelligence that your precious mother has gone. My heart has gone out to you in deepest sympathy every day, for I have had no hope for her recovery since you first announced Typhoid fever.

I wonder if her spirit will take its flight upon this bright and beautiful memorial day, while our whole nation is engaged in the beautiful service of paying tribute to its dead heroes. Her life has been pure and holy and doubtless she is glad to hear the Master's call to her reward. You will never have to blush on account of any act committed by either your father or your mother. This is a comforting thought to you dear heart. They will spend eternity in that beautiful companionship commenced on earth so many years ago. Their life will be a constant inspiration to their children and friends left behind. . . .

The ladies of the M.E. Church have announced a social at our house next Friday evening. They serve cream and strawberries (Harold calls them hay-berries) for 10 cents. I presume the size and condition of our lawn is one chief reason for the request to hold it here. Our bank gives open air concerts every Friday evening, on the street, and have done so for several years past, during the summer months. This being the night of our social, we shall probably secure their attendance after about half past 8 o'clock.

But these matters do not interest you now precious heart. You have long been shut out from the gay social life, and your time fully occupied in the care of your parents, the last sad duty of which you are so soon to perform. I hope and pray that you may be given strength and courage to bear up under your great sorrow.

With renewed assurances of love and esteem I am

Sincerely,
Frank

MAILED JUNE 2, 1897, FROM NORTONVILLE, KANSAS. [ENVELOPE IS BORDERED IN THICK BLACK LINING, AS IS NOTE PAPER.]

F. M. Wilson, Horton, Kansas
Sunday afternoon, May 30, '97

My dear Mr. Wilson,

My precious Mother passed away at 5:37 o'clock this morning—the end was perfect peace and she is now with my sainted Father.

We will lay her to rest tomorrow—Thursday—afternoon. I should like to have you attend the funeral—but I think a visit a few days hence would be better.

In Sorrow,
Irene

MAILED JUNE 2, 1897, FROM HORTON, KANSAS.

Miss Irene Webb, Nortonville, Kansas
Wednesday Morning

My Darling Irene,

Dear heart be assured of my profound sympathy in this your second great sorrow. I have rather been expecting to attend the funeral in case you expressed a desire for me to do so, but have concluded to wait a few days and pay you a visit whenever it may best suit your convenience. I wanted to forward a floral tribute from here this evening but I find it impossible to reach you in time. If I send it via Topeka tonight I fear it will not leave Topeka until tomorrow evening. I cannot get it to St. Joe in morning early enough for morning train.

Mr. and Mrs. Alton may conclude to join me in this tribute of respect to the memory of your precious mother....

With sincere love and sympathy,

Frank
Wednesday, June 2
8 P.M.

MAILED JUNE 8, 1897, FROM HORTON, KANSAS.

Miss Irene Webb, Nortonville, Kansas

My Darling Irene,

How sad and lonely you must feel today. Kind friends are doubtless doing all that can be done to lessen your sorrow, and reconcile you to the great loss which you have sustained, but alas how feeble do such efforts seem and how little do they accomplish.

Time alone can reconcile you to the new conditions which confront you.

No more can you lean upon Father and Mother in the battle of life, but alone you must fight it out. You are young and brave and strong and will overcome all difficulties that may be encountered and very soon adjust yourself to new conditions. I have been thinking of you all day and wishing that I might be with you.

I failed to receive my usual letter yesterday, and experienced the consequent disappointment but I cheerfully excuse you for the omission, knowing full well that your heart has been too full of sorrow to fulfill your obligations of this character.

I presume that some of your brothers and sisters have remained with you and that you prefer to be left alone with them, free from the intrusion of friends, for a few days. I shall be glad to hear from you whenever you feel inclined to write, but I shall not grow impatient with waiting. I would have made you a visit today had I been well assured that I was welcome, but I felt that you would rather have me postpone the visit.

Mrs. Alton writes me that Mr. Alton was absent from home last Wednesday and Thursday but that she forwarded the roses to you, and directed that they be delivered at your home. I hope they reached you in good time, and good condition. . . .

Now my dear sweetheart, with much love and esteem I must say

Good night,
Frank

F. M. Wilson, Horton, Kansas

My dearest Friend,

Please accept my thanks for the box of lovely roses which you sent as a token of love to the memory of my beautiful Mother. They were delivered in the forenoon sometime and were very fresh and fragrant.

I never saw so many beautiful flowers. My Mother's room was like a beautiful white garden. I remember but little about the flowers. I saw only the dear face in that casket. The past week seems a strange sad dream to me. I have the feeling that I shall awaken from it and find life the same again.

I have never become used to the change since my Father left us, but before he passed away he told me to be brave and strong for Mother's sake. When the end came and ever since then I put my life and soul into trying to help and comfort her. Now she is gone. Gone from the home she loved so much and from her children whom she loved so dearly and who worshipped her. I can't understand it. I appreciate the beautiful sentiment through it all.

My Mother was never happy or contented a day after we laid Father to rest. The only tie that held her to life was her children and especially her baby as she lovingly called me to the last. She did not want to leave me alone and clung to me as long as life lasted.

With her seven children around her bed and her hand clasped in mine she passed sweetly and peacefully into the Great Beyond to join her loved companion who she told us was standing with open arms to welcome her.

Our good Father and our good Mother are gone. We children have been nobly born. Whatever of goodness any of us may possess comes as a just inheritance. I only pray I may become as good a woman as my Mother. I have no higher aspirations.

We laid her to rest as beautifully as we could. The service was conducted by Dr. Emory and was the exact in every way as Father's. The same pall bearers, music, hymns and all. My same girl friends arranged the grave and now she sleeps close beside my sainted Father. Everything has been in confusion since the funeral. My brothers were anxious to get back to their work and it was very necessary that business arrangements should be made before they separated. Everything has been arranged most satisfactorily without carrying anything into court.

The excitement of everything has kept me up and it is only now when the members of the family are one by one leaving that the awful reality seems to come. It is not that I shrink from any responsibility that may come to me now. I know I have much to be thankful for in my perfect health and all. My brothers and sisters are tender loyal and true. It is not this. It is the great change and the utter loneliness that seem to completely overwhelm me. If you can I should like to have you spend next Sunday with us.

I take it for granted you will come and shall ask you to let me know which way you will come.

I thank you for your kind words of sympathy.

Sincerely and Lovingly,

Irene

Tuesday Morning

MAILED JUNE 10, 1897, FROM HORTON, KANSAS.

Miss Irene Webb, Nortonville, Kansas
June 9, '97

My Darling Irene,

I rec'd your letter this morning. I had about concluded that you were sick, and unable to write, and had made up my mind to write and find out if such was the case, if I had not heard from you today. I am glad to know that you are well, and I shall be delighted to visit you next Sunday.

I find it impossible to reach Atchison Sunday morning in time for the Nortonville train so that I shall be obliged to start Saturday evening. I will drive to Willis after supper Saturday evening and arrive at Nortonville at 9.54 P.M.

If you are not at train to meet me, I will stop in town, and call on you Sunday morning.

If the weather is unfavorable I will not expect you to meet me. If it is not convenient for you to meet me do not do so.

I hope that the weather will not interfere with my trip.

It seems almost an age since I last saw you and I am getting very anxious for a visit with you.

Until then believe me

> *Your sincere lover,*
> *Frank*

IN ALL THE CONFUSION her cousin Charley had left his collars on the sleeping porch dresser when he left. Irene came across them as she commenced restoring order to the farmhouse ten days after the funeral. She knew they were Charlie's because she had given him the collar box for Christmas four years ago. She would add this to the packets of other left-behinds to take to the post office. Except for Charlie they all belonged to sisters-in-law. She was beginning to miss them. To think, not that long ago, she missed having the house empty.

Downstairs things looked pretty much as they did on June third at the service. She was in no hurry to pick up from that. She took a comfort from the great cluster of chairs, even empty. The spent flowers she had put in the garden to simply return to nature. She took a comfort in that gesture as well as in seeing such an abundance of them. She had put his roses under the pear tree. She stepped to the window to look at them again.

She thought about the journey the roses had made, from St. Joseph, Missouri to Nortonville, Kansas, and then carried by hand from Mr. Engels of the livery stable. He had ridden his favorite, Cleo. He didn't feel he was dressed to come in the house, but Jerret McVey insisted that he stay for the service if he wanted. The place was bursting, but everyone was respectful and solemn.

Twice now she had been with her family in a deathbed vigil. She wondered, years from now, would there be one at the farm for her? Or would it be somewhere else? Horton? Valley Falls? Not Belleville; the die had been cast.

With so many there, she had not spent the time or said all the words to her mother on that last day. She had said it all before then, though. Nothing was left unsaid between them. That was a comfort.

No one had talked about the trip to Houston, but it was on everyone's mind. Too painful. If only we hadn't gone. If only we had just stayed at home. That kind of life is not for us. No, Irene thought, it gave her a lift at the time. Mama saw her kin and talked over the past. Can't go around moping over something nobody could have predicted. God, that train ride. That hotel.

She stood at the window looking out at the pear tree. Rose stems had tumbled into the yard in the wind, their flowers shattered. Brown petals curled in cracks of the bark of the tree. This is not dreary, she thought. It's actually cheery. If this were a novel—really, Irene, a novel of Nortonville— well, then a story, the symbolism would be unmistakable. Death and decay. Shattered hopes. Withering romance. But actually, what she saw cheered her. To Irene the roses spoke of love.

CHAPTER EIGHT

I AM RATHER AT A STANDSTILL TO KNOW WHAT TO DO

MORNING FOUR

In the dim, predawn light of the morning of Sunday, June 13, 1897, Frank was told, "She has expired." *But I already know that. Why does he tell me again, I already know that. I can see that for God's sake, right there in that bed!* He blinked his eyes open. Then the aftershock hit him and he reexperienced every feeling of that moment: knee-buckling pain, horror, astonishment, and an exquisite upwelling of deep love for his wife. He let out a moan of considerable volume.

He was in a brass bed, in a room he had no recollection of. He sat upright. He saw his valise but no one else in the room and no other bed. He sank to the pillow again and thought, *Nortonville Hotel. Here to propose to Irene. How could I forget? Ha. Fool.*

Frank had been free of the morning terrors for exactly twenty-five nights until just now. He thought that this would be the right time to move forward and to propose engagement to be married. He had followed Fowler's procedures and there was no better time than this very day. If anything, it was later than he first sketched out in his mind. That, of course, couldn't be helped when her mother fell ill. This would be the day. From the looks of early light it would be a brilliant day. He had a feeling she would accept, maybe even that very day. More likely she would take the time prescribed by convention. After all, that was all in Fowler's book, which she said she had read.

He dressed in gray tweed pants, a collarless shirt with bloused sleeves, sodbuster boots, and a straw farm hat. He packed yesterday's clothes, closed the valise and stepped into the hallway.

Sunday breakfast fare at the hotel was lots of coffee and not much else. Frank got downstairs before any of the other guests and could claim a piece of cornbread from the basket before walking to the livery stable. He hired a saddled chestnut mare for the day.

"What's she called?"

"Balky by some. Cleo by me. A lot has to do with who's on 'er. Who would that be?"

"Frank Wilson, Horton. Visiting the Webb place. I'll have her back an hour before the last train east. Mind if I leave my valise here?"

"Engles. Nice to meet you. You sent those roses for the service. You tell Miss Irene we are so sorry for her losses. It's been a hard, hard winter for that girl."

Cleo turned out to have a quick pace as Frank trotted her. He then slowed her to a walk to enjoy the spring field flowers and to let the morning's work on the farm get underway before intruding. He brought Cleo to a stop and let her graze. He stayed in the saddle since he was alone and this was his first time out with the horse.

He and Allie had always liked riding at dawn. Now, in this moment, sitting Cleo in bright, warm sunshine, he could think of those times without so much as a clutch in his throat. He could do so and still anticipate the excitement of the moment he would state his proposal to Irene. But, in bed this very same morning, memories of Allie had blotted out his awareness of where he was, what he was doing, and all feelings other than ten-month-old ones.

He knew the spells could come at any time. He understood their cause but not their meaning. He also knew that he couldn't let them govern his life. Or take over his free will. That honored no one, least of all Allie. He spoke aloud as if he were on a stage in a full theatre: "Allie, I am going to propose marriage to Irene Webb." He waited for the earth to swallow him. He looked up for a thunderbolt. Nothing moved except Cleo leaning for a clump of foxtails. All right, then. Let's go, Cleo. He kept her at a walk until the Webb farm came into view. At the sight of it, Frank clicked Cleo into a trot again.

Irene was gathering lettuce near her pear tree when he arrived. She stood up quickly but waited for him to come to a stop so as not to alarm his horse.

"So, they gave you Cleo. Good girl, let me pull you a carrot."

"And what do you have for this vagabond lone rider?"

"What are you hungry for, Senor Vagabond?"

Frank said nothing. He dismounted, and with his free hand around Irene's waist he drew her against him. She exhaled against his throat, wrapped in his strong embrace. He kissed her. Irene brought both hands to his cheeks as she kissed him. She flicked the straw hat to the ground and pushed her open fingers through his short auburn hair. Over and over.

Frank looked at her, his eyes searching every quarter of her face. Then he bowed his head and said, "Irene, I am still devastated over your mother's passing. It's not good enough to say she is with Hiram. I ache for her to be right here, with you."

"I know. Come over here, to the pear tree. Not much left of them now, but see those stiff stems? That's what's left of the roses. They were good messengers of your sentiments."

Frank felt his throat close. He had to blink and look into the distance. He walked back to pick up his hat. When the tenseness subsided he said, "Looks like I need to get you fresher ones."

Irene brightened up and said, "How about some cattails and black-eyed Susans instead? I thought we'd take a ride to Grace Lake. It's four or five miles east, over by Dunavant. I'd love to get away from this farm and solemn reminders. You want one of our horses or are you all right with Cleo?"

"That sounds perfect on a day like this. I'm happy with Cleo. She might like to graze a new pasture."

Irene put together a light picnic for them. She was already dressed for a ride in black boots, dark-blue cotton pants, and a cowboy shirt with bone buttons. Frank thought she was the most feminine creature he had ever seen. Her hair was out of its coils and buns and went in every direction the breeze did. Frank felt waves of conflicting urges about the proposal he carried under his tongue. Just when he felt it was the perfect thing to say on such a perfect day, something inside him wondered if he was absolutely sure beyond question. Nothing is absolutely sure he thought. Why did Allie die again this morning?

Irene and Bluebelle led the way, first down the Section road, then through fields and pastures on paths engineered by cattle. After an hour or so they came upon Grace Lake, a spring-fed body of water the shape of a willow leaf, about a hundred yards long and half that in width. It sat in the swale of a small hill which held redbud trees and bowers of wild lilacs, all in full blossom. On the hillside stood the fieldstone walls of an abandoned barn, its roof now collapsed to a jumble of dry-land driftwood.

The shallow end of the lake held cattails, which, in turn, held marsh wrens and red-winged blackbirds. As they approached they alarmed a mallard pair who launched themselves to a quieter spot along the creek seeping from out of the cattails.

Bluebelle headed to the water's edge. There the horses leaned to drink, shook their heads and manes, and stamped, jostling their riders. Frank and Irene led the horses to the shaded side of the old pioneer barn to graze, and walked along the edge of the lake. They stopped at a sunny, grassy bank and stretched out to enjoy Irene's picnic.

"This spot is idyllic. How do you know about it?"

"Oh, all the Webb kids have come here over the years. This place is not far from Hickory Point. Ever heard of it?"

"No, I haven't."

"It's part of local lore about the days before the War, when Free-Staters were pouring into Kansas. Thirty-some years ago, a posse of Free-State men caught up with a Missouri gang who had marauded Valley Falls, which was called Grasshopper Falls back in the day. The posse sent for the army in Lawrence and when they came the fighting broke out at Hickory Point. A half dozen on each side were wounded. One died. One of hundreds of such days at the time."

Frank stood up, loosened his shirt buttons and fanned his face with his straw hat in the strong sun. Irene watched him and gave a little gasp. Frank raised his eyebrows.

"Nothing, really," she said. "Just then, seeing you there, I was reminded . . . well, I got to thinking, anyway . . . Frank, you look just like a boy I saw working on the tracks outside Guthrie. And he looked so much like you but younger. He was smiling out in that sun. Feel like a twenty-year-old? You have the frisky legs of one. You're not smiling," she said and pushed his knee playfully. He fell to the ground and rolled over twice like a log.

"Now who's frisky?" he shouted to the sky.

"Come on, Frank. Angels fly because they take themselves lightly."

Neither spoke but soaked in the sunshine, the whispers of long grass in the breeze, and the warmth of being together. Irene said,

"My father brought me here when I was, oh, twelve, I suppose. It was a whole lot colder then, just after Christmas. We were out because I had to try out new riding boots I got from Santa Claus. Not a cloud in the sky. We'd watered the horses, just like now, when Papa looked up. Then I heard it too. Way off. I mean way, way off. And up. Papa said, 'Sandhill cranes,' but neither one of us could find them in the sky. Papa said they'd risen over Nebraska and on their way south. He told me a flock will form; then, as they fly, more and more birds will join them, and then other flocks will join that flock. They wheel around in the sky as the flocks make a bigger flock. And they rise as they circle, higher and higher till they're too high to see. These are birds as tall as Maggie Rea but they get to circling and rising until they are out of eyesight. And the sound they make, Frank. Papa heard them again late last fall—soon after your first visit, actually. It's a continuous warbling, prettier than geese. And at that distance it is magical."

After a long pause she said, "That day I looked into the sky, I thought I was hearing angels."

Frank lay very still, eyes closed, as his mind explored what he had just heard. He, who had never heard the cranes, imagined that first time Irene had heard them with Hiram, and that last time Hiram had. Great, ancient birds rising to migration; slowly rising; calling; smaller flocks and individuals joining; eventually a great chorus of cranes circling upward until they were out of sight; and then all that reached the ground were quavering voices beyond the visible.

"Who's to say you didn't?"

Frank then thought about the present, this perfect day, the water brilliant with sunlight. He thought, She lives in paradise already. He thought about cranes here and trains there in Horton, where they manufactured noise and called it locomotives. He looked intently at the lilacs and listened intently to the song of the blackbirds. Can I really propose marriage? Take her to Horton to watch it replace lilacs and cattails with more bricks and mortar? Am I enough? That's the real question. No, it's not. It always comes back to one thing. It's irrational. It's the feeling that I'm still married. I need to rethink this at home.

He said, "Emerson was right. You are a diamond morning."

"You! We should probably start back."

They rode side by side from Grace Lake directly to the livery stable. Frank opened up to Irene about his nightly torments. He said, "I had no idea the spells, as I call them, would keep coming back."

"Frank, I hope you haven't become superstitious over these dreams."

"So do I. I'm sure it's something like Marley appearing to Scrooge: 'A slight disorder of the stomach . . . a blot of mustard, a crumb of cheese.' But it spoils the night to start the day."

He turned to look at her. "Irene, please indulge me with time to try to conquer this."

This time it was Irene who was unsmiling. As they rode in silence, she was thinking about her own situation. She could understand grief, all too well. But this sounded different, or at least like a different kind of grief. For me, she thought, losing Mother and Father makes me yearn for this man even more. For the frantic routine of a household and his boys. Even dueling grandmothers. Reading a play after dinner. Right now, I feel incomplete and unfinished. For him, it seems grief is a moat and a wall between us. What if he just goes on being Allie's husband? How much better would that be than Abelard and Heloise? Time, he wants. Well, "to every thing there is a season, and a time to every purpose."

At the Nortonville Station, standing next to Frank and his valise, Irene took his hand and said to him, "Frank, if you want me, I am here for you. I will be here when you are ready. I'm in no hurry for anything. And I'm not going anywhere. I only ask one thing: tell me your mind when you know it, one way or the other."

MAILED JUNE 16, 1897, FROM NORTONVILLE, KANSAS.

F. M. Wilson, Horton, Kansas

My dearest Friend,

I received yesterday a second communication from the School Board at Belleville. They have heard through my cousins there of my recent bereavement and knowing I am now free from home responsibilities, they again offer me the position of H.S. Principal.

All the teachers there have been employed and this position will be filled within the next few days. They will wait to hear from me. I am rather at a standstill to know what to do. I feel that since your recent visit and the understanding existing between us that it would hardly be right for me to accept the position without first telling you and learning your opinion. The position is a good one and I would have a pleasant home with my cousins who are very anxious to have me. Will you please write me at once your opinion regarding the matter? I hesitated before writing you but I have done only as I would wish "to have other do to me."

I have been lonely indeed since you left tho I try to make the best of conditions as they are, tho change seems harder and my great loss greater each hour that I am left to myself.

I think I shall take Maggie Rea to Iowa with me and we will hardly get off before the very last of this week or first of next.

Lovingly Yours,

Irene

Tuesday, June 15th. My parents' 46th wedding anniversary.

Miss Irene Webb, Nortonville, Kansas
June 16, 1897

My Darling Irene,

. . . Precious heart, I have always admired and respected you, and since my first visit to you last Dec. this esteem and admiration has been ripening into love. I have from the beginning had but one object in view, viz: To ask your heart and hand in marriage, if after a seasonable courtship, we found that each could bear to the other, that full measure of love essential to happiness, and without which marriage would be a disappointment worse than death.

When I left home last Saturday, I expected to ask your consent to our marriage, before my return, but somehow my heart failed me, and I could not have the courage to do so. I obeyed the promptings of my heart and came home without telling you of my purpose.

Dear sweet heart, am I right in thus delaying my suit, until I can have that unreserved assurance of my heart, that I should proceed. God knows that I do not wish to wrong you. I have shed tears over these lines.

I pray that you may not judge me harshly, but believe me to be prompted only by the highest motives for your best welfare. I wish that I could see you every day. Perhaps I could soon overcome the feeling which I have referred to. My greatest regret since our courtship begun has been that you were not living in Horton, where we could meet under various circumstances and conditions every day.

When I visit you, I always prolong my stay as long as possible, and then regret that I cannot remain longer. I love your society, and am no sooner gone, than I wish that I might return to your presence, and yet when I would say the words, which would seal our fate for life, I confess to that feeling of fear and doubt to which I have referred.

Perhaps I have reached that period in life when one is confronted with more doubts and fears than during the earlier periods. Perhaps this same feeling would come over me, no matter who might be the object of my affections. Of this I am not sure. I cannot blame you if you should get entirely out of patience with me, and yet I do not feel that I can give you up. I have never strived more earnestly to settle a question. I have not given it up, but have redoubled my energies since last I saw you, and it will be the one absorbing question of my mind and heart until disposed of.

Now as to the question of the Belleville School. You have not solicited this position. It has been once offered to you and declined. Again it is offered to you. It is seldom that so good a position comes unsolicited, when so many teachers are striving to secure them. It is a compliment of a high order from a source of which you should feel proud indeed. If you feel that you would like to be employed this fall and winter I would advise you to accept the proposition for I am sure it will be pleasant for you there. No great harm can come to the school if you should accept the position now, and resign it, either before or after school opened, giving them due notice in time to secure another teacher. This is often done by teachers who after accepting one position keep on looking for a better one fully intending to resign the position if a better one is found.

Your high sense of honor would not approve such a course, nor would I suggest it, but in this case, if you accept and resign I believe you would feel fully justified in the act.

I am sorry that I cannot see you tonight. I would so much prefer to talk to you, than to write you about this matter. I hope you will have a very pleasant trip to Iowa and that you and Maggie Rea will enjoy it to the fullest extent.

Now my dear I must close. I am almost tempted to destroy this letter and try to write you another. I do not like to send this, but I am sure you will forgive me, for you cannot doubt its sincerity. I am very sorry indeed that I am not with you tonight.

God bless you until we meet again.

In Sincerity and love,
Frank

IRENE WALKED THE FIVE miles to Grace Lake. Or rather, she stomped most the way. She walked because she had to make her legs ache and, as her oldest brother would say, to blow the stink off. She was beyond furious. She ached everywhere from months of accumulating grief, and now wounding words from a mouth she loved. She was crushed.

Grasshoppers lurched into the air from the browning grass as she strode to the old barn. The redbud and lilac blossoms had been dashed in spring storms.

For two days and nights she had searched within herself for blame. She had found none. Today, as she sat staring at wind puffs on the water's surface, she attempted to bring her logic to bear on the irrational. All right, she thought, if I'm not to blame, what are the possibilities? Well, he could have been just toying with me all along. Possible, but I don't believe it. I know what I felt and saw. I'm not that gullible. Maybe he feels too much pressure at work or that trip to Hades and back. Maybe he feels crowded by my Belleville offer. Or he could have found someone else; someone he always had in the back of his mind and was weighing along with me. Yes, that's a possibility but somehow not likely. I think that for the same reason, and there's no proof of it. He would have said something to me. Delia Alton would have heard. Or maybe that's because there isn't someone else *now* but he wants to keep looking. So, I don't have a real, live rival but a phantom he thinks might be just around the corner. That is distinctly possible. Glory, how do I cope with that?

Be all that as it may, the plain fact is he does not feel towards me as strongly I do towards him. And the logic of that is he doesn't love me enough to commit. Maybe he doesn't know me, really; the deepest, most private me. Those classical readings in his living room never included anything ripe from the Renaissance. He has fond memories of when I was only a glorified houseguest; then nothing for three years. Then came the letters. Our letters took on a life of their own, and we became characters in a collaborative book. I wouldn't mind something more intimate. He has never seen me so much as take off my shoes! All he knows and loves is the writing part. It really is Abelard and Heloise.

I refuse to give up until he hits me square between the eyes with a fence pole. I refuse to let him straddle that fence like a toad forever. It might be safer to simply let it all wilt right now, but I'm going to stay with it to the bitter end.

That's more like it, she thought as she trudged back to the farm. I need to compose something with great care. It would do me no good to plead. That would not be my character. He says he would rather talk to me than try to express himself in a letter. I will take that as a good sign because what he says in that letter punctures my heart. This letter of his is from a wobbling Hamlet. I can't push and I can't pull because he leans in both directions at once. He clearly can fathom a finality that I cannot. I can't appear defeated.

I have to demonstrate my heart is still his if he will only take it. That's my purpose for tonight.

MAILED JUNE 21, 1897, FROM HORTON, KANSAS.

Miss Irene Webb, Nortonville, Kansas

My Darling Irene,

. . . I have wanted to recall that last letter of mine ever since I dropped it in the office, and I am very anxious to see you and beg your pardon for any pain that it may have caused to your feelings.

My regrets have doubtless given me more pain, than the receipt of the letter caused you. I spoke from the depths of my heart, and having only your best welfare in view, but the words were better left unspoken. While I cannot recall the words, I do ask you to return me the letter that I may destroy it, for I am ashamed of it. I wanted to say in that letter, that I would call on you today, but did not wish to delay you on your start for Iowa. You said you expected to start the last of the week or first of next. . . .

Now precious heart I do hope and trust that you will forgive me, and write me a good long letter very soon.

Believe me your sincere lover,

Frank

MAILED JUNE 21, 1897, FROM NORTONVILLE, KANSAS.

F. M. Wilson, Horton, Kansas

My dearest Friend,

Never have I felt more profound respect and admiration for you than I have felt since I received your last letter. I have studied its contents until I feel that every word has been carefully considered and weighed. I have given my whole mind and heart to it and I now feel in a measure competent for the task of answering it.

I postponed starting to Iowa last week that I might be more alone with my thoughts and entirely undisturbed in my reflections. There is no place where I can be as free from interruption as here in my sadly quiet home.

Let me state in the beginning that there is nothing but the kindest feeling in my heart and I trust sincerely you may take what I write in the spirit it is written. I told you that I hesitated before sending my last letter to you. The reason I hesitated was that I feared you might think it presumption on my part to write as I did. The more I studied over the matter however, the more I felt sure you would not consider it in that light but only in the way I meant it is: to obtain your opinion as to the advisability of my teaching this coming year. I looked at the matter this way— would I after the recent conversations we had had together think it considerate of you to make a business engagement for a year which would of necessity occupy the greatest portion of your time and attention, without at least telling me and learning my opinion—especially when such an engagement was considered by me out of the question. This and this only was my motive in writing you about the matter.

The content of your letter is no surprise to me except the portion in which you state the purpose you had in mind in making your last visit. I am truly glad you "obeyed the promptings of your heart" and did not tell me. Why? Because you do not love me sufficiently to ask me that question. I have the conscious assurance that you admire me and esteem me—and you love me but for the virtues and the lovable characteristics which you think I possess rather than for myself. I feel this and tho you were to tell me with your lips it were otherwise—it is your soul that speaks to me.

Your misgivings as to the future are but natural and not at all to be wondered at; even the little things which we undertake often occasion much doubt and uncertainty as to the outcome; how much more then should your mind quail before the realization that upon this venture depends the entire happiness of your future. Your doubts and fears are but the proper outcome of your serious reflection and but the proper respect for the magnitude and sacredness of the undertaking. I have never revealed my whole soul to you. I have wondered if the time would come when I could. I know now it cannot so it is perhaps better so. I could never be happy unless I knew absolutely that I possessed the entire heart and soul of the man I married.

I am assured you cannot give me this feeling. Why then consider the matter longer? The only right course to pursue is for you to cease caring for me in the way you do. Find someone to whom you can give the feeling you have to give and make her life happy. I do not think that I am lacking in the quality of patience when patience is required—here I think it out of place. While to me it is not pleasant to think of our fruitless courtship, and yet, actuated as it has always been by the highest, noblest and purest motives it can hardly harm either of us.

I pray you do not let the thought of injustice to me enter your mind. It has never entered mine. I trust that the friendship which has been very dear to both of us from its beginning and which has stood the test of years may be preserved always. Its associations are indeed sacred to both of us as it links in its chain the memory of your beloved wife and my beloved Father and Mother.

And now I trust, my dearest Friend, that your mind and heart may be relieved of the struggle they have been undergoing. To my mind there is but one cause for that struggle—you are trying to persuade yourself to do something impossible. I would have that restless feeling vanish and in its stead I would have one of quiet contentment.

I wish you were by my side tonight that you might read my heart and prove to yourself the sincerity of my words. I would smooth from your brow any lines of care or worry and impress thereon a kiss of loyal friendship. In conclusion I will say that I shall be pleased to hear from you, tho' I shall not expect letters of the same tone as heretofore.

I think I shall not start to Northern Oak before Thursday of this week. A letter written after that day you will please to address there.

I do not go through St. Joe either way—and were I to I should not like to go to Mrs. Alton's as I am already indebted to her. I want to have her make me a visit before my home is broken up.

The School Board at Belleville have notified me they will not now elect the H.S. Principal till the first week in July, thus giving me a little longer time to consider the matter. I appreciate the courtesy and kindness they have shown me and if I decide to accept the position I shall endeavor to give value received.

I must now close.

Believe me

Sincerely Yours,
Irene Webb
Sunday, June 20, '97

FRANK SLOWLY LOWERED THE tissue pages of the letter to the green blotter of his desk in his bedroom. He felt numb. His clumsy attempt to cancel the effect of his letter with a retrieval letter had not had any effect at all. He had said it badly and now he could not un-ring the bell. Certainly not by writing yet another letter which he would surely bungle. I can't leave it like this. Look how carefully she has expressed her sympathetic understanding of my oafish words. Look how her dignity shines, and no disparaging words.

Still, she says she has not revealed her whole soul to me. Yet she puts it this way, "I could *never be happy* unless I knew *absolutely* that I possessed *the entire heart and soul* of the man I married. I am assured *you* cannot give me this feeling." Assured her of that? I suppose I did. Just by being who I am. How do I assure her otherwise? It's a mixed question: her "whole soul" unrevealed; my "entire heart and soul" not conveyed. Irene, the stark truth is that I can't get Allie out of some part of my heart. Does that make me imperfect as a man you could marry? Take me as you find me, Miss Webb.

No, she probably doesn't mean it that way, don't be disingenuous. Don't read her letter as you read a statute. Probably not seeing it clearly myself. We both present ourselves in ambiguous terms. Can we at least agree on what the other is trying to say?

There's only one way to find out.

MORNING FIVE, JUNE 22, 1897

"Franklin Miller Wilson! What are you doing on my front porch on a Tuesday after sundown? Not even one of your chatty telegrams."

"I came for a kiss."

She looked at his earnest face, fret marks firmly set, lips drawn tight, and thought, Well, that'd be a cold one.

"And this orphan girl, alone and unprotected in her empty farmhouse, out of earshot of anybody for three miles, is where you think to get one? Well, come right in. Where's your valise?"

"Didn't bring one. I just got myself to the station after the bank closed and came straight here."

"How'd you get from town down here?"

"I walked. A full moon. Nice night for it. Didn't bring a bicycle either."

She raised her eyebrows. "Just as well, those things frighten me. But I can see you on a high wheel, rolling around Mission Township of Brown County baying at the full moon." Frank lifted his head, and gave a banker's impression of a dog. Both burst into laughter. "I can't imagine having you and a dog *and* a wheel around the place at the same time. At least you and the dog could be trained to fetch. But the wheel?" They laughed again.

"So, now that you're here, what brings you to me tonight?"

"For some straight talk. To straighten out what I've managed to mangle in my last letter. And to set you straight on who I love and why. For that, I'd walk to the Colorado mountains and then climb the highest one, and walk back again."

"All that impulsive walking gives me a thirst. I'll get us some water. Sit down and rest those frisky legs. And take a deep breath, Mr. Wilson. Your face looks positively in turmoil."

When Irene returned to the sitting room with water and cold chicken on buttered day-old biscuits, Frank was looking over sheet music at the piano. He held up the cover of "Oh Promise Me" and looked at her expectantly.

"Frank Wilson, if you have something to say to me then do so in your own voice. Don't be handing me sheet music or old books or old letters to do your talking. Take another deep breath and a bite of chicken and just say what got you over here on such an impulse."

Frank did, indeed, take a deep breath. He reached for her hand and held it. In a voice as slow and quiet as a prayer, he said:

"That letter I mailed says the dumbest things I have ever thought. I never should have sent it. I want it back. I am sorry I caused you such grief on top of everything else you're grieving over. I love you, Irene. I'm not here because of what's best for your welfare, or mine, or my sons. I'm here because I want to live with you for the rest of my life. I am here to propose marriage and I want you to accept my proposal."

"Well, that's what you had made up your mind to say to me nine days ago. But you couldn't stop digging inside of yourself looking for more ore. Yours certainly is not an unexamined life, so Socrates would say it is well worth living. Your relentless self-reflection keeps on digging after you've found the ore that's there. After that the only thing left to bring to the surface is rubble, like that letter. Maybe that letter wasn't as dumb as you make out, but neither did it say your mind plainly. You don't go switching your mind so quickly, Mr. Wilson, not on something like that."

He squeezed her hand and said, "You're right, and that's why I had to get myself here now. I didn't 'switch my mind' at all. I just gave in to fear in that letter. But I didn't say that the right way in the letter. The only good thing that came out of the letter was your reply, which is the single most beautiful piece of writing I have ever read."

He paused. He moved his jaw but nothing came out. He looked at her and tried to project his thoughts into her mind without having to use words. Finally he said, "Irene, you know that I am a widower."

Irene recoiled. "Frank! How could you even ask me such a question?"

"It's Allie who died, not my love for her. I want you to say you understand that."

"Oh, Frank, of course. I could never expect otherwise. I love her too and have struggled over my feelings for you and her. What you and I have in common here is that she has, in fact, died, and that we were above reproach when she lived."

Frank closed his eyes. There is only one more step. There is only one way to finally reach "assurance" on this. If a proposal of marriage is not enough assurance from me, then nothing is. If I'm not enough the way I am, she will simply have to say no. He opened his eyes and said,

"I love you, my precious darling. I love you sufficiently to ask you this vital question, and I am asking it now: Will you marry me?" He kissed her hand and held it against his cheek. She could feel him tremble.

Irene took her time to choose her words.

"I accept what you say, and I accept the question as sincere and real. I can accept nothing else right now. I do not reject your proposal, but I wish to consider it just as I would have had you made it when you came here June thirteenth. I believe convention allows up to a month, and I shall adopt that time for consideration. If that is satisfactory, then we can dismiss your previous hesitancy as a thing of the past, or at least something not born of insufficient love. Something out of fear, as you say. But that can wait. What cannot wait is the kiss you came for."

Frank thought, She didn't say no. That means my heart is enough the way it is. Gathering her in his arms for a lingering kiss, Frank imagined that he could hear cranes.

THE NEXT MORNING, JUST at daybreak, they rode in happy silence back to the Nortonville station. The sun broke though for an instant to illuminate droplets of rain on field flowers left over from a cloudburst in the night. The damp loam of fields two months plowed and planted in corn gave off an aroma of assurance and well-being. And it was in silence that he kissed her before stepping from the buggy to the station platform. Her words, "Git, Bluebelle," punctuated by a slap of harness reins over flank, sounded like birdsong to his ears. Bluebelle must have heard it differently, however, for she had lurched and was nearly a runaway, causing a commotion in the street, a fright to Irene, and an end to the morning's idyllic reverie.

"A month, Bluebelle. Why did I say that? Dignity, you say. Not exactly dignity, but I suppose I thought I needed to heal from the way he'd hurt me. And convention, you say. Yes, that's what I told him. Get back to the normal course of things—his Fowler procedure. Maybe I shouldn't have let dignity or convention hold me back. I thought I'd lost my whole future, Bluebelle. When I sat down and wrote that letter he admires so much, I knew I was fighting for my life. When he dropped in like that from the blue last night, it was the providential gift of all the Webb angels and the crane angels as well. Providential? It means heaven-sent good luck. Sorry, horse. You're thinking anything can happen in a month. You're thinking I should just snap up that proposal in a heartbeat. You are persuasive. But, no, another month won't hurt. What can happen? So, Bluebell, what do you and I do for the next thirty days?"

MAILED JUNE 24, 1897, FROM NORTONVILLE, KANSAS.

F. M. Wilson, Horton, Kansas

My dear love,

I have time for only a short letter as Maggie Rea is going to town and I want her to mail it for me. Mrs. McVey is better. She now sits up most of the time but is not able to do anything. She has had a pretty hard time but a few days of rest and quiet will restore her to her usual health. I am sure I am truly thankful she is not to have a siege of fever. I feel that I could not endure to go through another time of sickness. I shall not start on my trip until she is stronger and has someone to help her with the work. I want to take Maggie Rea for the child has her heart so set on the trip that the disappointment over not getting to go would mar the pleasure of my own going. How are you, my dear? I have thought of you constantly ever since you left me. I feel highly honored by your words to me. I consider it the greatest compliment you could possibly pay to my womanhood. I would rather be the queen of a good man's heart than queen of a Kingdom.

I have been pondering and shall ponder well over the question you have asked me and dear heart mine, I hope that you, too, may consider well all parts of the question. I know you have, but there may be things you cannot determine. Please feel free to ask me anything and tell me if there is anything you would have different about me. I hope you weren't very tired Wednesday. I tried to sleep in the afternoon but a still sweet voice kept whispering in my ear "I Love you my precious darling" somehow I couldn't sleep. Even last night in the wee small hours I could hear that Frank Wilsonan voice of yours. Now pet, I hope I shall hear that voice, but I object to being kept awake in the very sleepiest hours of the night.

I hardly think I shall start away now till Monday—so you can send my birthday letter to Nortonville. If you send it Saturday evening, I will get it Sunday morning. I wish you could come over, but as Mrs. McVey is not well, perhaps we would better postpone your visit until my return.

Well, well, this is a very short letter.

Good Night—

Lovingly and sincerely,
Irene

Miss Irene Webb, Nortonville, Kansas

My precious Sweetheart,

Your very anxiously expected and highly appreciated letter, came to hand this evening.

As this is a delightfully pleasant evening, and I am alone at home (the remainder of the household having gone down town to the band concert, which takes place every Friday evening) and not knowing whether or not the conditions tomorrow evening will be so favorable, I have concluded to improve my time by writing you so that you will be sure to receive it not later than Sunday.

I forwarded to you by express today a slight token of love and esteem, which I trust will reach you in good condition tomorrow. To insure its delivery, I mailed you a postal card, which could be read by any member of your household who happened to call for the mail, but mindful of your antipathy to postal card correspondence, and your early instructions to me along that line, I carefully omitted everything which might disclose the identity of the author.

Tell Maggie Rea that I dared not send you a bicycle. In the ecstasy of my joy last Tuesday night, I neglected to ascertain your favorite wheel. Fully aware of the sensitiveness of most people upon this most important subject, I dared not take the risk of giving offence in presenting you with a wheel other than your favorite.

Tell Maggie Rea, that I hope ere your next birthday anniversary arrive, I shall have had every opportunity to know your likes and dislikes, in the matter of wheels, and I have also thought that possibly a tandem wheel would then please you best.

Then when Maggie Rea comes to visit her Aunt, Uncle, and cousins, she can have her choice between a ride on the bike, or in a 4 wheeled vehicle drawn by the family horse. We will always be glad to have her visit us, won't we?

I enjoyed my return trip last Wednesday morning, which was made promptly on time. Arrived at home at half past 8 o'clock, found the family at breakfast, and after another cup of coffee, I arrived at the bank before opening hour.

It being a warm day, I confess to a drowsy feeling all afternoon, which disappeared after a long night's rest.

I hope that "still sweet voice" will continue to whisper in your ear "I love you my precious darling" until you give your consent that its author may love you always.

When I left home last Tuesday evening, I thought I could not return satisfied, until I had obtained your full consent to be my wife. I yielded to your earnest request for more time, only because I felt that some lingering doubts remained in your mind, as to whether you could give me full return for the love which I proffered you.

Precious heart I do not wish you to give me your answer until fully satisfied that you can give to me your whole heart and soul.

I offer you as much, and am anxiously waiting for you to speak the word which will enshrine you the queen of my life and heart.

Since I left you Wednesday morning I have been perfectly happy in the assurance of your love, and in the thought that you would soon consent to be mine. You have been almost constantly in my mind and your sweet smile haunts me always.

You ask if there is anything I would have different about you. I answer no. I would not know where to suggest an improvement. I believe that you possess the charms which I crave, and while I do not feel worthy of you, I do earnestly desire to become so. If you would know more concerning me I beg of you to make free to enquire of any one, assuring you of my response to any questions you may wish to ask me.

If your mind is as free from doubt as mine, and you love me, as I love you, I beg of you, upon this the anniversary of your birthday, that you give me the answer which I crave.

How I would like to be with you Sunday, and take from your lips the words which can render me so happy. I shall anxiously await the coming of your next letter which, I hope will bear me the precious words of acceptance.

Yet, again let me repeat it darling. If you think you might love another, better than you can love me, then I beg of you, decline my offer, or take more time to consider as may seem best to you.

With only your highest welfare at heart believe me to be

Lovingly thine,
Frank

MAILED JUNE 28, 1897, FROM NORTONVILLE, KANSAS.

F. M. Wilson, Horton, Kansas
June 27, 1897

My dear Sweetheart,
Yesterday morning I sent with a neighbor woman for the mail. She came through the rain with it and among the budget was your postal card "Please call for package at express office."

Now if there is anything in the world that excites me it is to know there is something for me some place and I do not know what it is—only there is something. Mama said when I was a child

I would search everything and every place to find my Christmas presents. Well, to resume It was almost noon and I hurried thro with my dinner intending to make a trip to town at once. Maggie Rea was almost as excited as I was. We both hurried and do you know about the time we were ready to start the biggest, blackest old cloud covered the sky and the rain fairly came down in sheets. We waited hoping it would cease but there was no ceasing—it rained all afternoon and all evening. A very good thing for the corn crop but a hard experience on us. It dampened our ardor, or it would certainly had we gone out in it. I tried to preserve my soul in patience. I tried to read but the lines would waver there tho the letters would form themselves into "Please call for package at Express office." I tried to play and the music would read "Please call for package at express office." At last I tried to sleep and I actually dreamt of that card "Please call for package at express office."

This morning bright and early Maggie Rea and I drove up town. We found the package and your dear letter. As we were coming by Mrs. Kellog's she came out to tell me she is going to Kentucky on a visit and insisted that we come up on the porch for a call. All this time that precious package was unopened. I told her I had a birthday present I hadn't opened and I couldn't wait. She insisted on "seeing, too" so we opened the box to find the beautiful rose bowl. It is perfectly lovely and I am so pleased with it. I think you exhibited excellent taste and I thank you so much for it. Cut glass is something I appreciate and admire very much indeed. It is a luxury I have never been able to indulge in, however. I have only one other piece—so you couldn't possibly have selected anything I would like so well. Again I thank you, dear heart. It is sweet and kind of you to remember my birthday. Only I think you are not quite fair. You went and had a birthday and did not let me know about it till a long time after. I will forgive you for past offenses, but do not let such a thing occur again.

We always kept up the custom of giving little tokens on birthdays. This morning it was indeed a sad reminder of the past when I failed to find my Father's and Mother's note by my plate. Dear, faithful loving hearts. I wonder if the time will ever come to me when I shall not miss them so so much. . . .

—Later—

I put aside my writing to go for a ride. We went to the cemetery. The flowers I placed on the graves Friday were still fresh owing to the late rains. I wonder if I am really the same girl who sat here in this chair and wrote to you last Sunday evening. My darling I wish you were here tonight. Writing is such a poor substitute for talking. I have read and reread your dear letter today and it lies open before me now.

Dearheart, I am so glad you did not think of sending me a wheel. Why Pet, I should have felt dreadfully if you had. You know what I said about it was only in jest. I cannot ride a wheel and have never cared especially to learn or to have a wheel. I like the idea of a tandem. Indeed, dear love, I care for nothing but what you can share and enjoy with me. Darling mine, I wish I could write you what you would have me tell you on this my birthday, but I would rather not tell you until the time I asked you to wait. Three weeks is not very long—Three weeks from tonight I will tell you and will also tell you why I asked you to wait tho' I can tell you that now. I want you to think that much longer as well as myself. If you are sure now that your mind and heart are free from doubts, you will not be less so in three weeks. If there is any tendency to doubt that time will give tendencies an opportunity to develop or disappear. Therefore, my dear sweetheart, while I appreciate your words and while they prove to my mind and heart that you do really and truly love me with your whole soul, I would ask you to be content with knowing I love you and that I only ask for this time to make myself more sure if possible, that I can give you all you can ask. Darling mine, sometimes I think that were my parents living you would not have asked me the questions you did when you did. Please do not let that make the least difference. I appreciate your manly sympathy in my great loss but do not let this hasten you in anyway. This thought was suggested to me by your saying you had my best welfare at heart.

I have just found this is my last sheet of paper so I will have to close, tho' I am not ready to. Maggie Rea and I start tomorrow. I will write you on our arrival. I would willingly and gladly wait till after the 4 prox. but we have written we are going. Good Night,

Irene

MAILED JUNE 30, 1897, FROM ATCHISON, KANSAS.

F. M. Wilson, Horton, Kansas

My dearest,

Maggie Rea and I came down to Atchison Monday evening intending to go on to Northern Oak yesterday. My sister however, persuaded us to wait until today. We leave at 12:15 P.M. over the K.C.S.J. and Council Bluffs to Hamburg, Iowa where we meet my brother's train over the CB and I.

The weather is so extremely warm. It seems so much warmer here than at home. I presume the main reason is one has to fix up more. I attended a wedding this morning. The Bride is a friend of my nieces. We were invited only to the church. It was a beautiful wedding. The Bride looked so sweet in her cool white Organdie. The music was beautiful. The large pipe organ at St. Benedicts is played by a colored man and he is fine indeed. I never heard the wedding march rendered more exquisitely. During the service the organist played very softly "O Promise Me" and selections from the Bohemian Girl "Then You'll Remember Me" and others.

I shall be glad to have a letter from you as soon after I reach Northern Oak as possible.

I will write you a line as soon as we arrive. Maggie Rea is not a very good traveler. The motion of the train makes her sick.

Good morning dear heart.

Yours lovingly,
Irene

MAILED JULY 2, 1897, FROM NORTHERN OAK, IOWA.

F. M. Wilson, Horton, Kansas

My dearest,

We reached Northern Oak at 6:15 P.M. yesterday. The ride from Atchison was hot and disagreeable, but Maggie Rea stood the trip pretty well. She feels tired out this morning but will be all right in a short time. My brother has a large cool house and a pretty lawn. I am sure we shall enjoy the rest and visit here.

I am now ready to receive letters and I hope to get one from you very soon. Please do address me care of M. S. Webb as there are other Webbs here I understand.

Good Bye, Love till next time.

Sincerely,
Irene

P.S. I told you a fib. We did come through St. Joe. I did not think we would and did not know different till the brakeman called the station.

Irene

Miss Irene Webb, c/o M. Webb, Northern Oak, Iowa

My dear Sweet heart,

This is the glorious 3d of July. Wallis went to Holton yesterday morning to attend the races. This morning my mother and Harold also went to Holton, while I remained at home. I spent the entire forenoon pushing the lawn mower at home and at the cemetery. I started to the bank immediately after dinner, to spend the afternoon in writing to you as I felt that it would take the remainder of the day to square the account with you. Your three letters lie before me, all having arrived in due time, and were read with much pleasure.

I intended to write to you last night so that you would receive it today but could not find the time.

I am really sorry that my postal card "Please call for package at Express office" caused you so much annoyance. I remember that you cautioned me against the use of cards in our correspondence and I studied some time before deciding to send it, but it looked like an innocent, harmless thing, after it was completed and I concluded to take the chance.

Little did I dream of the disastrous consequences of that innocent looking card. Only think of it, for one whole day and night it kept you in awful suspense, not to say suspenders. That during this whole period of time you could not read, sing, write, talk or sleep, for thinking of that message.

Darling forgive me for this my first offence and I promise you it shall not occur again. The next time I will telegraph, telephone, or tell somebody else to tell you, or something along that line.

Aside from the many annoying consequences above enumerated, there is another bad feature of it, which had not occurred to me until too late. The receipt of such a message would naturally cause you to expect a very valuable package, as for instance a house and lot, a bicycle, or a shetland pony. The feeling of disappointment which would come over you upon receiving a tiny piece of cut glass, after having your expectations wrought up to such a pitch, would more than offset the pleasure of receiving a birthday present.

I wonder all these things didn't occur to me before I sent that card. But men always blunder in such matters. N.B. The above is a huge joke.

Now I had thought of sending you for a birthday present something in the line of fine stationery, handkerchiefs, or hosiery, knowing your weakness along those lines. But it occurred to me that the life of such articles of usefulness and beauty is short at best, and I might not live, or rather they might not live to see me again. I wonder if you have failed to notice that Jay Gouldian idea which has governed me in the selection of the few presents which I have presented to you. You see if I should be fortunate enough to secure you for a wife, I will also recover these valuable presents. N.B. The above is no joke.

My remarks in my last letter about a wheel were intended for a joke, as I fully understood your remarks upon the occasion of my last visit concerning the wheel.

Jesting in correspondence is a dangerous practice unless carefully labeled.

I hoped and expected that you would give me your yes, to my question, but dear love, I cannot wish you to do so, so long as there is a lingering doubt in your mind. You have asked me to wait, and I will be content with your love for two weeks more. Then darling I will come for your answer.

You surprise me with the statement that you sometimes think, were your parents still alive, I would not have asked you to be my bride. I remember using the expression that I had your best welfare at heart, but you misunderstood my meaning.

I did not mean that I would be willing to marry you on account of my sympathy for you in your misfortune and to provide you with a home.

This I would not consider for your best welfare.

Dear soul I only meant this. That if you believe your greatest happiness would be promoted by your marriage to someone else, then I will give you up, not desiring to wrong you by pressing my suit.

This is not wholly an unselfish feeling, because if you are not happy, how could I as your husband expect to be.

With love to Maggie Rea as well as yourself.

Sincerely,
Frank

F. M. Wilson, Horton, Kansas

My dearheart,

Your letter reached me Saturday and I was delighted to hear from you. I intended writing to you Sunday or yesterday but the children claim about every minute of my time. My brother has three very nice children. Obed, the eldest is a bright boy of seventeen, handsome and well-behaved; a little listless but a very nice boy indeed. He is the eldest grandchild and is named for my Father, Obed Hiram—the Hiram only is for Father. Earl, the middle child, is almost eleven. He bids fair just at present to become a cowboy or a highway robber. He is full of life and as mean as he can be but a dear boy just the same. Little Elaine is a sweet baby girl three years of age. She is her papa's idol and really she is a very sweet, bright little woman. She talks all the time and keeps me busy making doll dresses and helping her with her things. Just now she is standing by my side wanting "to write, too, please, Lady Tot." She has always called me "Lady Tot." No one knows why but altho the other children call me Aunt she never uses any other than the Lady title. Her mother and all of us think it is so cute we have never corrected her.

Maggie Rea is having a lovely visit. Her cousins are devoted to her and aside from a few little "scraps" she and Earl have had they get along beautifully. Our stay has been very pleasant and I already feel much rested and refreshed.

Monday was observed here as the Glorious Fourth. The children began celebrating Friday evening and have just finished the last box of fire crackers. For which my sister in law and I feel devoutly thankful. There is a very fine race track here and

a number of fine horses are kept in Northern Oak. Alex the finest trotting, or rather, the fastest trotting horse in the world is
owned by a man here and is exercised on the track Tuesdays and
Fridays. Brother Man took me out to see her. She is a beautiful
animal. I'd like to have her! Man said a one third interest in
her was purchased two years ago for only $30,000. Wish I were
going to have another birthday—maybe you'd purchase Alex
for me instead of a bicycle. No dear heart I must confess I had
never thought of your two-fold motive in presenting me with
such expensive gifts. Come to think of it tho it was a pretty safe
investment for you anyway. You see if I should not become yours
I would not feel right in keeping the things and they would be
all yours then—while you run a big risk of having only a half
interest in them as matters are. As Artemus Ward says, "this is
a joke." ...

I hope to spend a good part of the summer resting and trying
to forget or rather become used to my great sorrow. At times I feel
quite reconciled then it will all come like a great wave and I seem
almost buried under it.

Dear heart I wish I could see you today. It will not be very long
tho' until I do. No, Love, I did not mean that you would never
have asked me the question you did. I think I said you would not
have asked me what you did <u>when</u> you did. Were those not the
words? I am not too busy these days to think much about you
and about the future. Oh, I haven't told you of another birthday
present I received after coming to Iowa. This one is not in the
form of cut glass but a very pretty little pup. A water Spaniel dark
brown with curly soft hair and long curly brown ears. Man has
a very fine Water Spaniel and she has four babies. The pups are
two months old and the cutest little things. I am not particularly
fond of dogs but these are beauties. ... If Harold were about to

have a birthday I think I would send him my dog. Guess I'll have to keep him till he does have a birthday.

You will have time to send me a good long letter before we leave Northern Oak.

Lovingly Yours,
Irene
Tuesday, July 5th-97

MAILED JULY 11, 1897, FROM HORTON, KANSAS.

Miss Irene Webb, c/o M. S. Webb, Northern Oak, Iowa

My darling Irene,

. . . Yes darling you have correctly quoted the language of your former letter, and I see that it was my mistake in placing the emphasis upon the "what" instead of the "when." . . .

. . . To answer the question as I now understand it I shall be compelled to say, I do not know how soon I should have asked you the question, had your parents lived. Perhaps I would have seen you oftener, and under different circumstances and conditions, and might have asked you sooner.

It's a great problem darling, and the individual who approaches it without fear and trembling has less caution in their makeup than I find in mine.

. . . I shall count the days until next Sunday, when I shall hope to be with you and receive from your sweet lips, your answer, upon which so much depends.

Until then dear heart be assured that I love you with all my heart and soul. Awaiting your next letter, which I will expect to announce the date of your return home, and that a visit from me will be agreeable I am

Lovingly thine,

Frank

Sunday, July 11-97

⌒ ⌐ ～

MAILED JULY 6, 1897, FROM NORTHERN OAK, IOWA.

F. M. Wilson, Horton, Kansas

Good Morning, dear heart,

We start home tomorrow—Tuesday—morning. Arrive at St. Joe about 2:30 or 3:00 o'clock P.M. I think we will stop there and wait for the Santa Fe which leaves about 8:10 for Nortonville. This will give us a few hours there instead of at Armour where the regular change is made.

If you have business (?) in St. Joe tomorrow evening it would be very pleasant for us to see you there. I think the best plan would be for you to call at the parlor of Pacific Hotel as soon as you arrive if you go. We will be there about six, the time you will probably arrive. I think we will hardly go out to Mrs. Alton's this time. I hope to receive your Sunday letter today—

Lovingly,

Irene

Monday Morning

Miss Irene Webb, Nortonville, Kansas

My dear sweetheart,

I rec'd your letter this morning, and later your telegram which I answered at Hamburg.

Am sorry indeed that I cannot leave home today as I would like very much to see you even for the brief time which would be left for us between trains. This is pay day on the railroad, and our busiest day in consequence thereof. We always open the bank after supper on pay days.

I telephoned Mr. Alton to place at your disposal a carriage, and have Mrs. Alton show you the city, and to accompany you himself also if convenient. I trust you will enjoy your brief stop in St. Joe and reach home in safety.

Hastily but lovingly,
Frank

MAILED JULY 14, 1897, FROM NORTONVILLE, KANSAS.

F. M. Wilson, Horton, Kansas
Thursday A.M.

My dearest,

Maggie Rea and I—and the brown dog—have just reached Nortonville. We spent a very pleasant afternoon in St. Joe thanks to your kindness. I was greatly surprised to find Mrs. Alton at the train as I had not expected at all to even see her. The carriage you sent up along that telephone line came safely and we all enjoyed a lovely ride over the city. We came to Atchison on the evening train, remained over night at Mrs. Miller's and came out to Nortonville this A.M.

My dearheart, please do accept thanks for your thoughtful kindness yesterday. I love you for your loving consideration always. I shall expect to see you Saturday evening at 9:54. Until then Sweet love Good Bye,

Irene

You know my weakness for nice stationery—hence this.

Irene

TELEGRAPH TO IRENE WEBB,
NORTONVILLE, KS, JULY 17/97 FROM F. M. WILSON

Impossible for me to leave home

F. M. Wilson

Miss Irene Webb, Nortonville, Kansas

My Darling Irene,

Please don't scold me for disappointing you last night for I can't bear to be scolded, and besides I don't deserve it this time. I wired you about 1 o'clock yesterday afternoon that it would be impossible for me to leave home. I trust and hope that you received my message in time to save you a trip to town last night.

For more than a week I have been unwell, and scarcely able to attend to business. It has been with great effort on my part that I have kept out of bed. For several days I have wondered if I would recover sufficiently to present myself before you today, for I didn't feel like doing so, in the condition I was then in. Yesterday morning it was hard for me to make up my mind whether I ought to abandon the trip or not. Had it been any other occasion than this, I should have easily decided to write you that I was unable to go, in time so that you could receive it before starting to meet me. Owing to the importance attached to this visit, I decided to wait until the last moment and go if possible, even though not feeling perfectly well.

About noon I received word that several parties from Holton would be here on the evening train to transact some important business, which I felt sure would require several hours' time. It was then that I decided to wire you that I could not leave home. Had the business with these gentlemen been of such nature that it could have been postponed I should have tried to do so, but it involved so many different persons, and has been dragging along so long, that I considered it my duty to remain and get the matter settled.

You will perhaps wonder why I could not drive over today. I do not feel well enough to drive so far, and return in the same day, and of course I would be obliged to return tonight as Mr. Henderson and Mr. Latham are both absent from home.

I came to the bank yesterday morning at 8 o'clock and did not leave for home until half past nine last night. The gentlemen from Holton came in at half past five, and remained here until the 9 o'clock train, this time being wholly occupied by the business in question. I came to the bank this morning and worked until 2 o'clock, stopped for dinner, and returned at 3 o'clock and have plenty of work to keep me busy, and out of mischief until bed time. I have stopped long enough to write you this my apology and to ask you to pardon me for any disappointment which I have caused you. I am sorry darling that I could not spend this day with you, and feel perfectly well, so as not to appear too dull and stupid in your sight.

. . . I wrote you last Sunday and you should have received my letter before leaving Northern Oak, but did not mention it in the note written upon your return to Nortonville Wednesday. I have had no letter from you this week excepting the note referred to so I wonder if you failed to receive my last one. I also mailed you some views of our home. I presume you will write me today, and I trust you will make it unusually long and interesting to partly compensate for the great disappointment I have experienced in being unable to visit you. It was also a disappointment to be unable to meet you in St. Joe, and especially so when I had suggested such a meeting to you several times before you started to Northern Oak. I am very glad that Mr. and Mrs. Alton were so kind to you. I feel greatly indebted to them for many kind acts, and trust that I may have an opportunity to return the kindness soon. I hope in the letter which you will doubtless write me today, you will say all that you would have said to me had I called on you. "Give me your answer true love." I shall look for it in the long nice letter which I will expect tomorrow.

Now dear love if you will excuse me I will get back to work again. I shall be glad when Phillip Latham returns to assist me with the work, though I do not wish to interfere with his vacation or cut it short.

I am feeling better today, and hope to be myself again before many days.

With renewed assurances of sincere devotion and love I am

Yours forever,
Frank

Chapter Nine

YOU HAVE OFTEN ASKED
ME TO CALL YOU FRANK

Mailed July 19, 1897, from Nortonville, Kansas.

F. M. Wilson, Horton, Kansas

My Darling Frank,

You have often asked me to call you Frank but I have never felt until now that I had a perfect right to call you that. Henceforth my Love, you are Frank to me.

Your dear letter has just reached me bringing sunshine with it and clearing up the clouds of the past two days. Darling I can hardly write fast enough to tell you all. In the first place your telegram reaching Nortonville at 3:16 Saturday afternoon did not reach me till late last evening Sunday. Owing to the stupidity of the post master here, it was not taken out of the box and it was by the merest accident that I received it at all. Saturday afternoon I sent Maggie Rea for the mail. There was nothing from you. Mrs. McVey and I drove up to the train and you can imagine my disappointment when you failed to appear. I had never thought of you not coming. I made up my mind at once you had missed connections at Atchison and would telegraph me. I went in to the telegraph office but "no message for Miss Webb." We came home and I sent Maggie Rea to the train at 9:34 yesterday morning. She returned without you and without word of any kind. I then said He'll drive over. I watched till noon for you then gave up in despair. To all questions and expressions wonder I only replied that it was not your fault someone else was to blame. I know you must have sent me word but where was it? Late in the afternoon Mrs. McVey and I went for a drive and stopped for the evening mail from Topeka. Still no message from you. We started home when I—I don't know why I did it—turned and drove back to the post office. I asked Mr. Hillwood to look again in our box. He looked at me rather strangely, but did as I requested and said "nothing more Miss Tot." I said I'm sure you must be mistaken and he looked again and there pressed close against the wires of the side was your telegram. The mistake on his part was inexcusable and I had to stretch my conscience a good deal to say it's all right to his apology. But dearheart it is all over now and your letter this morning explains everything. I have been hugging it ever since it came. Darling never, never for one moment did I think it was your fault or that you were in anyway negligent. I knew everything would be explained and I knew as well as I do now that you had done all you could to let me know. You see what confidence I have in you. I do not believe you are capable of doing wrong. Yes you are capable of doing wrong but what is far nobler you would not do wrong.

My dear Pet, I am so sorry you are sick and you have been working so hard too. I wish I were able to help you someway; be assured my Frank that if my love and sympathy can help you, you will be well right away. My heart is so full of love for you and I do so hope you are better even now. I am so sorry you could not come yesterday or Saturday rather. So much seemed to depend on your coming. My Uncle Dr. Webb is in very poor health, he has asthma. He is going to try a change of climate and intended going the last of the week or today. I hope and trust he may be benefitted. I love him next to my dear Father now. He has been so good and tender to me since my Father left me. I have made a confidant of him and told him everything I would go to Papa with. I wanted so much for you to see him before he goes away. I am assured from the great care he is taking to have everything left so well arranged that he fears he may not return to us. Since I came home I have been doing a great deal of writing and copying for him. If he does not go today or this week I should like to have you invite him and me to spend a day with you. It would be a great comfort to me, dearest, to have him see the home you have asked me to share and to visit Wallis and Harold. He has met you and likes you. I will let you know when he will start. I am afraid he will not think he can go to Horton but maybe he will for me. I have not mentioned the matter to him.

I shall expect you next Saturday evening and if you can't come, please write, telephone and telegraph and send a messenger boy over with a note. May be I'll get one of the messages. The best way tho is for you to write me a nice letter telling me to meet you.

Yes, Love, I received your letter and the photos of your home the evening before I left Northern Oak. I enjoyed both. The photos are very good I think for outdoor ones. I showed them to my brother and his family. My brother wanted me to remain in Northern Oak over Sunday and he would send you an invitation to visit me there. I know you could not leave for even that short trip or it would necessitate your being absent from the bank Saturday and Monday and that would not be possible when the others were gone. Your telegram reached me at Hamburg. It was short and not very sweet. "Can not come" as I wanted to see you. . . .

Now Sweetheart, I do not know whether I have told you every-thing or not. Not all I intended to tell you yesterday but the rest is sweeter spoken than written. So will you wait till I can whisper the words in your ear?

I hope Father Time will hustle a little this week. Five more days!

Write and tell me you are well again and that I may expect you Saturday evening.

Believe me

Your devoted
Irene

MAILED JULY 22, 1897, FROM HORTON, KANSAS.

Miss Irene Webb, Nortonville, Kansas
Monday, July 19-97

My darling Irene,

It's bed time and I shall not attempt more than a short note for I feel that I need my rest during this warm weather.

I was delighted to receive your nice long letter yesterday morning, but sorry indeed to learn of the annoyance and trou-ble to which you were put, by the failure to receive my telegram. It's too bad dear, but as the intentions of all concerned cannot be questioned, we can only pass it by as one of the unpleasant epi-sodes of our courtship, of which there have been but few. Had I anticipated such delay in delivery of my message, I would cer-tainly have sent a messenger across the country. It was certainly annoying and embarrassing to you, to be upon the lookout for me for the greater part of two days, with no idea of why I did not put in an appearance and I assure you that I am very sorry to have been the cause of it. . . .

. . . I think you may look for me next Saturday night, but I will advise you later if I can go.

OO

Good night darling.
Your devoted
Frank
Wednesday, 7-21-97

MAILED JULY 23, 1897, FROM NORTONVILLE, KANSAS.

F. M. Wilson, Horton, Kansas

My dear love,

Your letter of Wednesday evening reached me this morning and was read with pleasure. It has just a little tinge of disappointment in it tho' where you are not quite sure of coming tomorrow evening. . . .

My Uncle Dr. Webb left on Tuesday for Eureka Springs where he hopes to receive some benefit from the climate and water. He will remain for some weeks if he feels that he is being helped— otherwise he will return in a week or two days. I thank you, my dear, for your kind invitations for us to visit you and when he returns home I hope that we can arrange for the same. . . .

I want to send this on this evening's train so must close.

With fondest love,
Irene

TELEGRAM TO MISS IRENE WEBB, NORTONVILLE, KANSAS, DATED JULY 24, 1897, FROM F. M. WILSON, HORTON, KANSAS

Will be there tonight—on train 9 o'clock.

F. M. Wilson

MORNING SIX

On the morning of Saturday, July 24, 1897, Irene could barely restrain herself from trotting Bluebelle as she went to town, but in the oppressive heat she did, indeed, hold the mare to a steady walk out of prudence. The trough at the post office was dry. With muttered commentary on governmental productivity, she drew pails of well water and poured them into the trough for her horse and any others that might happen into the center of town on market day. After a slow amble to the window she asked, with a smile, "Anything for Webb?" What was delivered to her was not a letter, but the shortest telegram of her short life, containing a message larger than the largest library.

After the slow plod back to the farm, Irene spent the rest of the day fussing over the house. She first set about to de-clutter the parlor where too many piles of sheet music had accumulated along with some of Hiram's condolence letters and small cards that had been stuck to floral arrangements. Those documents had been overlain with similar letters and small cards attendant to her mother's death. As she sorted each written reminder she remembered the feeling of helplessness with which she had tried to dispense cheer to each parent in their illnesses. Her mother's sickness was especially poignant because it had been preceded by such fun in the waters of the Gulf. All in all, the room was more a shrine than a music room, and the air was a generation old. She opened up the entire house. She brought in fresh clusters of peonies, sunflowers, daisies, and dried sorghum stalks. She realized that she would come to miss having a full house of family around as much as she would miss her parents.

A steady breeze kept the air moving but at a temperature that would bake bricks. She had made a large bowl of her father's favorite salad, sliced cucumbers and dead-ripe tomatoes sprinkled with sugar and dressed sparingly with white-cider vinegar. The pitcher of milk in the somewhat-cooler root cellar was fresh that morning, as were the eggs Irene had gathered, hard-cooked and shelled.

ON THE TRAIN THAT day Frank sat stiffly, making the ride even more noticeable to his spine. Why am I going? For an answer. Six weeks ago I couldn't ask the question. Four weeks ago I could, but she couldn't answer it. That makes a pattern. What does that signify? A cooling off? No other explanation. So what can she answer now? Am I cooling, too? I'm not even sure what I want her to say. Which is worse, no answer or one I don't want to hear? She has to say something. I don't think she will accept.

BY THE END OF the day Irene had settled on the arrangement of bowls and vases and books laid open and sheet music on the piano after many experimental trials. The upstairs rooms were adorned with vases of field flowers and ready for company. Birdsong finally ceased in the gathering darkness. Mr. McVey would have met the train by now to hand over a horse and rig for Frank to use until he returned to catch the train on Sunday.

Irene re-pinned her hair and sat with a stiff, paper palm-leaf fan remaindered from the last funeral. But at least he did commit, she thought; he did ask. And what did I do? Uh-huh. I did absolutely nothing. I told him to wait one month. He went to that Hades of his so that stretched it out.

She had decided on acceptance of Frank's proposal before a day had elapsed, never mind a month. In fact, she could not hold in her mind a thought to reject it. She had even written out various ways of saying yes, which she did not intend to put into a letter but to speak with passion the next time he held her tenderly.

In this last month, perhaps his resolve has weakened? Did that new pretty teacher tell him she didn't need a month, and shamelessly fling herself on him, and tell him he was well-enough sexed for her? Is my one and only engagement going to die aborning? Yet another death this year, but with no fair notice?

She heard the rig being eased into the stable. She offered up a prayer to the angels, and then arranged herself along the love seat with a book. She knew Frank would tend to Mr. McVey's horse before coming to the door. When he did call out to her from the porch, she feigned surprise and exclaimed,

"Oh my! That's right. It's today you said you'd be paying a call."

Frank pushed his way through the screen door with his valise in one hand and a grin on his face. "I hope I'm not catching you at a bad time." He took her hands and then drew her for a kiss, but a near-frantic brown spaniel pup leapt between them. It took several minutes for the two of them to quell the hops and wriggles of the pup, who was finally coerced into the backyard on a lead clipped to a clothesline wire. And it took several minutes more for them to reach consensus that it was, indeed, hot enough for each of them and that the corn looked parched. Nothing was parched when they kissed.

Irene rested her temple against his shoulder and said, "What brings you to me tonight, Frank?"

"To collect something you owe me. An answer to that offer I dropped off the last time I was here. Shall I review the terms?"

"I think I have the main parts in mind." She sat, fanning herself.

"Irene, on the drive out here from town I had a prayer conversation with your father, Hiram. It helped to clear my mind. I said, 'If I may have your Irene as my wife, I will spare no effort to make her happy in my home for as long as our days allow us.' Irene, please tell me that you accept my proposal of marriage."

Something mischievous got into Irene; maybe it was from the pup. "Did Papa say anything about the cooking up there?"

"Now, Irene, this is not a subject of mirth."

"Well, I just can't help it, Frank. You should try it. Remember what I told you, angels fly because they take themselves lightly."

Frank had come here to be solemn and he was determined to remain that way. In a solemn and patient voice he said,

"Irene Webb, will you be my wife? Will you spend your life with me?"

"Yes, Frank. Absolutely yes. Without hesitation. I am overjoyed. I only hope that I will be able to fulfill my duties and your expectations." She ran to him with her arms spread wide and squeezed him against her. Then she released him, smiling. His eyes beamed in a rush of relief and victory.

Frank exhaled and tried to think of just the right thing to say. Perhaps it was the heat. Then he tried to think of anything to say.

"I hope I don't disappoint," Irene blurted.

Frank smiled and said, "You gave the answer I came to hear."

Neither could think of anything profound to say.

Frank ventured, "It'll be hot upstairs."

"Mmm, not on the sleeping porch. But if you want we could go to the cellar."

"That's an interesting suggestion. Primitive. Feral. Deep, even. Back to our roots."

"You! How about the sleeping porch then?"

"How are the kisses on the sleeping porch?"

"We need go there to find out."

FRANK WAS RAVENOUS ON the morning of July 25, having slept like a stone until awakened by the roosters. He discovered Irene had already milked the Guernsey and collected the morning's eggs. He chuckled, recalling his urbane host's breakfast order in St. Joe of shirred eggs, "mind, three minutes," and reached for a cold, hard-cooked one. Irene was singing a hymn and Frank attempted some serviceable harmony but kept going off the beat, giving it an unintended ragtime lilt. The conversation turned to details which neither had given serious thought before.

"What about your mother?" Irene wondered.

"Oh, she and Cora Henderson are talking things over right now. And when they get to talking, be advised that Horton will be talking."

"I remember Mrs. Henderson very well. She seems like a strong partner for your partner. I look forward to spending more time with her."

Frank nodded enthusiastically. "Who all in Nortonville knows?"

"Well, when Maggie Rea knows it'll be news all over Norton Township and Valley Falls."

For some reason that observation compelled Frank to kiss her.

"Frank, we can't really ask people to come to an August wedding on short notice. And some will be planting winter wheat after that."

"So October's looking promising then?"

"Or even later. But not into Thanksgiving."

"No, not that late," Frank said. "You need to tell the folks in Belleville . . ."

"I've already composed a letter. You must put it in the mail at the station."

"Remind me later."

"Men!"

Frank said, "We should consider honeymoon destinations. Have you thought about that?"

"I have not but it is you, not I, who needs leisure time. In November the mountains are surely out. If we do go anywhere I would think it would be a city, one with theatre in full swing."

"Good thought. We both have family in the East. We could use the trip to visit with them."

"But not use them to provide us a honeymoon," Irene said as a mock scold.

"I would make such social blunders without you, Irene," said Frank with a wry smile.

Nothing definitive came in terms of travel planning and the two fell silent again. Irene decided to tread cautiously onto sensitive ground and ask about the spells. Frank shrugged and said they still hit unexpectedly with cyclonic force, but he could snap back more quickly these days after they subsided. Frank had adopted a certain fatalism over the matter. Irene was momentarily stumped as to what she could do about that.

"Frank, do not attempt to reply to what I'm about to say. I can guess your responses, and it is really more about my own outlook than any assurances you might attempt to give. I want you to simply listen to what's on my mind. I do worry over your spells. I admit that much that gives me worry is the recurring presence of Allie in those spells. What does that mean to you, in making another marriage commitment? I am trying to find my own peace with such worries. No, don't attempt to say anything. After all, your spells are involuntary.

"But I have other concerns as well, about you and about Horton. You and the Altons keep talking about Horton gossip. Believe me, I scoff at gossip, but wonder about what fire might cause the smoke. I know the fine relationship in which we all lived under one roof. And I know that each of us is above reproach. Yet even my very own mother asked me questions about those days. There is always innuendo in such questions. I already know that there is no substance over which to carry any measure of remorse. I have no concern from my own standpoint, but we have to think about the effect on your business. And what people say to your fine sons. How shall we face that atmosphere together? I want you to think about very exact forms of conduct, maybe public charitable works or services, or frequent social gatherings. It simply won't do us any good to ignore ignorance, dear. We can't just ignore prejudice and gossip. Do I even come down to Horton before the wedding? I think not. What we can do is live exemplary lives. Reflect on these thoughts. These misgivings, if they are such, are entirely over what specific future actions we can take. They are not misgivings about my commitment to you."

Frank nodded. He did not attempt to answer. Instead he said,

"There is no denying the plain truth that you are not moving into a new home. You will be moving new to an old home. There are prejudices going all the way back to my parents' divorce. There is the ill will of Mrs. McCall. There are the petty jealousies of some who would like to live at Mina and High. And the town banker in every town is unpopular. No matter how helpful he may try to be, resentments build up. Frank Wilson, as a person, is generally well liked, but I'm still the banker. And you will be the banker's wife so you will get a taste of that. Even more so because I hope eventually you will take part in the business of the Homestead Bank. Allie did, with her practical approach to everything. She and I learned to be bankers as we went along at the Havensville bank. She was invaluable at Homestead. Cora Henderson certainly knows it inside and out. We turn to her all the time. Her wisdom is worth as much as the capital Scott Henderson put in the bank. I want your wisdom on the board of directors at some point. On this, I depart in philosophy from that of your father who preferred the farm business to stay out of the lives of your mother and you. But your position will set you even farther apart from other Horton women. It is bound to create frictions."

"My mother spoke to me of pioneer Webb strengths. I have them. You are welcome to them."

She then began to ask about rugs, furniture, and fall clothes for the boys, and again brought up the topic of their wedding trip. Frank brightened and became animated on each of those subjects. He said he wanted to see the Gulf waters for himself. She told him she had no interest in returning to Houston. He said a wedding trip to New York or Chicago, where he had important friends, would expose her to society there and help establish her standing in society at home.

Her repeated questions about the costs of joining a party telephone line were met with nothing but grunts from Frank. "Can't you at least find out?" He acknowledged he would look into it, and in the meantime, she could always reach him by calling Horton Central and they would send someone to fetch him for a call.

When it came time for him to take Mr. McVey's rig back and go to the station, Irene said, "Look over on that table. What is that?"

He stepped over to look, and quickly tucked the envelope into his breast pocket, to be mailed at the station.

MAILED JULY 30, 1897, FROM NORTONVILLE, KANSAS.

F. M. Wilson, Horton, Kansas

My Beloved Sweetheart,

And how are you tonight? This has been an extremely hot day here—scarcely a breath of air stirring. I have spent the entire afternoon lounging around En Ne'glige' trying to keep cool but I made a failure of the attempt. Mr. and Mrs. McVey and Maggie Rea went to Valley Falls.

. . . I find myself thinking constantly of you and of our future. Dear heart I pray Heaven to make me ever worthy of your best love and confidence. My highest aspiration is to be all you would have me to be in a devoted companion. You seem so good and so true to me. So strong and tender. I believe I love you enough to desire your happiness above my own or above anything else in the world. I want you to be contented and happy. I want everything and everybody around us to be happy. My darling—I have a chance to send this to town so will close that you may receive it tomorrow.

Devotedly,

Irene

Wednesday Eve

AMANDA WAS SEASONING THE pot of sauerkraut when Frank came in the kitchen. It was a dish she favored, Frank tolerated, and his sons were evenly divided on. Harold would need some coaxing tonight.

"Mother, I have acted on your wise counsel of nine months ago. You always said I was a fast learner, but in this case I fear you must find me slow and dull. But better late than never. I have been accepted by Miss Irene Webb and we are now betrothed." Frank beamed at his mother and rocked back and forth on his heels, his hands thrust into his pockets.

"Frank, don't do anything rash. Don't you think you should study this further? Perhaps consult with Forrest and Nettie? Perhaps see a specialist in Topeka?" She winked.

Frank threw back his head and laughed like a blacksmith. His mouth began to water as he watched her cut the connective strings between plump, bark-colored brats that would be tossed in the pot in the last ten minutes.

Amanda wiped her hands on the dusty blue apron she had brought with her from Holton and kissed Frank on the cheek. "You are a good sport to put up with a bit of teasing. This is very welcome news. However, your story was scooped by Mrs. Cora Henderson. But you already know that since you conspired with her to inform me while you were away in the next county. Congratulations, Frank. Maybe these nightmares of yours will subside now. I couldn't be happier with your choice."

"Mother, do you think they'll remember you back in Holton?"

"Oh, I have a notion they will. Don't pay me any mind. Do you think I'll grieve putting some distance between me and Mrs. McCall? Have you told her yet?"

"You may have that honor if you wish, Mama."

"Don't *you* wish, you mean! No, Cora and I think Pearl should be the one to tell her mother first so she won't be surprised, then you tell her yourself so she won't think you're neglecting her."

"That is brilliant."

"Thank Cora Henderson. She thought it up. Saves us all from unpleasantness. She'll be glad to see me leave and angry to see a new Mrs. Wilson in this house. I'll hate to miss the show. Call the boys for supper."

"Could you hold off serving for half an hour? I haven't told them yet."

Frank went out the front door. Harold was on the swing watching Wallis play catch with Tonya Thornton. He hated to break up the game, but if he didn't talk to the boys now, together, it could make things more difficult. He walked down the steps and called out, "Over here, Tonya."

Tonya checked her throw to Wallis, turned and tossed it to Frank, who had to jump to snag it with one hand. Twenty years ago he had been a member of the Cyclone Base Ball Club of Holton. "Good catch, Mr. Wilson. Sorry for the throw. You keep it and play with Wallis, I have to get home now."

"Would you like to stay for supper? You could play after supper. It'll still be light."

"No, thank you, I'd better go home. Thanks, Wallis. Bye-bye, Harold. Thank you, Mr. Wilson, I'd like to check rain on supper."

"A *rain check*," Wallis enunciated. She stuck her tongue out at him and in a swirl of blonde hair she lit out for the corner. She avoided cutting across the lawn, and waved as she ran down Mina Street.

Frank turned to Wallis and said, "Come up on the porch, son. I want to talk to you and Harold about something." When Wallis plopped himself on the swing, he gave Harold a shove. Harold shoved back. Wallis started to laugh and push harder when Frank said,

"Settle, you two. You can play after supper. Right now, I want to talk to you. Things are going to be different around the house soon and I want to explain."

"You getting another horse?" asked Harold. Wallis sat very still. He thought he had an idea of what was coming next.

"Harold, be serious for a minute. Look, you both know that I have been writing letters almost every day to Miss Webb in Nortonville. And visiting her. Well, she's all alone on that farm after her folks died this year. So I've been thinking. How would you like it if she came here to live?"

Harold looked puzzled. Wallis just looked at Frank. Then he asked, "Papa, where will she stay? How long?"

"Boys, I have asked Miss Webb to marry me, and she has said yes. We'll probably get married just before Thanksgiving. Then, she'd move in here permanently. It's a big change, but everything about the two of you would be the same. She is very fond of both of you. You liked going to her farm, didn't you, Harold?"

"Yes, Papa. Would Maggie Rea come with her?"

"Well, not to live here, no, but I'm sure she would come for visits. Wallis, what do you think?"

Wallis shifted his jaw slightly. "Would we call her Mama?"

"She would never take the place of Mama in our hearts. She would be my wife and the lady of the house. She's coming into the family, Wallis. I want you to call her what is most comfortable for you. It's probably simpler to call her Mother, but you can decide that later. Right now, I just want you to start getting used to the idea that she will be moving here, and Gramma Wilson will be going back to Holton."

Wallis began to tear up. He looked around the porch. He looked at Frank. "Everything has changed. Well, it's a good thing for you, Papa. And we'll get along fine."

Harold asked, "Is that sauerkraut I'm smelling?" Wallis punched his arm. "Stop hitting me. Make him stop hitting me."

MAILED JULY 30, 1897, FROM HORTON, KANSAS.

Irene Webb, Nortonville, Kansas

My darling Irene,

I must first tell you that I got home safely Sunday night. . . .

. . . Mr. Henderson returned from his long absence Tuesday evening. He had a very pleasant trip, and advises me by all means to take my wedding trip to New York and surrounding points of interest. Some of our good friends in New York also sent word that they would make it very pleasant for us if we would come there. I have made confidants of Mr. and Mrs. Henderson, and they are fully acquainted with our engagement and intentions.

I have also confided in Dr. Ralston our secret, and likewise to Phillip Latham, so you see it will soon cease to be a secret I fear. Mrs. Henderson assures me that my mother will be very much pleased to see me happily married. During my last visit to you Mrs. H. had a talk with mother about the matter.

I shall be glad to hear that you and your Uncle are coming over to visit us. I thought I would not mention the matter at home until assured that you were coming, but I feel assured that Mother will be very glad to see you and to get acquainted with you. I hope that she will like you darling and that you will like her.

It will be a trying ordeal for you my dear, but I am sure that you will act nobly your part, and I shall endeavor to make your visit as pleasant for you as possible.

. . . I am so sorry that I cannot drop in and see you every day, but dear love the weeks will soon roll around and the time arrive, when you will be wholly mine, and you will come to abide with me and brighten the home with your cheerful presence.

We will count the weeks and soon be counting the days until that happy event to which we are looking forward with such interest.

Good night love,
Frank

MAILED AUGUST 2, 1897, FROM HORTON, KANSAS.

Irene Webb, Nortonville, Kansas
Thursday, July 29, '97

My beloved Irene,
I have been thinking of you all day and cannot close my eyes in rest until I have sent you a short message of love, though I am not sure that you will expect me to write tonight. I rec'd your sweet letter Friday morning. Sweet indeed is the sentiment expressed therein and I assure you my darling that I fully and heartily reciprocate the feeling.

We have but a few more weeks of preparation until you will bless and comfort me with your constant companionship. May you never have cause to regret the step you are about to take.

I wish that I were with you tonight love. I would not ask you to excuse me and permit me to retire, but would be perfectly willing to sit with you for several hours longer.

If you will excuse me now I will try to get started earlier the next time.

Lovingly thine,
Frank

P.S.

Sunday, Aug. 1st

When may I expect to receive that long promised photograph of your own sweet self? I hope you have not quite forgotten it.

MAILED AUG 2, 1897, FROM NORTONVILLE, KANSAS.

F. M. Wilson, Horton, Kansas

My Beloved Sweetheart,

This time last Sunday I was sitting at your side talking to you. How hard it is to be content with letters now isn't it?

. . . Charlie came home last evening and he and Uncle Dan stopped this morning and took me with them for a little ride. I confided to them our engagement and received from them sincere wishes for my happiness. Charlie told me, Darling, that since he had known of your visits to me he has taken the privilege of learning as much as he could about you. He told me also that he had learned only good things of you and he believes you worthy of my heart. My Uncle too has informed himself all he could. I knew nothing about their actions but I know they had only my interest at heart and were not prompted by any other motives. I have told no one else except my brothers and sisters. By the way Love, if we go East on our wedding trip we must arrange to spend a short time at Pittsburgh with my brother.

I am very much afraid he cannot attend my wedding. He has been home twice during the past six months and I fear he will think he cannot afford the trip again. However, he may come. He is in New York now. Darling mine; I cannot help picturing the preparations for my wedding with my loved Parents here. They would have done everything I wished—they loved me so—If only my Mother could have been spared! And yet darling while it would have been a great satisfaction to both my Father and Mother to see me in my own home, the change for my Mother after Father left us, would have almost killed her. She used to tell me that she wanted me to be happy and she would not ask me not to leave her yet she did not care to live when Pa and I were both gone.

I wish you knew how deeply I feel over the step we are about to take. I crave above all things your whole soul's love. Not a mechanical love when duty is the controlling element but a deeper broader and truer affection which is natural, honest and sincere.

I must close now. When are you coming over again darling?

With fondest love for thee my dear one,

Irene

MAILED AUG 2, 1897, FROM NORTONVILLE, KANSAS.

F. M. Wilson, Horton, Kansas
Sunday, Aug. 1-'97

My darling,

I called you to the telephone this morning to ask you to come to Atchison and spend this evening with me at my sister's. When you told me you were not well I thought I would better not urge you to come. I should like to have you meet my sister and her family and thought this would be a favorable opportunity. I am disappointed to know you are not coming but I did not want you to make the trip when you were not feeling well. I am going home tomorrow morning and expect to come back Monday and spend most of the week here. I shall probably go to St. Joe Thursday or Friday—possibly you can run down some evening next week. . . .

With love I am

Your Sweetheart,
Irene

Chapter Ten

I SOMETIMES BECOME DESPONDENT AND DOUBT IF I EVER WILL BE WELL AGAIN

Mailed August 6, 1897, from Horton, Kansas.

Irene Webb, Nortonville, Kansas

My darling Irene,

. . . One year ago today, we removed Allie to the St. Joe Hospital. Little did I think she would never return to her home. Almost a year has rolled by since her spirit took its flight and now I find myself preparing to receive her dear friend as her successor to my love and affections.

My precious darling I shall love you as I always loved her and I believe that if we could communicate with her spirit she would approve our course and bid you welcome. I shall give to you that full complete and unreserved love which you demand, and which you offer me in return. My soul's desire is to make you happy and to provide always for your comfort. I am asking of you a great sacrifice, and I often wonder if you fully realize the responsibility which you are about to assume. I know that you are very thoughtful and have given the question much serious consideration. You seem to be perfectly willing to share with me the joys and sorrows of life, and I shall endeavor to see that the former exceed the latter.

As to the time and manner of our wedding I have left it all with you, desiring your pleasure above all things, but I believe when you consider the effect which the hot weather has had upon me this summer you would prefer to wait until October.

I want to take a wedding trip, but have no decided preferences, and would be glad to know your wishes in the matter. Inasmuch as I have never been East of Illinois, nor west of the Kansas line, a trip in either direction would be equally interesting to me. I shall ask you to plan a trip of 15 or 20 days and I am sure it will please me. About your visit to my home I also want to leave that matter entirely with you. I shall be glad to see you if you feel like coming. Please consult your own feelings and act accordingly. No doubt you would feel embarrassed to some extent, and I would not expect that you would entirely escape criticism but how far this should influence you I must ask you to determine.

With constant love believe me.

Yours forever,
Frank

MAILED AUGUST 6, 1897, FROM HORTON, KANSAS.

Irene Webb, Nortonville, Kansas
Aug. 5, '97, 1 AM tomorrow

My darling Irene,
I wonder how you have spent this beautiful day. I feel quite sure that you have devoted a portion of it to my correspondence. I did not go to Haddam yesterday as expected, but expect to go tomorrow, and return about Wednesday evening.

I will take Harold with me. Wallis is so enthusiastic over his recent camping out experience and the preparations which he is now making to start out tomorrow morning for another week at the same place, and with the same companions, and three new ones, that he does not care to go with me. The boys came home Friday night about 10 o'clock, having been out since Monday, in all the rain which fell during the week, but claimed of course that they didn't get wet. They spend most of their time fishing and hunting. They start out again tomorrow better equipped than before and will no doubt enjoy the experience hugely. They do their own cooking, and talked about doing their bread baking, but we have persuaded them to give up this idea and take bread with them. It would make you laugh to hear them making plans for the trip. Harold is wild to go with them. I have promised to take him out to the camp someday, and let him remain until the following day, and give him a taste of it. I shall have no fears, for he is a brave, little man, and would willingly remain with the boys in camp all week I think.

I am feeling much better than I have been, and hope that I shall continue to improve and reach my normal condition before I see you again. The boys are always whole and hearty. Neither of them has ever been sick.

I hope you will have a nice little trip outlined for us when I see you next Sunday. I am sure the day will not be half long enough for you, we will have so much to talk about when we meet next time. I am so sorry we cannot see one another oftener. I wish I could be with you tonight darling mine.

I will try to content myself with the thought that after a few more short weeks you will be wholly mine, and constantly present to comfort and delight me with your charms. I love you darling and shall try to be good to you. I want you to have a comfortable and happy home and will try to lighten the burdens and cares whenever it can be done. I cannot promise you a life of luxury and ease and I know you do not crave or expect it. I assure you that you will find much to do, but I trust that it will prove to be no serious tax upon your energies. I do not want you to be a drudge with a careworn look calling for universal sympathy, but I desire to preserve the strength beauty and freshness of your youth. I have never said much to you sweetheart along this line, because you lived with us long enough to know about what I can afford to do for you. Since we came to Horton our household expenses have varied from about $1,600 to about $2,800 per annum.

I hope the time will never come when we shall be obliged to reduce living expenses but I feel assured that if misfortune should overtake us, I would find in you a brave and true helpmate ready and willing to take up the battle of life without complaint.

Darling, I must close and put Harold to bed. I have been trying to persuade him to go and permit me to continue my writing, but he insists on remaining with me. As we are to start to Haddam tomorrow I must put him to bed at once.

Now darling just imagine that I have given you a hug and a good night kiss, and until you see me next Saturday night.

Believe me your own,
Frank

MAILED AUG 9, 1897, FROM NORTONVILLE, KANSAS.

F. M. Wilson, Horton, Kansas
Sunday, Aug 8, '97

My Beloved Sweetheart,

Your precious love message came Friday evening and was greatly enjoyed. I had spent the whole afternoon in the dentist's chair and I needed something sweet and comforting. Your letter was just the thing.

My darling lover boy, I thank you for your loving compliments on my letters. I am glad you enjoy them; if they please you, I am satisfied. You must not expect a very long letter tonight sweetheart. I am tired and sleepy and must get to bed early. The past two days have been sad ones for sure. An intimate friend of my mother's and a woman I have known all my life died suddenly Thursday night. She leaves a large family of children—two girls of whom are about my age and are among my most intimate associates. Poor girls, they are so sad and lonely. I feel that no one can realize their feelings as I can. I have been with them the greater part of the time since their mother left them. It was very hard for me as it brought my own grief back afresh. I wish I had known that Mrs. Graham was so near death that I might have sent a message of love to my parents. They are happy and contented now; free from earth's sorrows and cares.

I am expecting my friend Maggie Russert of Lawrence tomorrow evening. She will spend this week with me and accompany me to St. Joe Thursday. We will probably spend two days there. My dress maker will go up Friday to help me in the selection of my dresses. I think I shall return home on Friday or Saturday and perhaps return as far as Atchison with you Sunday evening or

Monday morning. I cannot say definitely yet, but will write you later about it. I want very much for you to meet Maggie and I shall keep her over next Sunday if I can. She wrote me she would have to return Friday but I may prevail on her to stay.

She was my roommate at school and has been my true friend for years. I want her to be my bridesmaid—that is a promise of years standing. I want you to select your best man—anyone you may desire to have assist you thro the ceremony will be welcomed by me. I should like to know, darling, how many and who of your relatives and friends you desire to attend our wedding. Please do feel that any and all whom you desire to have will be very cordially received.

Under the circumstances I feel that our wedding should be a very quiet affair. I shall have only my immediate family, my Uncle Dr. and wife, my Uncle Dan and cousins Jennifer and Charlie and my friend Maggie Russert. I shall have no invitations issued— only announcement cards. I shall be pleased to write informal invitations to your relations and friends when I have your wishes and when the proper time comes. I trust you will have Miss McCall or at least invite her. I am very anxious indeed that there shall be no feeling of bitterness existing and that if there is any now it shall soon vanish.

I am sure I shall be pleased with my ring. I will trust to your usual good taste and judgment in the selection and I know I shall not be disappointed. Please guard against getting it too small.

Yes, darling, I believe you love me and desire my happiness. I have given the subject of our marriage the best and most earnest consideration of which I am capable. This one thing decided my mind. I know I love you more than anyone else in the world and that my life is not complete without you. I did not love you so dearly until you proved to me that you truly and sincerely loved me. Fears and misgivings have not entirely left my mind. I do not know how I shall succeed in my new home. I only know that my devotion and affection for you are strong enough to justify me in taking the step. About our wedding trip darling, I prefer to leave that entirely with you. My traveling has been very limited and I shall enjoy a trip any place or any direction. I have only one suggestion and that is that our trip may be made to some spot where you can enjoy a good rest. The rest I leave to you. (I mean the rest of the suggestions and planning—that pun was entirely unpremeditated. I was surprised myself to notice it.)

Now Pet, this short letter is lengthening out and I must say Good Night. I hope to say it next Sunday night.

Your loving and devoted

Irene

MAILED AUG. 11, 1897, FROM ATCHISON, KANSAS.

F. M. Wilson, Horton, Kansas

My darling Sweetheart,

Maggie came Monday evening and at my sister's request we came in to Atchison last evening. We have spent today very pleasantly working on some work of mine. We go to St. Joe in the morning where we shall spend Thursday and Friday. I wish very much indeed that you might spend this evening with us here, but I fear you will not return from Haddam in time to come else I would telephone to you this afternoon. I want you to meet Maggie before she returns home and the only opportunity I see is for you to spend the evening with us tomorrow—Thursday—in St. Joe. She is obliged to return to Lawrence Friday. I shall spend all day Friday in St. Joe returning home either Saturday morning or

Saturday evening when I would meet you here on the nine o'clock train. I shall go Saturday morning if I finish my shopping. Now darling I will ask you to call me to the telephone at the Pacific Hotel tomorrow at 11:45 A.M. and tell me that you will spend tomorrow evening with us. We shall go there for dinner and that will be the only way to hear from you at so late an hour. I would suggest that if you think of having Mr. Latham for your Best man at our wedding it would be very nice for him to accompany you and meet Miss Russert. You will both like her. She is a lovely girl.

Until tomorrow, good bye—

Lovingly Thine,
Irene

MAILED AUGUST 12, 1897, FROM HORTON, KANSAS.

Irene Webb, care Mrs. M., 307 South 7th St.,
Atchison, Kansas
Wednesday

My darling Irene,
I have been sick ever since I arrived here and have spent most of the time lying around on a couch. I felt so badly yesterday that Mrs. Henderson wanted to put me to bed and send for a doctor, but I would not consent to it. I feel much better this morning and shall go home today. My health has been so poorly this summer that I sometimes feel despondent, and doubt if I shall ever again enjoy good health.

At other times I feel better, and begin to hope that a few days will find me in my usual condition, only to again be disappointed and to receive another setback.

I have been wondering if I should be able to visit you next Sunday, and fearing that I would not. Today it seems reasonable to expect that I shall improve, and feel well enough to enjoy my visit and if you do not hear from me to the contrary you may expect me at the usual hour Saturday night. If unable to go I will surely advise you by letter, telegram and telephone. When I commenced this letter I thought I would have time to finish it, but here I am interrupted, and as it is now but one hour until my train leaves I shall be obliged to close, and tell you the rest of it when I see you.

Precious sweet heart be assured of my constant love and devotion and believe me

Your own,
Frank

NIGHT MESSAGE TELEGRAPH TO F. M. WILSON, DATED AUG. 13, 1897, FROM IRENE WEBB, ST. JOSEPH UNION STATION, MO

My darling,

My plans are working out beautifully except your coming last evening. Mrs. Alton urgently insists upon my spending Sunday with them and writing you to come up Saturday eve to spend Sunday here. I can arrange to stay if you would as soon come here as to go out home. Please telephone Mr. Alton sometime today so that I may know whether or not to go home on the morning train.

In great haste—
Irene

MAILED AUGUST 13, 1897, FROM HORTON, KANSAS.

Irene Webb, care E. K. Alton, St. Joseph, MO
Friday morning

My darling Sweetheart,

... I have been feeling miserably all the week, and have spent most of my time lying around the house. I sometimes become despondent and doubt if I ever will be well again.

I shall be with you tomorrow night if well enough to go, and until then believe me your own.

Frank

MORNING SEVEN

On the morning of Saturday, August 14, 1897, Frank thought, I have no business sitting on this train, going to St. Joseph, one year to the month of Allie's dying in that hospital. At least I won't be going to the same house and front parlor and attic. But I can't keep saying no to everyone's invitation. The purpose of this trip is to deliver the engagement ring to Irene.

And so, with a force of will that nearly spent him before he even arrived at St. Joe, Frank fought the familiar start of a spell. He had developed better means than his original, No, please, God. He could now force his mind away from Allie's pale stare. He could put lilac bushes in his mind now, with effort. He could stifle the clenches in his throat. He could force from his mind the nurses and the parlor and that box. Then, with practice, he had been able to force his eyes to read whatever was at hand, and he always carried with him something he could open at a moment's notice. Today, it was the pages with futures prices from both the Chicago and Kansas City papers from a week ago. The commodity prices didn't matter, just the columns of figures. This morning, he concentrated on summing the column of numbers in his head. It all helped.

St. Joseph terminal was a frightful place to embrace a fiancée amidst steam clouds, and horrendous, staccato chuffs as drive-wheels slipped in surges. But there she stood, seemingly above it all, beaming her broad smile as she stood beside Delia Alton, whose father was in charge of this chaos. Irene and Frank embraced, and that improved Frank's outlook considerably. Irene was startled to see how gaunt and thin he looked from less than a month before.

During the ride from the station to the Alton house with Irene, Delia Alton recited the news of the nearby world that newspapers miss, that is, pregnancies sorted by wanted or unwanted, affairs sorted by confirmed or suspicioned, and new merchandise to be traded to new settlers. Frank and Irene, however, registered little of Delia's commentary. Frank looked for traces of feeling in Irene's face and was immediately rewarded. Irene found signs of strain in Frank's face. It bore the pallor that had earlier tasted clammy to her kiss. He took her left hand, examined her third finger, pursed his lips, and whispered, "Looks rather bare."

Later, sitting on the front porch with Irene, both Altons, and two neighbors, Frank began to sink. It was best that he not attempt conversation, he told himself, especially on warmed-over politics, which Alton and his neighbors were absorbed in. "It is better to remain silent and be thought dumb than to speak out and remove all doubt," his mother had drilled into his mind.

"... the Republicans made a mistake in re-nominating Morrill ..."

"... McKinley had a handsome majority ..."

"... bitter dregs in the cup of political happiness ..."

"... Kansas went over to the enemy again ..."

"... vote for the party and not the man ..."

"... Demopopocrats ..."

"... Popodemocrats ..."

"... a few nice chickens now in exhibition coops ..."

"... about your Indian Territory adventure?"

Frank became aware that an uncomfortable silence expected something from him. Irene whispered, "Hayden ... Tell about Hayden."

He stood slowly and asked if he could be excused to lie down in the sleeping porch for a few minutes. Irene rose to follow him, but he shook his head. She did anyway.

Sitting beside him on a bed in the porch, Irene tried to gauge the physical facts. Forehead warm to the touch, skin slightly clammy, eyes clear, breathing steady. She said, "What do you want to do, Frank?"

"I'd like to lie here for a minute or two. I'd like you to go to the folks on the porch below and tell them I'm all right and just trying to shake a summer fever. Then, I'd like you to return so we can talk. A glass of water would be welcome."

When Irene returned, water glass in hand, he said, "Irene, I'm sorry to be so wobbly."

She sat at the edge of the bed and cuddled his hand in both of hers. "In the carriage today you judged my ring finger to be bare," she said slyly. "Indeed it is. Did you have in mind something to cover it up?" She smiled. Then, with a mock pout, she said, "Or is that something you need more time to think about and talk about and write about? Or perhaps the love level has not reached that point."

"Irene . . ."

She rolled her eyes to the ceiling and let go of his hand. Her voice was quiet as she said, "Well, I just get so . . . so itchy at times when you are being introspective and putting prudent icing on a prudent cake."

Frank rolled his legs off the other side of the bed and went to his valise. He smiled and said, "I endured that train ride on this stifling day for one purpose. I actually do have something for you." He stepped back to her side of the bed. "Give me your hand."

She giggled.

"The other hand, Irene."

The slender, yellow gold ring mounted by a solitary diamond slid easily over her finger. She trembled as he told her that he had now performed the act he had set out from Horton this day to do, and renewed his proposal.

Irene turned four circles with the back of her hand in front of her. She launched a rush of words as strong as a flash flood,

"Frank, you are my lover and fiancé! My F-I-A-N-C-E! I want a short engagement, Frank. In fact I want it to last no more than two hours. Less if possible! I am ready to locate an official *right now*. We can be married this afternoon. It only takes twenty minutes. Tomorrow at the latest. Skip your gritty train and be my husband before high noon tomorrow."

He smiled, and held up his hand. But she kept building on the theme.

"We should go to a judge's house, interrupt his supper, and get it done then and there. The Altons will be witnesses. These nice neighbors of theirs will throw rice."

"Be sensible," he pleaded. Before she could start in again, he said, "Remember the questions you gave me as homework at our last meeting, the ones about how you can help thwart gossip? Dear Irene, an elopement while I have a fever might start more tongues wagging than before. They would commit me to that hospital in Topeka where you want to put Maggie Rea."

Irene stopped whirling and sat down, a little dizzy. "Frank, fine. No elopement till your fever breaks." She looked up and fairly shouted, "So *when*? Tell me a date . . . you *must* have thought about a date. At least give me your date. Surely you can say a date if you truly feel as you say you do. Do you truly feel that way? Now is the time for brutal honesty. And for a date!"

Frank continued in the most prudent voice he could muster, "I mean all that I have said. No, I don't have a date in mind. I don't see how you can equate the two."

In fact, Frank could not name a date because he could not even give himself the same unconditional, absolute, open-hearted declaration of commitment Irene had given him a month before at her farm. He could almost do it, but he knew it was not brutally honest to say either yes or no.

"Irene, here is what is brutally honest: I'm not even up to dinner with the whirlwind Altons tonight. Ralston has me on medicines that rob my appetite and sap my strength. I am on-again, off-again in sleeping and eating. I don't concentrate at the bank. Do you suppose you could make my excuses and then be doubly charming at the table to fill in my absence?"

Irene knew that it was a nonanswer but did not want to jump to awful conclusions when it could simply be a fever. She was in no condition for a long talk. She thought she, too, might be coming down with something.

"They will worry, you know," she said. "Still, there is no doubt they will understand. This gleaming ring will take your place! We will be very happy at supper just knowing you are in a bed a few steps away. Mr. Alton will want to administer sherry or something more manly. Shall I decline? What a sour face! I will tell him that you would otherwise like nothing better but Dr. Ralston has given strict orders."

MAILED AUG. 16, 1897, FROM ST. JOSEPH, MO.

F. M. Wilson, Horton, Kansas

My Precious darling,

I cannot close my eyes in sleep tonight until I have a little talk with you. My own dearheart I am so grieved to know you are feeling so badly. It seems like a dream that I have seen you again. I have been so happy the past three weeks and darling only to think how worried and unhappy you have been during that time.

Believe me my own love, I do not consider your condition as serious as you do. Understand, darling, that I realize you are not well and that you have been suffering intensely, but what I mean is that I do not think you are going to be any worse and that you will quickly get back to your normal condition again. I believe, too, that your loss of flesh is not due to your physical condition but to the strain and worry you have been going through. Now darling let us be reasonable about the matter; I think I realize exactly how you feel. You are anxious that our marriage should take place yet you feel that it would not be just to me for us to be married when you feel as you do. I do not honestly believe you will get better until you do.

Our marriage can be postponed indefinitely, or if you feel that you want me near you to care for you, the ceremony can be performed and I will do everything or anything within my power to help you. When I surrendered my heart to you I gave it wholly and unreservedly. My place in life shall be over at your side to comfort, cheer and bless you in every way I can.

Darling love, please do not think about me. Melancholy is a characteristic of your disease and you should fight against it with your whole will. I know you will soon be yourself.

... My own true love, I understand now why you hesitated last night when I asked you if you loved me enough to place my engagement ring on my finger. At the time I saw only one reason for your hesitation and that was that you could not answer my question in the affirmative—I knew nothing of the perplexities you had gone through. Forgive me darling mine for my hasty words will you? As I write my beautiful ring glistens on my finger....

Goodnight Sweetest dearest love,

Your devoted
Irene

MAILED AUGUST 17, 1897, FROM HORTON, KANSAS.

Irene Webb, Nortonville, Kansas
Sunday Night

My darling Irene,

Your loving letter rec'd this morning, and I hasten to reply briefly as requested. I felt somewhat better yesterday but today am back to the condition in which you last saw me.

Some days I feel a slight improvement but it does not last long enough to encourage the belief in a speedy recovery. Your offer to postpone our marriage indefinitely, is characteristic of your generous and loving nature, and the strongest proof of your love for me. I accept the offer, and we will consider the postponement to be indefinite thus relieving my mind of the matter for the present.

I started on this letter an hour ago, here in the office, but have been constantly interrupted, and shall be obliged to stop, as I see

about a half dozen customers in the front room waiting. I shall
write you more at length at first favorable opportunity.

Believe me

Sincerely,
Frank

~ ~ ~~~

F. M. Wilson, Horton, Kansas
Aug 17-97

My darling,

Your letter reached me this morning and I was so glad to have it.
While you are feeling so badly I know it is a task for you to write
and I shall be content with only a few lines but please darling
keep me advised every few days of your condition. I shall be in
Atchison until Friday night or Saturday morning. Have been busy
sewing all day. Do not regret anything about the preparations I
have made for our wedding. I have made none but what will save.
The selections I have made are those I would make for any season
of the year except possibly in hats and they can be exchanged if
necessary. I think I shall postpone having my dress made next
week and week after.

I left the Altons well. They were very kind to me and asked me
to insist upon your taking treatment of Dr. Briggs at St. Joe. They
have great faith in him. I think Precious heart I would not delay
commencing a vigorous course of medicine too long. You are going
to get well and strong again and the only question is how soon. "If
twere well twere done then twere well twere done quickly."

I must close now with fondest love and eager hopes for your speedy recovery. Remember my darling you are but pleasing me when you are least thinking or worrying about the future.

Lovingly,
Irene

F. M. Wilson, Horton, Kansas
Wednesday Evening

My Beloved Sweetheart,

I came out home yesterday morning and was disappointed not to find a letter from you waiting for me. I am going to take it as a good omen, i.e. no news means good news. Hasn't the weather been delightful the past week? I do so hope that the pleasant change has helped you and that you are feeling ever so much better. How I wish I could talk to you tonight. It seems so long since I saw you—the weeks are beginning to seem like months—soon I fear "each day of absence will seem almost a year." We did a good deal of sewing the four days I stayed in Atchison. I have my pretty comforts all done. I am so proud of them and I knew you will say they are pretty. I had engaged Jennifer Johannas for two or three weeks' work but I shall have her only one week now, and the other week I shall have done later. I would not have her do any work now but she is going to be married sometime this Fall and does not know that she can do all my work later. She takes such an interest in my sewing and there are some things I would rather have her do than to take the work to a city modiste.

I scarcely know what to write you tonight darling. In spite of my best philosophy I have been a little lonely and blue today. I believe your expected letters not coming had a bad effect.

Things are beginning to seem like Fall. I love the somber Fall days altho' there is a tinge of sadness in everything. I think we shall have some hot weather yet but not so many continuous days of course.

Maggie Rea is pleased to have me at home again. She was very lonely while I was gone she said. She will start to school the 20th prox. How are the boys? Maggie Rea's birthday is the 24th of September—but as she will be in school at that time we will give her a party the last of Aug. or first of Sept. She is already planning for it. She will be pleased to have Wallis and Harold attend and we will all try to make the boys feel comfortable and at home.

I dreamed of Harold last night, the sweetest dream. I will tell you it sometime.

My precious love, I must close now and go to sleep. I wonder if you are writing to me just now. I hope that you are for I am very anxious to have a letter from you. With constant love and devotion, believe me

Your loving
Irene
Sunday Evening

P.S. I told Mrs. McVey how badly you were feeling and she joins me in an urgent invitation for you to come and spend a few days in absolute rest and quiet here with us. Truly we will be glad to have you and I will sign a contract to send you to bed at 8:30 every evening. Tell me you will come and when—

Irene

MAILED AUG. 25, 1897, FROM NORTONVILLE, KANSAS.

F. M. Wilson, Horton, Kansas

My Precious darling,

Another day and no letter from you. My own darling are you so ill? I have been expecting a letter for nearly a week but I did not become fully alarmed until yesterday. That was the first Monday I have failed to hear from you for many months. Darling mine if you are too sick to even write me a brief message won't you please ask Mr. Latham or some one to write for you. The suspense is dreadful. I feel that I must hear something from you.

Do please my precious darling let me have some word. My whole heart's love and sympathy are with you.

Your loving and devoted
Irene

MAILED AUGUST 25, 1897, FROM HORTON, KANSAS.

Irene Webb, Nortonville, Kansas
Tuesday Night

Darling Irene,

I know that you are wondering why you do not hear from me.

You have received from me lately, little else than apologies and I shall not inflict another upon you for this neglect. I received your Sunday letter today and am ashamed of my neglect. You have been so good to write, whether indebted or not, and your letters are so nice, that I realize that I shall always be your debtor. Some days I feel better than when I last saw you, and at other times I find myself in much the same condition. The past three days I have felt miserable. I do not hope for rapid improvement, nor do I expect to get much worse.

By a careful diet I presume I shall be able to prolong my existence much beyond the period of my usefulness, but I do not hope to regain health and vigor, or to be of much account in this world.

This is no rash conclusion hastily reached. I have often had the same feeling, and for several years past a sense of my weakness and unworthiness has been impressing itself upon me, but never with such irresistible force as during the past few weeks when I have become fully convinced that I am disqualified for the responsibilities confronting me.

I seem to shrink and shirk from duty whenever and wherever possible, and to no longer take the same interest in the affairs of life that I once did. It is utterly impossible for me to look upon the bright side of life, and make it pleasant and agreeable for those around me.

I have frequently expressed to you this feeling, and you have seemed to underrate its importance, while I am becoming more fully convinced that it is all important. It seems to me that I could never be to you all that you must demand and require to make you happy, and the greatest injustice that I could possibly do you would be to bind your life to mine.

With all of my faults, I have been sincere and honest with you from the start, having none but the highest motives, though very fickle and changeable, and at times wondering if I really had or was capable of having a true and constant affection for any one again.

In my wavering and faltering state of mind I would be doing you a great injustice to make you my bride. I cannot escape the conviction that you would be disappointed and unhappy and regret the step taken when too late.

You cannot regret more than I do that I have not understood myself better from the start, but how much better to make the discovery now, than when it is too late to avoid the dreadful consequences.

Irene if these lines have caused you pain, forgive me, and believe that my high regard for your best welfare has prompted them.

Hastily but Sincerely,

Frank

Tuesday, Aug. 24-97

MAILED AUG. 28, 1897 FROM NORTONVILLE, KANSAS.

F. M. Wilson, Horton, Kansas

My darling—

Your letter of Tuesday's date lies before me. I cannot answer it now. I write this to ask you if you are feeling well enough to come and spend Sunday with me. I shall endeavor to make the time spent as restful as possible. Will you kindly write me or wire me tomorrow if I shall meet you Saturday night.

Sincerely Yours,

Irene

MAILED AUGUST 28, 1897, FROM HORTON, KANSAS.

Irene Webb, Nortonville, Kansas

My darling,

I just rec'd your note a few moments ago and have barely time to drop you a line saying that it will be impossible for me to visit you tomorrow. I have arranged to go to Holton tomorrow if I feel well enough. The weather is oppressive and I would much prefer to remain at home.

Hastily,

Frank

MAILED SEPTEMBER 1, 1897, FROM NORTONVILLE, KANSAS.

F. M. Wilson, Horton, Kansas
Aug. 28-97

My darling Frank,

I am sorry for my seeming neglect in not writing to you Sunday. I have been greatly depressed for the past week and Sunday this feeling reached its climax and as a result I spent nearly the whole day in bed with the most intense nervous headache I ever had in my life.

The more I read your letter the more I am impressed with your noble and generous nature; and while I appreciate the position you take on the subject of our marriage, I will say darling, that you are wrong. You are not acting for my best welfare in speaking as you do. My best welfare and greatest happiness can be secured only by our marriage.

Frank, I have given to you all that a true girl can give the man who has asked her to become his wife. Do you think for one minute that my love and devotion for you have wavered since you told me and wrote me that you were not well, that you are gloomy and despondent and that life seems hardly worth the living? My affection has not decreased but rather increased an hundred fold.

Our love has the solid mason work of friendship for its foundation and I know it will stand the storms of life. We were conventional friends four years ago. When Allie left you, my heart went out in profound sympathy to you in your loss; then, as if to repay me you were my devoted and sympathetic friend when my time came to lose the best parents a girl ever knew. You stand firm and reliable through all; then after my grief had had its sway you asked me to become your wife. I knew I loved you but to make doubly sure I asked you to wait a month for your answer. During that month I analyzed my heart thoroughly and when I gave you my answer it was with the full assurance of my whole nature that my heart and soul were yours. I concealed nothing from you. I had not a selfish thought or motive in my mind or heart.

I am happy and contented with you. I believe you are good and true, and in you I find a safe harbor from every ill.

One sentence in your letter has caused me much pain. It is this, "I have wondered at times whether I had or was capable of having a true and constant affection for anyone."

Darling with all the love I bear you I ask you for mercy's sake not to speak that way again, or if you are convinced that you do not possess that feeling for me tell me honestly and cancel everything between us forever.

I do not disregard the gloomy and despondent feeling you have regarding your health and regarding life in general. I believe tho' firmly that this feeling can be overcome or at least modified.

Dear soul you are lonesome. You have no one to freely open your heart and feelings to. No one to understand and appreciate and love you for true love's sake. You are wrong in the conviction you have that I would not be happy with you. You show that you do not know me very well yet. The greatest injustice you can do me is to feel that simply because you do not feel able to take a long wedding trip to place me in a position to go in society and entertain etc. you must not bind my life to yours. Darling you know as well as I do that while these things are pleasant enough in their way they are hollow and vain. I love you because you possess a lovable nature, you are honest and true and I love to be with you.

Think of the lovely winter before us, separated as we are. What tho' an engagement does exist between us, you are sick and I cannot be near you. I might as well be a million miles away. "The dreadful consequences" you speak of are those that will come to me if you are taken from my life. I see absolutely nothing in life without you.

I must close this vehement letter. I have written just as I feel and just as my heart dictates.

Dearheart I hope you are feeling better.

Your loving
Irene

F. M. Wilson, Horton, Kansas
Wednesday, Sept-1-97

My darling,

This is another hot day. My sisters are busy with fruit this week and I have been assisting them a little. Mrs. Miller is with us at present. Maggie Rea has been almost sick for the past two days but is much better now.

How are you dearie? I have time for only a brief note this morning as I am being dispatched to town for sugar and the girls are in a hurry for it. I hope to receive a letter from you this morning.

With fondest love

I am

Your devoted
Irene

Friday Morning

Dearest, I have a little present for you that I am sure you will appreciate when it is finished. At least you have been requesting it for a long time.

Lovingly,
Irene

LETTER FROM CORA HENDERSON,
MAILED SEPT. 4, 1897 FROM HORTON, KANSAS

My dear Miss Webb—

Your letter just received and its contents carefully noted. I hardly know what to write to you, or how to advise you. Mr. Wilson has been and is now in a very depressed state of mind, and as you say, his condition seems to be a mental, rather than a physical sickness.

As far as I can diagnose his case, his disease seems to be a kind of mental despondency and melancholia brought about by a feeling of uncertainty as to the possible outcome of your impending marriage.

The fact that he has asked for a postponement of your wedding is conclusive proof that he is not sure of himself. As to the best course for you to pursue, I hardly know how to advise you. You have shown a beautiful spirit in this matter and Mr. Wilson thoroughly appreciates it. If it were my case I believe I should change my tactics entirely, by letting him severely alone. You have been too kind to him and man's perverse nature requires a dose of the bitter to fully enjoy the sweet. I shall not tell Mr. Wilson that you have written to me at least not at present. And I would not advise you to write to Mr. Latham.

I appreciate your confidence Miss Webb, and I only wish it were in my power to help you—

Very Sincerely,
Cora Henderson

MAILED SEPT. 6, 1897, FROM NORTONVILLE, KANSAS.

F. M. Wilson, Horton, Kansas

My darling Frank,

I think not an hour has passed since I saw you on that train at St. Joe that I have not thought of you. I have tried with all the mental faculties I possess to penetrate the mysterious cloud that has come between us. That there is one you will not attempt to deny.

You are sick and miserable and all that, but if you were confined to your bed and almost at death's door you could send me some kind of a message when you know how eagerly I watch every mail for a letter. It isn't that—There is something beneath it all and darling, I believe I know what it is. It came to me almost intuitively last night while I was trying so hard to solve your seeming indifference. Since I promised to be your wife I have tried to fit myself in every way for a worthy companion. When Uncle Dr. came back from Eureka I told him the matter was settled between us unless he knew or could ascertain some good reason why I should not marry you. He gave me permission to take from his library any work I chose and I have informed myself all I have had time to from scientific works. Last night when the revelation mentioned came to me I consulted the authority I had at hand and believe I have diagnosed your case correctly. I cannot write more on this subject, but I will not leave it without telling you that if I am right the knowledge does not alter my love for you one iota. I would not presume to even mention this to you were it not that I am your promised wife and I regard the relation of an engagement second only in sacredness to the marriage vow. The pledge of your fidelity glistens on my finger as I write. This were a poor pledge indeed did I not have in my heart the consciousness of your honor and sincerity.

I cannot write what I want to say to you. I believe I understand your letter that has been so strange to me. Now darling, I want you to dismiss from your mind the idea you may have that I am an unsophisticated country girl and look upon me as a woman capable of womanly sympathy. I know I am unsophisticated in many things for a girl of my age but what is right and proper for me to know I should know.

I want to see you and I trust you will not disappoint me in coming over.

Whatever is the cause of this growing estrangement between us I want to know. I ask only this that you will be perfectly honest and perfectly frank with me. This is your nature, now come to me and tell me all. Believe me, dear, you will feel so relieved and so will I. Let us not prolong this uncertain unhappy existence. Let me assure you that my soul even now goes out in sympathy to you forgetting myself. You are not natural. I know you are wretchedly unhappy. You are carrying the burden of whatever cause it may be. You know that you are causing me pain and distress at a time when I should be the very happiest. My dearheart I plead with you for both our sakes to come and tell me everything. Throw pride aside and come. If you have experienced a sudden revulsion of feeling toward me, if you have found that you are mistaken in the love you thought you bore me, if you think I have been too kind to you, that I have been too easily won to be worthy of possession. If you are not sure of yourself or of the possible outcome of our marriage anything, please tell me. You owe me this.

I must know something definite about our wedding.

The time has come for the first time in my life when it becomes necessary for me to earn my own living. Thanks to my good parents, I am capable of doing so and I do not shrink from the undertaking. A home with each of my brothers and sisters and with my numerous relatives far and near has been offered me—all of which while I appreciate, I have positively declined to accept.

You will now appreciate the condition of affairs and see how necessary it is for me to know about our wedding. I sincerely trust that you will not let what I have written you in this letter cause you any worry or unhappiness. Never was my love stronger for you than at this moment. If you love me as sincerely as you should I am willing to do anything for our mutual happiness.

I will ask you to set some evening this week to come over. The evenings are lovely and light and I can meet you any evening. Please let me know at once when to expect you.

With sincere affection,
Irene
Sunday, Sept. 5th '97

P.S. Mrs. McVey told me she would have to go to V.F. next Friday so I shall ask you to come before that day.

Irene

MAILED SEPT. 7, 1897, FROM HORTON, KANSAS.

Irene Webb, Nortonville, Kansas

Darling Irene,

I have been absent from home since last Thursday morning, returning today. Your letter of last Wednesday was rec'd just before I started away. It is with much regret that I learn of your depressed spirits and consequent illness and my regrets are intensified by the thought that I have caused it all, and to you who have been so good, kind, and true, to me under all circumstances, so careful and considerate of my feelings, as to merit only the kindest treatment in return.

Irene—however unjust my conduct may appear to you I beg of you to credit me with sincerity of purpose in each and every step I have taken since our friendship began when I asked you to become my wife. I was never more earnest of purpose or more certain of my affections. You very naturally wondered at my sudden change of heart, and asked me to wait and make sure that my love was real and abiding. At the end of the 4 weeks probation, I was less certain than in the beginning, as you no doubt discovered, but I did not have the courage to reveal, except in part, the doubts and fears under which I labored.

I accepted your answer and came away, in the belief and hope that with the question settled, I could overcome my doubts and fears and be assured of the constancy and fullness of my love for you. In this I was mistaken, for strive as I could, I was troubled with perplexity and unrest, and a dreadful feeling that I was about to take a fatal step would come over me at frequent intervals.

When next we met, and I placed the ring on your finger, I did not have the courage to truthfully answer your question, and therefore evaded it.

I realize that it would be unjust to longer conceal from you my feelings. You require a love stronger and truer than I can give. I feel myself utterly incapable of loving constantly and truly. I am unworthy of the love which you bear to me and I would do you great injustice to accept it until I know that I can fully return it.

I am not well, but little if any better than when I saw you last. I have changed doctors and am now under treatment of our old family physician in Holton in whom I have very great confidence. If he fails to patch me up I expect to try Dr. Briggs of St. Joe though as before stated I have no idea that either of them can do more than afford temporary relief, from a trouble which is likely to always remain with me.

Though our engagement is now cancelled, under the terms proposed in your recent letter which I accept as the only alternative, I trust and hope that our friendship will continue stronger than ever. It is with much sadness and regret that I have penned these few lines. I have hoped that I might in some way avoid it. That my feeling would change.

I am in no condition to write you, and have hoped that I might be excused from the task, which seems so hard to me, but you demand that I speak, and I feel that I must do so.

I cannot proceed farther tonight, dearheart, but will write you again when I feel that I can do so, as I have much to say to you which I cannot speak tonight.

Until then believe me to be sincere,
Frank

Irene Webb, Nortonville, Kansas
Sunday, Sept. 5-97

My Dear Irene,

Your letter of Sunday lies before me and demands a prompt reply. I cannot go to see you at present, and beg of you to excuse me.

When I accepted your offer to postpone our wedding indefinitely, I did so that I might be left to myself for a time until I could regain my health and my reason in neither of which am I able to report much gain

. . . Last Sunday I felt that as you had demanded from me a full statement, that I must respond. Accordingly I wrote you an honest and truthful expression of my feelings, which I did not have the courage to mail, but laid it aside.

Today I received your Sunday letter, in which you demand in stronger terms, that I tell you all, reserving nothing. I cannot longer deny your request . . . and I am sorry indeed that I cannot at this hour speak the words that would cheer your heart and soul.

You have been constantly in my mind, and that you have been unhappy since our last meeting has caused me much sadness. But dear heart, if I were called upon to decide between a speedy marriage, and my funeral, in my present state of body and mind, I declare to you that I am not sure how I should choose.

Irene, you seem to attach but slight importance to my physical weakness, and to believe that you understand my case. I confess that I do not thoroughly understand my own case, but I feel that if I could remove myself to some distant spot where I would be entirely free from every duty and responsibility for a time, that my opportunities for improvement would not be lessened. I could well be spared from business, and from home, for I have been of but little account in either sphere of late. I am undecided whether I shall try the expedient or not.

I shall try to find time to write you again soon.

With love and esteem,

Frank

Chapter Eleven

I DESIRE TO CONSIDER OUR ENGAGEMENT UNCANCELLED

Mailed Sept. 13, 1897, from Nortonville, Kansas.

F. M. Wilson, Horton, Kansas

My dear Frank,

Your last two letters lie before me. It would require much time and paper to describe the emotions that have stirred my soul since I first read them. I realize now the strain under which you have been and your weakness of body and mind. My recent letters have harmed more than they have helped you. I wrote as I did thinking only to cheer and help you. When I said I must know something definite about our wedding I desired only an expression from you on the subject that I might know what to do. Many things conspired to cause me to write as I did: First of all my anxiety— about you—then the situation in which I found myself; nearly every day brought messages of best wishes for my happiness from friends of yours and mine—many from my personal girl friends accompanied by tokens of love and offer of assistance in making preparation for my wedding. Mrs. McVey's decision to return to Valley Falls and throughout all your unusual silence.

I hardly knew what to do. I was almost desperate when I last wrote to you. I did not know you did not want me to write to you. You didn't tell me so. I realize now that in trying to be good to you I was anything else. I understand the feeling you have of desiring to be left entirely alone. I have experienced the same. But you see I did not understand that was what you needed last week else I should not have written as I did.

No, I did not discover that you were less sure of yourself when I gave you my answer. Had I discovered it I should have insisted upon waiting longer.

I did not in my recent letter nor do I at the present time mean to place before you the two alternatives viz: a speedy marriage or a canceling of our engagement. I am sorry that you had that impression as it has caused you unnecessary pain and worry. I suggested a speedy marriage only to assure you of my devotion and sympathy and my willingness to help you.

I do not desire to cancel our engagement.

I have never questioned your sincerity. I attribute this wavering feeling that you have to your state of health. I fear that I have not attached enough importance to your illness. I have felt that you would soon be better and my heart's desire has been to cheer and comfort you.

To prove my faith in your sincerity I desire to consider our engagement uncancelled and our wedding postponed. I cannot believe that you desire our engagement cancelled. Your letters reveal your unsettled, unhappy state of mind and body. I would that I might help you—but what you need is absolute rest and quiet and I am willing to grant this on my part. Write to me only when you feel like writing. I shall not be unhappy now that

I understand this is what you need and desire. I cannot refer to your letters; they have caused us both pain. Let us forget them and hope and trust that all may soon be well.

Good Night and God bless you.

Your devoted
Irene
Sunday, Sept. 12-97

FRANK FUMBLED WITH THE keys as he stood on the stoop of the bank's front door. He had just received unwelcome news at Phillip Latham's house. Latham, it seemed, had discovered an opportunity to go in on a new bank in Indian Territory. He wanted out of Horton. He wanted return of his capital "as soon as reasonably convenient." Ha! Nothing convenient about this at all. And certainly not considering the way I've been feeling. Scant prospect of relief from that with the double load Latham leaves me. It would take weeks to fill his spot. Unless Cora Henderson would come in. That would be a delicate discussion with Scott and Cora.

Sometimes on a summer Sunday the bank was the only place he could find with peace and quiet. As he pushed the door open he heard a voice at the corner.

"Is that you, Mr. Wilson? I was just on my way to your house. Telephone call for you."

Frank snorted in annoyance, turned and walked to the boy from Central. "Thanks," he said and handed the boy a nickel. He strode to the Central building two doors down the block. Mrs. Hardin smiled and pointed over to the wall phones with the shiny plug of a long black cord in her hand. All but one were already in use.

"Beg pardon," he murmured to the heavy man next to him. He lifted the receiver and craned his neck to get closer to the mouthpiece mounted in the oak wall-box. "Hello? This is Wilson."

"Stand by. Here you are. Go ahead, Topeka."

"Frank? Hello? Is that you? It's Irene."

"Oh. Irene. Are you all right? Has something happened?"

"Nothing happened. I'm fine. I'm with Cousin Charlie. He says he saw you and that you are feeling better. I was thinking of you and wanted to hear your voice."

"Irene, it sounds like you're in a train depot. I'm at Central with a crowd of people around me. It is nice of you to call. I'll write soon. Tell Charlie hello. Look, I have to say, this is a real bad time for me to take a call."

"Ohhh. Charlie and I were thinking to make a quick trip to Horton so we can talk."

"I can't hear you . . . what?"

Strength left Irene's legs. Her knees sagged. She struggled to add volume to her voice. With effort she said, "Tonight I can come over. Hello?"

She hung up the phone and turned to Charlie. Her face was pale. She slumped against his chest and began to sob.

MAILED SEPT. 20, 1897, FROM NORTONVILLE, KANSAS.

F. M. Wilson, Horton, Kansas

My darling,

I was so relieved and happy when Charlie told me last night that you are better and that you are coming to see me soon. I am so eager to see you again. I thought I could be very brave in this matter, but darling, I find the strain is taking of me more than I realized. I have given to you the entire love and devotion of my intense nature. I already feel wholly dependent upon you so far as my peace of mind and happiness are concerned. The very thought of an estrangement between us breaks my heart. I cannot bear it.

Charlie, as you know, has always been to me a most devoted brother rather than a cousin. Yesterday morning I felt so lonesome and blue that I came down to spend the day with him. I had never confided in him anything except the fact of our engagement. When he saw me yesterday morning he discovered I was not myself and insisted that I tell him why I was unhappy. I had kept everything so long and had worried so that my nerves, I guess, were unstrung. I broke down and told him that you were sick, and what was worse I felt that an estrangement was growing between us and I couldn't stand it. He then told me that he was going over to Horton to see Miss Newton and asked me to go with him. I told him I would go only with your approval. I then called you to the telephone and I thought your manner not sufficiently cordial to warrant my going, tho' I then thought I must see you and would go. After going to the station with Charlie I decided I couldn't go.

I am going to my sister in law's this morning and will return home this evening or in the morning.

They all insist upon my remaining over next week, but I came intending to return last evening so must go not later than tomorrow morning.

I am writing in Charlie's room of which I have possession at present. They are typical bachelor's quarters.

Hoping to hear from you and to see you soon. I am with loving devotion

Irene

MAILED SEPT. 23, 1897, FROM HORTON, KANSAS.

Irene Webb, Nortonville, Kansas
Monday, Sept. 20, '97

My Dear Irene,

Although it is now 10 o'clock and I have worked hard since early this morning until this hour I must take time to write you a few lines before closing my eyes. I commenced a letter last night, but was interrupted by a business call and detained until too late to finish so I gave it up. I promised Charlie last Sunday to write at once to you and to visit you as soon as possible. . . .

Monday was our anniversary Celebration and of course I found no opportunity to write. Tuesday morning Mr. Latham resigned his position here, and I am now doing his work and mine. I had thought I could run over during this week to see you, but now that I am kept so busy and so close at work I fear that I shall be unable to do so until next Sunday, and I hardly know whether I can be spared on that day yet, but will endeavor to get away if I can. . . .

I explained to Charlie that I was on my way to the bank last Sunday to write you when you called me to the phone. Then I gave it up expecting to see you that evening. The previous Sunday I was in bed all day and unable to write. I suppose I could go on and make excuses for each day that I have neglected to write you, but I must admit that I could have found time for a brief note almost any day, and also that I am heartily ashamed of my neglect. . . .

I had no thought of neglecting the matter so long, but have put it off from day to day, thinking I would find a more favorable time to write you what I wanted to say. Although our engagement is cancelled, I had no intention of thus neglecting the correspondence, and fully expected to visit you when I got to feeling better.

I am improving now, though far from being well, and am still taking medicine. In your letter of 11th, you express a desire to consider our engagement uncancelled, but postponed. To this proposition I am not ready to consent, and if you thoroughly knew the uncertainty of my affections I don't believe you would desire it.

To quote your own words you do not want a mechanical love, with duty as the controlling motive.

Unless I can be sure that I bear you that full, complete, and unreserved devotion which you crave, I would greatly wrong you by making you my wife.

Darling, it grieves me to say this, but I would not be true to you if I remained silent. I know that you want me to speak plainly, and to be perfectly honest with you. If the thought of an estrangement between us now causes you sorrow and grief, what would you imagine the consequences should such a discovery be made after marriage?

Lovers may mask their feelings, but husband and wife never.

Darling how I wish that I might write you a letter that would bring joy and gladness to your heart. I am sure that if I could have honestly and truthfully penned such a message I would have found time to do so many days ago, even at the neglect of other matters.

I am sorry that you have been worried, and would have been more than glad to be able to cheer you up. It is not my nature to desire to cause pain and grief to any one, much less to the one who has been so good, kind and true to me.

I wish that I were with you tonight that I might soften the effect of these lines and render them less cruel.

I shall endeavor to see you next Sunday if agreeable to you, though if I should be prevented and at the last moment send you word that I cannot come don't be surprised.

I will come as soon as I can if the time is agreeable to you. I will then attempt to explain why I did not urge you to come here last Sunday.

Sincerely Yours,
Frank

MAILED SEPT. 25, 1897, FROM HORTON, KANSAS.

Irene Webb, Nortonville, Kansas
Sept. 22-97

My Dear Irene,

Failing to hear from you this morning, and therefore not knowing whether I would find you at home tomorrow, or if my visit would be agreeable to you at that time I am now undecided what to do. If I hear from you today, and you seem to be anxious for me to come, I will endeavor to go though I may be detained at the last moment.

Think you had best not meet the train tonight; for if I do go I think I had better stay in Nortonville and go to your house tomorrow morning.

Very hastily,
Frank

MAILED OCT. 3, 1897, FROM HORTON, KANSAS.

Irene Webb, Nortonville, Kansas
Saturday, 10 a.m.

My Dear Irene,

I am very sorry that I missed seeing you in Topeka Friday night. I presume Grace Dunn told you that she saw me at the depot about 11 o'clock, when she informed me that she had spent the evening on the avenue with you and that we were only a block or two apart.

On the way down to Topeka Nerva told me that she hoped to meet you, but she was not sure about your being there. I had no idea that I could find you in the short time that I had to spend there, for I took it for granted that you were lost in the great multitude on the avenue, and although I met Charlie on the street, I considered the chance of finding you so small that I didn't even ask if you were in town.

I presume you were as much surprised to learn of my presence there as I was to hear of yours for I believe I told you last Sunday that I had given up all thought of attending the festival. The special train Friday evening after office hours afforded me the only opportunity, and taking the boys, and two of my neighbor's children, I went as a sort of an escort for Pearl McCall and another young lady milliner who boards at McCalls'.

I am very sorry on my own account that I did not meet you, and especially sorry that you did not get to see Wallis and Harold. I presume you accompanied the Dunn girls to Lawrence Saturday. I hope you did and that you have had a very pleasant trip and visit. I shall try to see Nerva tomorrow and hear what she may have to say of her visit, and especially if she hears any message from you.

. . . I am still improving in health. Am taking medicine regularly and feel that our old family physician Dr. Smith has done as much for me as could Dr. Briggs or any other physician.

I begin to feel like my former self, and as though the past 2 months has been a dream from which I am just awakening. It is still hot, dry, and dusty here and we are all hoping it will soon rain, and that summer will be ended. It has been a long weary summer and I will be glad when it is ended.

Life will seem to be worth living when cooler weather sets in I am sure.

With best wishes for your happiness and comfort I am

Lovingly Yours,
Frank

MAILED OCT. 13, 1897, FROM HORTON, KANSAS.

Irene Webb, Nortonville, Kansas

My dear Irene,

The tables seem to be turned, and now it is I who have been anxiously watching every mail for the past week for a message from you.

I wrote you a week ago last Sunday, and expected, and very anxiously looked for a reply before the following Sunday for I wanted to visit you at that time.

If I could have reached you by telephone last Saturday I would have called you up to enquire if you would be at home, and if a visit would be agreeable, but I had no assurance that I could reach you and so gave it up.

You now have me wondering if you are ill and unable to write. I rec'd the joint letter from Maggie Rea and Mrs. McVey last Saturday acknowledging receipt of my present, and incidentally referring to the cold contracted by you in Topeka, but I attached but little importance to the matter at that time. I now fear that you have been sick, and I regret very much that I didn't go to see you last Sunday.

I shall be very anxious to hear from you by return mail and if unable to write yourself, please have Mrs. McVey advise me by letter or wire of your condition.

I very much desire to spend next Sunday with you if agreeable to you, whether you are sick or well, and if you are sick I shall let nothing prevent my going. I think I can realize now the feelings which possessed you a few weeks ago when you were anxiously waiting to hear of my condition.

If you are merely trying to pay me in the same treatment I cannot complain, but beg of you to consider the punishment complete and let me hear from you speedily.

In love and esteem I am

devotedly yours,

Frank

MAILED OCT. 15, 1897, FROM NORTONVILLE, KANSAS.

F. M. Wilson, Horton, Kansas
Oct 13-97

Mr. Wilson,

I am pleased to know it will suit your convenience to come over Sunday. I was about to write asking you to come at that time. I was in no condition to talk with you on the occasion of your last visit. I am feeling much better now and I am sure your next visit will be more satisfactory to both of us.

I was quite sick last week with a severe cold and fever each day. It was nothing serious and I am now well except my cold persists in "hanging on." I have not been too sick to write to you nor have I been trying to pay you back in your own coin. It was simply a case of ignorance on my part. I didn't know what to say and I was waiting until I should.

Mr. McVey will meet you Saturday evening. I suggest that you bring my letters with you tho' they can be sent by express or freight later if you do not care to burden yourself with the load.

Very Truly,
Irene Webb

MORNING EIGHT

On the morning of Saturday, October 16, 1897, Irene finished rereading all of Frank's letters she had saved carefully in the blue-and-white gingham-covered box. She stared at the box and calculated it would not be of sufficient size to hold the addition of her own letters when returned.

Frank did not bring with him the bundle of Irene's letters because he could not bear to part with them, even though he knew he must, by convention, should the engagement truly end. Somehow, this Saturday, he had hopes, at least, that it would not end. He had given up attempting to formulate an expectation. He was content to wait and see. So, Saturday night, he would wait at the Nortonville Hotel to see the sun rise on a crucial day.

Irene's sprucing of the farmhouse had been rather perfunctory compared to earlier visits. She spent part of the day looking over the Fowler passages and making firm opinions about the book. Some sense and some nonsense still pretty much summed it up. She made the homestead clean, fresh and inviting, of course, but with little in the way of extra touches. Oh, how she ached for the sounds of other Webbs. This visit would mark a junction in her life, Horton being in one direction, and all other possibilities lying in the other. She had formulated no expectation. She planned to speak her heart, her mind, her opinion on his mental and physical condition, and her philosophy of living. That done, she would be content to wait and see. She did, however, think that Sunday would be hers for the making.

Sunday morning she was wakened by the Guernsey in need of milking. She had overslept. She never did that. That circumstance dictated her next actions around the stable and the henhouse, and shortened her time with her Christmas mirror.

Frank arrived on Cleo, again. Irene had garden carrots for both of them. When they had settled Cleo, they looked around the empty stall of the stable. Each of them recalled that first visit when they had a notion to get playful there. They glanced at one another and smiled the same smile.

They held hands as they walked to the house. They went in through the front door and sat at the dining room table. Irene had set it with the good china and silver. They lingered over Irene's farm coffee.

"You are still so distant, Frank." She did not show or express concern. She said it with a smile. There would be no sadness in her house on Webb land today if she could help it.

He began to unpack apologies, phrased as he might have done in a letter, but she interrupted, with a low moan.

"Please, Frank, I have read the letters. I sympathize with your obvious sickness and discomfort but I would rather that we talk plainly here. Together and alone. Please, just tell me what is so heavy on your mind."

He frowned and said slowly, "I'm confused why you've seemed to shun me for so long. I've written at least half a dozen letters and received nothing." Frank bowed his head.

Irene said in an uninflected voice, "Twice you told me in writing that our engagement is canceled despite my heartfelt sentiments to the contrary. Well, my mind's been elsewhere, Frank. I am for the first time confronted by the most commonplace business decisions of this farm which, as far as I currently have any reason to expect, shall now be my main purpose for the rest of my days. Mr. McVey tends to the hard work and he organizes everything for when we meet, but he won't make a decision unless I've thought about it out loud with him. He is the teacher and I'm the pupil. I don't see the need to skip his schooling to reaffirm to you in writing where my secret heart is, Frank. Nothing has changed in my heart. You insist our engagement is canceled, so something must have changed in yours." Irene settled back, her hands folded in her lap. She was content to wait and see. This would be the moment.

"My heart is numb. So is my mind, half the time. This isn't like those spells. Or, I mean, it's on top of the spells." His face tightened. "It's a weakness that comes over me. And I get to thinking this weakness is a weakness of soul. Of spirit. But I never doubt my secret heart and my love, Irene, you must believe me."

Irene stood to declare, "Frank you wrote me that there is 'an uncertainty in your affections' that I fail to appreciate. I call that a reason to doubt. So, have you taken an interest in Pearl McCall?"

Frank looked up in surprise. "No. Absolutely not."

Irene's voice found more volume. "Then maybe that milliner boarder of hers. Or Miss Nerva Dunn. That elusive inner strength rallied just in time for you to escort the three of them around Topeka for the Festival."

Frank slowly shook his head. "That is an unfair accusation. I deserve the pain of the sarcasm but not the accusation. Again, the answer is no, absolutely not."

Neither spoke during an antiphonal call-and-response between two meadowlarks in the field. Irene then looked away. Her face softened. "All right, I believe you."

She said with rising intensity, "Frank, I have never disbelieved you. And I don't believe there is really an uncertainty in your affections. Yes, you have uncertainty but it is about duty and what's right to do and what's best for the future." She exhaled sharply. "You are so inward looking!

"But I believe your affections are firm just as I believe we remain engaged. We should both accept that, and try to discover what is best for the present. Is it about Allie?" She turned to him, her brows pulled together. Her eyes searched his face. In a low whisper of incredulity she said, "Do you think this . . . that we . . . are going against Allie? Frank, I have learned a lifetime of grief in just six months, so I could understand that. I don't expect you to get over Allie or your life with her."

Frank clenched his teeth. He had to explain this. He *had* to be more specific. Right now. Otherwise Irene would never grasp how "getting over" Allie was so different in his reality from the words of such an everyday expression.

He had thought through specific descriptions of what heartbreak meant to him. He had never expressed them aloud. He had to now.

He began slowly,

"It's more than grief over Allie. I am clear-eyed about the reality of Allie being gone. I don't feel a passion or even a longing for her to be with me again. No, it's pain that won't go away, not passion. Or rather, a pain that jumps up from nowhere and is slow to go. Here's what I've come to realize."

He stood up and paced. He punctuated his thoughts with fingers tapping the other palm. "There are three kinds of pain when I think about her. I think, 'Poor Allie,' and especially her sickness and the fright of the hospital. And I think, 'Poor us,' and about the plans we had and not seeing her boys becoming men. And I think, 'Poor me.' Those are three separate kinds of pain and one or another of them will come upon me without warning. And then I get one of my crying spells that stops me in my tracks." He sat suddenly.

Frank looked around the familiar living room and parlor. He felt its emptiness, its aura of disuse. He looked at the quiet piano. He then looked at Irene and said, "You wrote me in midsummer that at times you feel reconciled to your loss only to have it all come like a great wave and you seem almost buried by it. That describes perfectly how it is with me. When you try to understand my condition just think of your own words and your own tidal wave."

Irene felt his words. She recalled the rolling surf.

"Then, there's something on top of that. On top of the spells. It's like the 'poor me' except that I wonder if I can even survive. I want to but I doubt myself, Irene. I don't think about ending my life, but I think about whether I am worthy of living it. Can I keep on marching? Where to? It settled in on me this summer worse than ever before. This is not a wave, this is like a long, hot drought.

"You don't need a husband who thinks like that. You need a husband with more vitality. You need a protector, a steady force. I'm used furniture. Damaged goods."

Irene would have none of his gathering gloom. It was time to go to primary sources. Time to prod. She stood up and went to a side table, opened its drawer, and picked up a book. She held it out, its spine facing Frank.

"*Creative and Sexual Science,*" she intoned, "*Manhood, Womanhood, and Their Mutual Interrelations; Love, Its Laws, Power, Etc.; Selection, or Mutual Adaptation; Courtship, Married Life, and Perfect Children,*" she paused to inhale, then, "*Their Generation, Endowment, Paternity, Maternity, Bearing, Nursing and Rearing; Together With Puberty, Boyhood, Girlhood, Etc.; Sexual Impairments Restored, Male Vigor and Female Health and Beauty Perpetuated and Augmented, Etc., As Taught by Phrenology and Physiology,* by Professor Orson S. Fowler. He is thorough, I give him that."

Fret marks etched Frank's brow.

"These places you marked up—when you gave it to Allie—they're mostly about what Dr. Fowler thinks men and women need, and that it's all been passed down by 'hereditary endowment.' What is your notion of a happy life, Frank? Every week, get a letter, write a letter, study Fowler?"

"Now, Irene . . ."

"You didn't mark this part, on page 352, about second marriages. Did you read this part? It's about a man who came up to him after a lecture and told him, 'after seventeen years living on the prairie, far from neighbors and market, where our isolation and mutual struggles but endeared us the more to each other 'til she just died of cholera in a day.' He told the Professor he had followed his mother's advice and courted a girl, and, 'My second marriage has obviously contributed immeasurably to the happiness of all parties, my own especially. Yet this contravenes that one-Love doctrine, already proved so clearly.'"

Irene paused and looked for his reaction. Frank's mouth was partially open as his mind groped to recall this anecdote. He knew he had not marked it. She continued,

"And Professor Fowler said, 'Only one Love at a time, is the natural law, as there stated; yet the death of one modifies it. Form a second love as soon as your first is given up. The cardinal rule in second marriages is to on no account whatever draw comparisons; for favorable ones disparage the dead, and unfavorable the living.'" Irene put the book down and stared at Frank.

"I was prepared for our marriage up to this summer, and then it got complicated—the anniversary of her dying in front of my eyes," Frank said. "I am reconciled, same as you with your parents. But I'm afraid I am not the marriage bargain for you that you think I am."

Irene kneeled in front of him. She took both his hands.

"My grand expressions of the noble husband have left you in doubt over meeting the measure of my expectations. Maybe that's who you can't find in there in your introspection: that man you have said I crave with 'full, complete, and unreserved devotion.' The more I think about it, the more I realize that the idealism I held when I first received your romantic letters is not the right way to look at marriage. You have years of experience with marriage and I have none. I realize it is not an abstraction. Neither is it a science. It is a risk. But the risk is worse when it is defined by lofty expectations and assumptions."

Irene rose and kissed him. She settled back in front of him and said, "Frank, you are just right for me. Your will and intent about me are all that matter to me. I believe that you love me well and wisely. You could not get any more right no matter how long you fretted or tried. At times I wonder if I am enough for you. Let's not be so introspective that we talk ourselves out of one another."

She stood up and paced to the front door, looking at cottonwood leaves trembling in a southerly breeze. She gathered herself and quelled her own trembling.

"My dear Frank lover, it's not love that's getting you down, it's the way you esteem yourself. That's what I realized after all the reading in Uncle Doctor's library. That affects your entire life, and it's got to the point that you've shed weight and suffer headaches. It seems to me that it is a sickness we don't understand yet. But we can come to understand it, together. And find a treatment. Sickness is to be expected. The vow we take between us is 'in sickness and in health.' So don't make a rash decision over being a burden to me. I might become a burden to you. That's destiny. Frank, if you were to go on and on like this alone, with no one to give you assurances and love, who knows but that it might just take you to your grave before your time."

She returned to where he was sitting and took his hand. She led him to the love seat and sat very close beside him. She spoke as if she were explaining her very soul to him,

"And life is so everyday. Marriage is everyday. I don't think about life as marching or soldiering, Frank, I think of it as everyday. I have often said that but now, after the last six months, I know it as a certainty. We need purpose but not a Crusade kind of purpose. A purpose on a small scale. It is a purpose for this very day. We live that purpose this very day, even though we also plan for the next day or the next year. The purpose doesn't have to be the grand plan of life. The purpose is putting our minds to what we have in front of us to do this very day. A grand plan is a star to follow, maybe. But it is what we do in a single day that is purpose. You wrote me last Easter you wanted to spend more time in the present, not worrying over the future. This is a wonderful day to start. Do you feel worthy of living this day, Frank?"

Frank exhaled and said quietly, "I am more alive this day."

Irene brightened. "Because we are together. I'm holding your hand, right now. You can feel my fingers right now, underneath your wrist. My touch is telling you something. I could write you letters for another year and they wouldn't tell you what my fingers do right now. Today. Together. Think to yourself, is there a better purpose for this day than to feel the touch of my fingers? Nothing more and nothing less than my touch."

Frank searched her face. He rediscovered rain-gray eyes. "I know I don't have insincere or false love. I don't lack the will or intent, when it comes to you. So, therefore it has to be something else. More complicated."

Irene touched his hand again. "We can do it together—make it simple, I mean." Then she sang, softly,

'Tis the gift to be simple, 'tis the gift to be free
'Tis the gift to come down where we ought to be,
And when we find ourselves in the place just right,
'Twill be in the valley of love and delight.
When true simplicity is gain'd,
To bow and to bend we shan't be asham'd,
To turn, turn will be our delight,
Till by turning, turning we come 'round right.

My darling Frank,

... Tuesday I went to see my sewing girl. She will arrange her work at her shop so that she can come to work for me the middle next week. ...

My precious Irene,

... I hope she will work fast and complete your work as soon as possible and I know of no reason for postponing the day beyond the actual time which you require to get ready for it. ...

My darling Frank,

... Announcement cards are almost a necessity as some of our numerous relations "back East" and elsewhere might not hear of the event at all. I should like to have Dr. Emory perform the ceremony. ...

My darling Irene,

... The date selected makes it more convenient for me to leave home than a week earlier because the Railroad Co. pay off the employees between 10th and 15th of each month and this gives us 2 or 3 very busy days in the bank. I can be sure to have pay day off my mind before our wedding day. ...

My Dear Love,

... I shall depend entirely upon you to furnish the names of Horton friends. My acquaintance there, as you know, is very limited. ...

My Beloved Frank,

. . . I have had a very satisfactory day. The ring I purchased at Jaccard's. I enclose the bill for same. I am afraid you will think me extravagant. . . .

My Darling Irene,

. . . The question of our announcement cards came up today, and the query was, if it wouldn't sound strange for us to announce ourselves at home after Dec. 1st, when as a matter of fact we were to hold a reception on 22nd Nov. . . .

Darling Frank,

. . . Today I discovered my wedding slippers are one size too small. I may have to be married barefooted. . . .

My darling Irene,

. . . I wrote to Dr. Emory several days ago . . . I told him we wanted the ring ceremony and also told him that the ceremony would take place about 7 p.m. thus allowing him to reach Nortonville about 6 p.m. and return at about 9:45 p.m., and that I would probably be on his train from Valley Falls.

My darling Frank,

. . . Next Sunday my loved darling you will be with me and the next or there won't be any next. Yes, I had the engraving done in ring thus: F.M.W. and A.I.W. Nov. 17 '97.

Frank and Irene lived together in the white-trimmed yellow house across from the school for forty-one years. A son, Web, was born in 1900. Their daughter, Frances, was born in 1903.

Frank predeceased Irene in 1938 at the age of seventy-nine, the dean of Kansas bankers according to newspaper reports. Irene collated and preserved their letters and presented them to Frances before her death in 1952. Frances later passed them on to her only child—the author, John Wilson Feist, who briefly lived in the Horton house as a young boy with his mother and Irene during World War II, and retains fond memories of Grandmother's special pear tree.

My Dear Mr. Wilson, #27

I realize this is no
time for letters and I know
you have no heart or
time to read idle words,
but oh, please, let me tell
you how my heart goes
out in sympathy to you
tonight. Your precious
wife was very true, loyal,
helpful friend - ever ready
to help and sympathize with
me. I loved her as a
sister - Her nature was
so true and beautiful - and I
know beyond a doubt that
tonight she is with her

Irene "Tot" Webb, left,
and below, seated,
clutching hands.

House Party at Hootville in June 1895—

Left to right — Top row — Rebecca Goddard. Will Drury. Nelle Morris, ? Grace Buff. Berry Van Lewin
Lower — Scott Johnson. Tot Webb, Dare Roberts, Nova Buff. Gertrude Elwon— Dr. Wilson

Frank Wilson with daughter, Frances, and, below, standing center with teammates.

Hollenbeak   Swarty   Wilson   Taylor   Taylor
  Kirkpatrick   Scott   Weiss   Canfield

Cyclone Base Ball Club of Hatton
1876

Horton Sunday Oct 4/96

Miss Irene Webb.

My Dear Friend:

I rec'd your
very cordial letter of 14th ult promptly,
having returned from my trip on
Friday previous, but not from Ills
as you supposed.

Before leaving home, I rec'd a
letter from my Aunt informing me
that she and her family were about
ready to start for St. Paul & Minneapolis
for a visit with old friends.

This decided me at once, for I
saw an opportunity to avail myself

*Incandescent Maggie Ray,
above, and Irene;
dates unknown*

*Opposite, Irene and
the author*

A A REIDERER

Elmer Willis,   Lawrence, Kansas.

ACKNOWLEDGMENTS

Had these letters not been passed from Irene's hand to Frances Feist, preserved by her for a generation and then bequeathed to me, we would not have the stories of their authors. Were it not for the transcription of the letters by my colleague, Tonya Rizzo, and her recognition of their potential, the letters would never have been read. Without the caring, brilliant, meticulous editing of Marcia Trahan, their stories would not be a novel. And, the book's design would not delight so without Domini Dragoone's insightful artistry.

I am also indebted to the work of Horton's History and Literature Club (Mrs. Herbert Campbell, Chairwoman) which published in 1974 the "History of Horton & Surrounding Neighborhoods." That booklet draws heavily from the archives of the *Horton Headlight* newspaper. *Farm Town: A Memoir of the 1930s* by Grant Heilman, featuring the photographs of J. W. McManigal (Brattleboro, Vermont: The Stephen Greene Press, 1974), supplied vivid glimpses of the people of Brown County, their farms, the town of Horton, and the open skies over northeastern Kansas. On page 63 is Wes McManigal's photograph of the interior of the bank Frank founded. The same photograph made its way into "The Great Plow-Up," Episode One of Ken Burns's documentary, *The Dust Bowl* (2012).

The Color of Rain: A Kansas Courtship in Letters (Winter Wheat Press, 2021) is Feist's debut literary novel. Set in 1896-97 and created from the complete courtship correspondence between Frank Wilson, a widowed banker in Horton, Kansas, and Irene Webb, a young schoolteacher in Nortonville, Kansas.

He has written three geo-political suspense thrillers set in Japan:

Night Rain, Tokyo brings Brad Oaks and Amaya Mori together amid sniper fire and abduction aimed at preventing Elgar Steel from realizing an innovative infrastructure pipedream.

Blind Trust, the second in the series, brings them back to Japan at the request of the first female prime minister to navigate political intrigue and restore the country's electric power grid after a domestic terrorist attack.

Doubt and Debt, set against the backdrop of a 2026 Iranian-North Korean nightmare alliance, pits Brad and Amaya against ruthless monopolists to rescue Elgar Steel from a hostile takeover.

Night Rain, Tokyo, Blind Trust, Doubt and Debt, and *The Color of Rain* are available in audiobook editions.

Also upcoming is his nonfiction *Pocket Japan*, a concise guidebook for business travelers to Japan. If you're headed for Japan on business and the prospect of navigating the traditions and cultural differences has you overwhelmed, then *Pocket Japan* can provide a concise and informative approach for conducting business and forming relationships with Japanese business partners. Visit the author's website for details on its release: https://johnwfeist.com

9 781735 749730